THE EVOLUTION OF TROTSKY'S THEORY OF REVOLUTION

Curtis Stokes
University of Michigan, Dearborn

UNIVERSITY
PRESS OF
AMERICA

Library of Congress Catalog Card Number: **81-40930**

For My Mother

Rosa Lee Linnen

iii

PREFACE

As the archetypical fallen revolutionary, many writers have
found it difficult to look at Leon Trotsky dispassionately. In
fact, much of the literature on him inclines towards either
hagiography or vilification. This work was undertaken as a result
of the virtual absence of any serious study of his ideas. But it
should be emphasized that there has been no attempt at producing
either a biography of Trotsky or an examination of trotskyism as
a movement. Biographical details and the quarrels within the
trotskyist movement were taken into account only insofar as they
had a significant bearing on the evolution of his ideas. This
is a study of Trotsky's political thought. And most importantly,
it is an exposition and analysis of the evolution of his theory
of revolution. There were four broad stages in the evolution of
Trotsky's theory of revolution: (1) The advancing of the theory
of permanent revolution; (2) The acceptance of the necessity of
the leninist vanguard party in the revolutionary process; (3) The
universalization of the theory of permanent revolution; (4)
Finally, the application of the concept of a political revolution
to a degenerated workers' state.* This examination of the
evolution of Trotsky's theory of revolution was undertaken--as it
could have only been--against the background of the theories of
revolution and socialism of Marx and Engels, Lenin, and Stalin.
Each of the following four main chapters then consists of an exposition and analysis of one of the stages in the evolution of
Trotsky's theory of revolution and shows the relationship that
each successive stage has with the ideas of Marx and Engels,
Lenin, and Stalin.

For the completion of this study, as will become clear, we
have relied primarily upon the voluminous writings of Trotsky,
Marx and Engels, Lenin, and Stalin. While much of this work was

---

*It should be noted that when narrowly defined Trotsky's
"theory of revolution" can be used interchangeably with the
"theory of permanent revolution." Furthermore, although Trotsky
universalized the theory of permanent revolution before he
adopted the concept of the political revolution, we have opted--
for reasons that will become clear in Chapter III--for theoretical
continuity and clarity over the rigors of chronological order.
Thus, our exposition and analysis of the universalization of the
theory of permanent revolution appears in Chapter IV rather than
Chapter III.

submitted as a Ph.D. dissertation in 1978, we have decided to publish it--in spite of the subsequent appearance of Baruch Knei-Paz's <u>The Social and Political Thought of Leon Trotsky</u>--because of the continuing relevancy of many of the themes it raises and the virtual absence of serious scholarship that is devoted primarily to an assessment of Trotsky's political ideas. And although they are not responsible for any errors contained in this book, I would like to thank all of my friends, teachers, and colleagues in Ann Arbor and Dearborn for the support that they provided. Finally, I extend a warm appreciation to my dearest friend, Michele, who offered unbounded encouragement during some difficult days.

TABLE OF CONTENTS

CHAPTER I

MARX AND TROTSKY ON SOCIAL REVOLUTION

I.   The Marxist Theory of Revolution

There is no clearly defined theory of revolution to be
found in the voluminous writings of Marx and Engels. We must
instead plow through their work and carefully put the pieces together. We use the word "carefully" precisely because their
collaboration extended over a period of several decades and, as
such, they were wont to make adjustments to the theory from time
to time. Furthermore, as will become clear in the course of this
work, the theory is not without its ambiguous and contradictory
sides. Nevertheless, there is a theory of social revolution that
can be associated with Marx and Engels.[1]

The immediate historical stage for the emergence of marxism
or what Marx and Engels preferred to call "scientific socialism"
--supposedly to distinguish themselves from their "utopian" pre-
decessors--was the social, economic, political and intellectual
ferment occurring in Western Europe, primarily in France, Britain
and Germany, roughly from the period of the French revolution to
the birth of the Communist Manifesto. Not for nothing did Marx
insist that he, like the emerging proletariat, was schooled in
different ways in Britain, France and Germany. And it was while
synthesizing or creating a "new whole" out of the disparate concepts and ideas then prevalent that Marx and Engels were able to
advance their theory of history. The "materialist concept of
history" would prove to be the starting point for their theory of
revolution.[2] Its basic proposition states that

. . . The production of the means to support human
life and, next to production, the exchange of things
produced, is the basis of all social structure: that
in every society that has appeared in history, the
manner in which wealth is distributed and society
divided into classes or orders is dependent upon what
is produced, how it is produced, and how the products
are exchanged. From this point of view the final
causes of all social changes and political revolutions
are to be sought, not in men's brains. . . but in
changes in the modes of production and exchange.[3]

Thus, "economic production and the structure of society of every
historical epoch" constitute the main lever of the movement of
history which, in turn, finds expression in the class struggle.[4]
Those who look for basic historical explanations in the ideas and
institutions of an epoch, said Marx, are victims of "false consciousness" since the ideological "superstructure" has at best a

certain "relative independence."* Yet, in spite of these and
similar assertions elsewhere in their writings, Marx and Engels
never really explained how these "reflexes and echoes" of the
"material life-process" actually took place. Was the church, for
example, merely an "echo" of economic forces during the European
Middle Ages? To respond by according "relative" independence to
the church or any other institution is an inadequate response
especially since it is immediately claimed that the "economic
movement [ultimately] gets its way." The relationship between
consciousness and "material life" clearly poses a major problem
for marxist theory. In fact, facing a nonrevolutionary proletariat under conditions of the most advanced capitalist development, this question would assume primordial importance
within the marxist movement towards the turn of the century.*[5]

Rather than systematically attempting to deal with this
question of consciousness, Marx and Engels "ascending from earth
to heaven" continued to assert that "history is governed by inner
general laws." Central to this conception of history is the
idea that there exists a fundamental contradiction between the
"forces of production" and the "relations of production" which--
when progressively resolved--ultimately results in a further
evolution of human society.[6] Accordingly, there have been
several

---

*Marx observed that ". . . changes in the economic founda-
tion lead sooner or later to the transformation of the whole
immense superstructure." And he emphasized that all "consciousness must be explained from the contradictions of material life."
Marx, The Poverty of Philosophy, p. 95 and A Contribution to the
Critique of Political Economy, p. 21.

*But it should be noted that Marx's theory of history--in
spite of its limitations--has been appreciated even by some of
his most determined critics. According to Hunt, "it has
exercised a profound influence and all modern writers are
indebted to him even if they do not know it." And Bober, one of
Marx's ablest and best known critics, said that "with all its
weaknesses, it remains true that Marx's interpretation of history
towers as a signal contribution to social science." R.N.C. Hunt,
The Theory and Practice of Communism, p. 45, M.M. Bober, Karl
Marx's Interpretation of History, p. 427 and Vernon Venable,
Human Nature: The Marxian View, pp. 28-34. The latter work is
an interesting and spirited defense of the marxist theory of
history.

socio-economic systems in the course of human history. Each representing, on the whole, an advance over its predecessor. "In a broad outline, the Asiatic, ancient, feudal and modern bourgeois modes of production may be designated as epochs marking progress in the economic development of society."* This contradiction between technique or forces of production--which tend to develop and are therefore considered progressive--and the relations of production is expressed politically by the class struggle which is "the immediate driving power of history." Marx, however, was primarily interested in the class struggle in modern society. "Bourgeois society is the most advanced and complex historical organization of production. The categories which express its relation, and an understanding of its structure, therefore, provide an insight into the structure and the relations of production of all formerly existing social formations the ruins and component elements of which were used in the creation of bourgeois society."[7]

While Marx did gain some "insight" into the nature of previous social systems by studying the capitalist system, what interested him most was the fact that capitalism was creating the conditions which--for the first time since the appearance of class societies--would remove exploitation, oppression, and class struggles from human history "forever."[8] And the coming "collision" between classes which has as its principal task the elimination of the "last antagonistic" social system in human history will be quite different from all previous ones in that it will be majoritarian. "All revolution up to the present day have resulted in the displacement of one definite class rule by another; but all ruling classes up to now have been only small minorities in relation to the ruled mass of the people. . . Even when the

---

*Criticizing a narrowly unlinear view of Marx's periodization of history, Hobsbawm informs us that "we ought. . . to understand Marx not as referring to chronological succession, or even to the evolution of one system out of its predecessor (though this is obviously the case with capitalism and feudalism), but to evolution in a more general sense." This statement is broadly acceptable provided that the idea of "inevitability"--which is central to the dialectical process--is not clouded over in an attempt to "explain" what Marx really meant. Commenting on the dialectical process Engels said that ". . . nothing can endure before it except the uninterrupted process of becoming and of passing away, of endless ascendancy from the lower to the higher." Within a phenomenon or "contradiction"--despite temporary setbacks--the positive or progressive side will ultimately "assert itself." Hobsbawm, "Introduction," Pre-Capitalist Economic Formation, p. 36, Marx, Contribution to the Critique of Political Economy, p. 21 and Engels, "Ludwig Feuerbach," SW, Vol. III, p. 339.

majority took part, it did so--whether wittingly or not--only in the service of a minority. . . ." The class struggle between the majoritarian proletariat and the bourgeoisie--the axis upon which modern society revolves--will be of a different nature.[9] Why is this so? What is it about the capitalist system--a system in which commodity production is now generalized--that not only impels the ruling class to create its own "grave-diggers" but even allows us, says Marx, to move beyond the realm of the "prehistory of human society?"

There are three basic components in the marxist theory of revolution sine qua non there can be no social revolution in the sense understood by Marx and Engels: 1) the existence of modern large-scale industry, 2) a large working class movement independently and self-consciously organized as a result of its economic struggles against the capitalist class and 3) the existence of an economic crisis--or sharp "contradiction" between the productive forces and their capitalist ownership--from which the only practical escape is the conquest of political power by the proletariat. Marx and Engels believed that capitalism was in the process of creating these conditions. We will now examine the components of the marxist theory of revolution.

Marx had a dialectical appreciation of the capitalist system. On the one hand, it represented a tremendous advance over all previous social systems but on the other hand--albeit as exploitative as previous social systems--it was sowing the seeds not only for its own destruction but for that of the history of class societies as a whole. It was, therefore, both necessary and useful for the working class--so long as capitalism had not "ripened"--to endure exploitation at the hands of the capitalist class. To be sure, Marx tells us that capital entered the world "dripping from head to foot, from every pore, with blood and dirt" but one will not find a more glowing portrait of the youthful bourgeoisie than from the pens of Marx and Engels:

> The bourgeoisie, during its rule of scarce one hundred years, has created more massive and more colossal productive forces than have all preceding generations together. Subjection of nature's forces to man, machinery, application of chemistry to industry and agriculture, steam navigation, railways, electric telegraphs, clearing of whole continents for cultivation, canalisation of rivers, whole populations conjured out of the ground--what earlier century had even a presentiment that such productive forces slumbered in the lap of social labor.

And it is only in this society where there is "equality before the law of all commodity owners" does a class appear which is capable

4

of putting all these productive forces to human use. "In proportion as the bourgeoisie, i.e., capital, is developed, in the same proportion is the proletariat, the modern working class, developed--a class of laborers, who live only so long as they find work, and who find work only so long as their labor increases capital."[10] Yet this same working class--whose ranks continue to swell--is brought together under the same roof, "socialized," disciplined, organized and even educated by the very system which obliges it to be exploited by a small minority of people who "privately" own the means of production. This parallel evolution of bourgeois society--growth of the working class alongside the growth of industry--is bound to reach a critical point at which the dam will burst "since the development of class antagonism keeps even pace with the development of industry."[11] But it must be remembered that the dam will burst only when the pressure becomes absolutely unbearable because "no social order ever perishes before all the productive forces for which there is room in it have developed." This is an extremely important observation. Marx is saying that "the new social order" can be established only after all possibilities for development have been exhausted by the current social order.

As such, only Western Europe and North America had reached that stage of economic development whence the "knell of capitalist private property" could be sounded; that is, these were the only regions of the world in which the continued capitalist monopoly of economic and political power constituted a "fetter" on the further development of the West and the world in general. There is no "insufficiency of production"* in the West. Indeed, the basic problem is one of waste, anarchy (resulting from the lack of coordination or planning) and artificial restrictions upon production--the result is the squandering for the sake of profits of enormous human, cultural and technological resources. The social revolution, then, can be successful only upon the material basis created by world capitalism in the "advanced" West. The Eastern peoples, in the process of being "civilized," will be

---

*"The separation of society into an exploiting and exploited class, a ruling and an oppressed class, was the necessary consequence of the deficient and restricted development of production in former times. . . . But if upon this showing, division into classes has a certain historical justification, it has this only for a given period, only under given social conditions. It was based upon the insufficiency of production. It will be swept away by the complete development of modern productive forces." Engels, Anti-Duhring, pp. 333-335.

swept along in the wake of the revolutions in the West.* As
Engels put it:

> [Large-scale industry] has brought all the peoples
> of the earth into relationships with one another,
> has lumped all of the small local markets into one
> world market, has everywhere paved the way for
> civilization and progress, and things have reached a
> point when everything that happens in the civilized
> countries has its repercussions in all other countries,
> which sooner or later will lead to emancipation of
> the workers there too.[12]

Since production in the bourgeois world has a "cosmopolitan"
character so too must the social revolution and socialism. In
fact, it is quite easy to get the impression--given the rather
sweeping language employed in The Principles of Communism and
The German Ideology--that Marx and Engels expected social revolutions to occur almost simultaneously among the advanced
Western countries.**

---

*It should be noted, however, that revolution was not to be
imposed upon any people. "One thing. . . is certain: the
victorious proletariat can force no blessings of any kind upon
any foreign nation without undermining its own victory by doing
so." Engels, "Letter to K. Kautsky," SW, Vol. III, p. 481.

**Yet a closer reading of their writings--most notably after
the failure of the German revolution of 1848--clearly suggests
that England was the country upon which most of their attention
was really focused. Marx, in fact, went so far as to say that
social revolution all over Europe would be like "a storm in a
teacup" without England. "It is the only country where, thanks
to its domination of the world market every revolution in economic
relationships must direclty affect the whole world." Hence, it
would be "a hollow and pious wish" to believe that there could
be a social revolution that didn't involve "the metropolis of
capital." Marx then went on to say that "the most important" task
of the First International was the hastening of the social revolution in England. Marx and Engels, Correspondence, p. 223,
Padover, ed., Karl Marx: On Revolution, p. 44 and Karl Marx: On
the First International, pp. 171-172.

On the other side of the ledger, however, any attempt at social revolution--as understood by Marx and Engels--without the material foundation would result in social disaster. The existence of the most advanced technique ". . . is an absolutely necessary practical premise because without it want is merely made general, and with destitution the struggle for necessities and all the old filthy business would necessarily be reproduced." Socialism does not mean the sharing out of scarce resources, however equally.* Both Marx and Engels stated unequivocably that regardless of the good intentions of the revolutionaries any preparation for a social revolution where the material basis for such action is wanting could only lead to the substitution of one form of exploitative domination by another. Marx specifically said that "if the proletariat destroys the political rule of the bourgeoisie, that will only be a temporary victory, only an element in the service of the bourgeois revolution itself. . . [so long as] the material conditions are not yet created which make necessary the abolition of the bourgeois mode of production and thus the definitive overthrow of bourgeois political rule." Engels, likewise, was concerned about the problem of a mere "temporary victory" over the bourgeoisie:

> The worst thing that can befall a leader of an extreme party is to be compelled to take over a government in an epoch when the movement is not yet ripe for the domination of the class which he represents and for the realization of the measures which the domination would imply. What he can do depends not upon his will but upon the sharpness of the clash of interests between the various classes, and upon the degree of development of the material means of existence, the relations of production and the means of communications upon which the clash of interests of the classes is based every-

_____

*The aim of socialism is the "abolition of all class distinctions" but its realization is premised upon the existence of an abundance of goods and services for which only modern large-scale industry opens up the possibility. Without this basis, only a "mere freak" of the new society is imaginable--a kind of "theoretical communism" at best. Marx and Engels, "German Ideology," SW, Vol. I, pp. 37 and 64 and Padover, ed., Karl Marx: On Revolution, pp. 37-38. This theme, of course, will be central to our assessment of the project of the bolsheviks.

time. What he can do is in contrast to all his
actions as hitherto practiced, to all his principles and to the present interest of his party;
what he ought to do cannot be achieved. In a word,
he is compelled to represent not his party or his
class, but the class for whom conditions are ripe
for domination. Whoever puts himself in this awkward
position is irrevocably lost [our emphasis].

Only when the abolition of class distinctions "can be lasting" is
there sufficient justification for a social revolution.[13] Is
there any wonder why the marxist theory of revolution has essentially no applicability for Eastern peoples?*[14] Marx and Engels,
in any case, drove their message home even more with their
assessment of the only class which is capable of "reorganizing
society."

The class whose "historical mission" (as Marx and Engels
frequently put it) is to carry out the "great social transformation" is the large working class population whose existence is
implied by the very existence of modern large-scale industry.
And, most importantly, the working class movement must be the
"self-conscious, independent movement of the immense majority, in
the interests of the immense majority." Since the working class
is "irrevocably pre-determined" to capture political power in
bourgeois society, its consciousness will flow "precisely from

---

*Marx and Engels observed in 1882 that "if the Russian
revolution becomes the signal for a proletarian revolution in
the West, so that both complement each other, the present
Russian common ownership of land may serve as the starting-
point for a communist development." This statement, however,
does not alter the basic Western orientation of marxism since
this "abbreviated process of development" for Russia must be
accompanied by proletarian revolution in the West. As Engels
put it, "the retarded countries" must see "how it's done" in
the West. As will be seen in Chapter Two, there were, perhaps, other reasons why Marx and Engels felt obliged to "modify"
their theory of revolution. Marx and Engels, "Preface to
Manifesto of 1882," SW. Vol. I, pp. 100-101 and Engels, "On
Social Relations in Russia," SW, Vol. II, pp. 403-404.

its economic struggles" against the capitalist system.*[15] Yet, while it is true that the emancipation of the working class must be the work of the working class itself, it is not true that this emancipation can be brought about without the existence of political organization. There must be a "previous organization" of the working class before it will be able to capture political power. Marx said that the "constitution of the working class into a political party is indispensable in order to insure the triumph of the social revolution and its ultimate end--the abolition of classes." But there are parties and parties. The party of the working class would be neither vanguardist nor conspiratorial. It would be merely an "outgrowth" of the economic struggles of the working class.** In fact, says Engels, "everywhere and at all times" revolutions are

---

*". . .capitalist society itself creates the material and the spiritual conditions, and by which alone can be achieved the emancipation of the working class and with it the emancipation of all members of society without exception." And it is further noted that "for the ultimate triumph of the ideas set forth in the Manifesto Marx relied solely and exclusively upon the intellectual development of the working class, as it necessarily had to ensue from united action and discussion" [our emphasis]. As the working class is "historically compelled" to capture political power, we see that the marxist theory of revolution is more or less saturated by an economic dimension that would be inconsistent with the revolutionary theories of the "Comintern marxists" of the twentieth century. A point that will assume increasing importance as we examine the theories of Lenin, Stalin and Trotsky. Marx, "Letter to F. Bolte," SW, Vol. II. p. 423. Engels, "Critique of Draft S.D. Program of 1891," SW, Vol. III, p. 439 and "Preface to manifesto of 1890," SW, Vol. I, pp. 102-103, Marx and Engels, "The Holy Family," Collected Works, Vol. IV, pp. 36-37 and "Manifesto," SW, Vol. I, p. 118.

**The role of the political party is not to bestow "socialist consciousness" upon an ignorant proletariat but to provide a certain coordination of the struggles of the proletariat since communists have no "sectarian principles of their own by which to shape and mould the proletarian movement." Marx and Engels bluntly observed in 1879 that "we cannot. . . cooperate with people who openly state that the workers are too uneducated to emancipate themselves and must be freed from above by philanthropic persons from the upper and lower middle classes." Thrashing conspirators and elitists, Marx said that "it goes without saying that these conspirators do not at all confine themselves to organizing the revolutionary proletariat. Their business consists precisely in forestalling the revolutionary process, in driving it artificially toward crisis, in making a revolution extempore,

9

essentially the "outcome of circumstances quite independent of the
will and the leadership of particular parties and entire classes."
But, if political parties are "indispensable" for the success of
the proletarian struggle, how can it also be said that revolutions
are "quite independent" of political parties? Marx and Engels'
observations on the role of the political party in the struggle
for the "new society" are sometimes ambiguous and even contradictory but it seems clear that their general orientation was
that the working class would need a political party but that it
would be neither vanguardist nor conspiratorial.[16]

    Will the proletariat--referred to as the "immense majority"
in the Manifesto--need any allies in the execution of its mission?
During the barricade days of 1848 and the rather "apocalyptic
note of urgency" of the Manifesto itself (published on the very
eve of the "revolutions") Marx and Engels did not give much attention to the question of allies. In the view of Marx and Engels,
the middle-classes--caught between the two basic classes in capitalist society and primarily concerned with holding back the
"wheel of history"--were "gradually sinking" into the ranks of
the proletariat. This belief and the context of the stormy
events of 1848 impelled them forward in their position that the
proletariat was the only "really revolutionary class" facing the
bourgeoisie.[17] Reality, however, would be just around the corner.
Shortly after the defeat of the revolutions of 1848 Marx observed that "on the side of the Paris proletariat stood none but
itself." What Marx is partly acknowledging is that without the
support of the peasantry--who were not "sinking" into the ranks
of the proletariat as swiftly as theory would have it--the social
revolution on the European continent would be unrealizable. The
historical mission for introducing the "new social order" remained, to be sure, exclusively the task of the proletariat but
in order to effect the revolution--where the peasantry is a
sizable section of the population--the proletariat could and
should attempt to convinve the peasantry that its best interest

----

without a condition for revolution. For them the only condition
for revolution is the sufficient organization of their conspiracy."
Any working class party seeking to "prepare" or "make" the revolution would thereby demonstrate its "contempt" for the working
class. The proletarian party must leave "the preparation of
revolution to general conditions and to the directly participa-
ting classes." Otherwise, the proletarian party would "renounce
its own party position and the historic tasks which emerge from
the general conditions of existence of the proletariat" [our em-
phasis]. Marx and Engels, "Manifesto," SW, Vol. I, p. 119, Correspondence, p. 307 and Padover, ed., Karl Marx: On Revolution,
pp. 55 and 58 and Karl Marx: On the First International, p. 150.

rest with the working class movement.* Though Marx maintained
that the peasantry was "absolutely incapable of any revolutionary
initiative," he, nevertheless, stated that the peasantry finds its
"natural ally and leader in the urban proletariat." Both observations were made just after 1848 and are not as contradictory as
might first appear. Initiative must come from the proletariat
in the forging of an alliance with the peasantry or the peasantry
will tend to gravitate towards the bourgeoisie. "It is self-
evident that the working class cannot leave its emancipation
either to the capitalists and big landowners, its opponenets and
exploiters, or to the petty bourgeois and small peasants, who,
being stifled by competition on the part of the big exploiters,
have no choice but to join either their ranks or those of the
workers" [our emphasis].[18] Even though the peasantry has "no
historical tradition" behind it the fact of the matter is that
England was the only country "where the great majority of the
population consists of wage laborers."[19] As a result of the increasing recognition of this fact--the absence of a large industrial proletariat on the European continent at least until the
last two decades of the century--Marx and Engels were to give considerable attention to the problem of proletarian allies from the
1850's.

----

*However, as "peasants will be peasants" they remained on the
whole narrow-minded, stupid and ignorant. "The isolation of the
peasant in a remote village with a rather small population which
changes only with the generations, the hard, monotonous work,
which ties him more than any serfdom to the soil and which remains always the same from father to son, the stability and
monotony of all his conditions of life, the restricted circumstances in which the family becomes the most important, most
decisive relationship for him--all this reduces the peasant's
horizon to the narrowest bounds which are possible in modern
society. The great movements of history pass him by, from time
to time sweep him along with them, but he has no inkling of the
nature of the motive force of these movements, of their origin
and their goal." This judgment of the peasant in 1848 as a
"barbarian in the midst of civilization" will more or less remain with Marx and Engels--despite their appeals for a worker-
peasant alliance--until the very end. Engels, "From Paris to
Berne," Collected Works, Vol. VII, pp. 519-520 and Marx, "The
Eighteenth Brumaire of Louis Bonaparte," SW, Vol. 1, pp. 404,
478-479 and 482.

But the existence of modern industry and a large working class population are only two of the basic conditions for social revolution. The third condition centers on the "rebellion of the productive forces" against the "fetters" placed upon their further expansion and development as a result of continued bourgeois ownership. Social revolution occurs when this "contradiction" has reached its sharpest point:*

> Along with the constantly diminishing number of the magnates of capital, who usurp and monopolize all advantages of this process of [capitalist] transformation, grows the mass of misery, oppression, slavery, degradation, exploitation; but with this too grows the revolt of the working class, a class always increasing in numbers, and disciplined, united, organized by the very mechanism of the process of capital production itself. The monopoly of capital becomes a fetter upon the mode of production, which has sprung up and flourished along with it. Centralization of the means of production and socialization of labor at last reach a point where they become incompatible with their capitalist integument. This integument is burst asunder. The knell of capitalist private property sounds. The expropriators are expropriated.

Marx and Engels would countenance social revolution only when the capitalist system "stands convicted" as it "breaks down under the pressure of the productive forces, its own creations." And as we have often observed, this possibility exists only in those countries "in which modern society exists."[20]

---

*Engels noted that the "elements" of a social revolution are "the development, on the one hand, of a class whose conditions of life necessarily drive it to social revolution, the proletariat, and, on the other hand, of productive forces which, having grown beyond the framework of capitalist society, must necessarily burst that framework, and which at the same time offer the means of abolishing class distinctions once and for all in the interest of social progress itself" [our emphasis]. To those who might be tempted to move ahead of the historical process he observed that "every premature attempt at an insurrection can only end in a new, perhaps still more horrible defeat" [our emphasis]. Engels, "The Housing Question," SW, Vol. II, p. 361 and "Program of the Blanquist Commune Emigrants," SW, Vol. II, p. 382.

Would the "expropriated" capitalists be simply shot or com-
pensated for their loss of property? Would the struggle for the
"emancipation of labor" be peaceful or violent? Marx and Engels
would not prejudge these situations. However, in their last
years, they tended to incline towards the ideas of compensation
for the former owners of the means of production and the peaceful or legal route* towards socialism. Marx pointed out that "we
do not deny that there are countries such as America, England,
and I would add Holland if I knew your institutions better,
where the working people may achieve their goal by peaceful means."
To engage in an insurrection would be "madness" where peaceful
means are sufficient.** After Marx's death Engels added France
and inclined towards adding Germany to the growing list of
countries in which the parliamentary road to the "new society"

---

*This is especially true for Engels since he lived until 1895
and thus witnessed the legal possibilities for the burgeoning
labor movement on the European continent during the last two decades of the nineteenth century. Marx died in 1883. And in fact,
it was Engels' Anti-Dühring which played a major role in shaping
this growing working class movement--especially in Germany. Most
people, said Mayer, "had no time to plunge into a book like Capital." It was Anti-Dühring in which "for the first time, the real
attitude of Marx and Engels was revealed to the clearest minds
of the younger generation of social democrats [marxists]--Bebel,
Bernstein, Kautsky, Plekhanov, Axelrod, Victor Adler, Labrioli,
Turati--men who did most to hammer marxist doctrines into the
proletariat of the continent." Some critics, however, might
charge that Engels' "vulgar" marxism marked the "death knell"
of the European labor movement--especially in Germany. Mayer,
Friedrich Engels, pp. 235 and 243.

**Though he saw the possibility for the "reconstruction of
society" through an "act of parliament" in England, "in most
countries on the Continent the lever of our revolution must be
force." Even in England, however, Marx edged away from his
belief in the possibility of the peaceful route to socialism by
declaring that "the English middle class [bourgeoisie] has always
shown itself willing enough to accept the verdict of the majority,
so long as it enjoyed the monopoly of the voting power. But mark
me, as soon as it finds itself outvoted on what it considers vital
questions we shall see here a new slave-owner's war." Padover,
ed., Karl Marx: On Revolution, p. 64 and Karl Marx : On the
First International, pp. 323-333.

seemed a possibility.[21] Marx and Engels, likewise, remained
flexible on the question as to whether the victorious proletariat would "buy out" the capitalist class. "We by no means
consider compensation as impermissible. . . . Marx told me (and
how many times!) that in his opinion we would get off cheapest if
we could buy out the whole lot of them." Not wanting to answer
all questions "in advance and for all cases" Marx and Engels
simply stressed that given historical circumstances would determine how the working class reaches power and how it subsequently deals with the capitalist owners of the means of production.[22]

The "transitional period" towards communist society begins
with the conquest of political power by the proletariat. "Between capitalist and communist society lies the period of the
revolutionary transformation of the one into the other. Corresponding to this is also a political transition period in which
the state can be nothing but the revolutionary dictatorship of
the proletariat."*[23] This "necessary" transitional period is a
period of proletarian class rule. Marx and Engels had a critical
but yet an appreciative attitude towards "bourgeois" political
democracy.[24] For them, however, genuine political democracy is
only introduced with the dictatorship of the proletariat.[25]
What would be the length of this proletarian dictatorship and
what would be its tasks? The length of this "transit point"
would depend essentially upon the level of economic and social
development that the working class finds upon winning political
power. Engels, for example, in 1891--perhaps considering the
advanced state of Western industry--thought in terms of a "short
transitional period" along the road to the abolition of all
class distinctions. And the basic task of the disctatorship of
the proletariat is to remove the "fetters" from the already de-

---

*It should be noted that Marx and Engels used the expression
socialist and communist society rather interchangeably and did
not consider the period of the dictatorship of the proletariat--
a period of class rule--as constituting either the lower or higher "phase" of the new classless social order. The basic difference between the lower or higher phases of the new classless
social order centered on the capacity of the new society to provide goods and services according to "work" or "need."

14

veloped productive forces so as to unleash the unimagined potential of modern industry and agriculture; in short, social ownership of the means of production and the planned utilization of
available material and human resources are introduced. During
the process of performing its "necessary" functions, the proletarian state will begin to "wither away" until it ultimately
joins the "scrap heap" of class history.[26]

Thus, communist society--premised upon the enormous wealth
produced by bourgeois society--begins to take shape upon the
"withering away" of the proletarian state. Only then, under a
classless existence, can it be said that humanity has moved beyond "the prehistory of human society."

II. The Theory of Permanent Revolution

We have indicated that the marxist theory of revolution was
neither systematically developed nor without its ambiguous and
contradictory sides. As a result of these facts a whole slew of
would be disciples of Marx and Engels have been able--with a
certain justification--to advance new doctrinal systems in the
name of updating the marxist theory of revolution. The trotskyist theory of revolution is one of these new doctrinal systems.
Trotsky, to be sure, would acknowledge his agreement with Marx
on the materialist conception of history, the nature and function
of the capitalist system and the conception of the future classless society.[27] The point, however, is that Trotsky--like Lenin
and Stalin--could always "justify" adding to or subtracting from
the marxist heritage simply from the standpoint of "concretely"
applying the teachings of Marx and Engels. In fact, he never
tired of repeating that "marxism is above all a method of analy-
sis--not analysis of texts, but analysis of social relations."
Is it not possible that in rejecting "textual marxists" Trotsky
might also be rejecting--however unconsciously--marxism as such?
Where does one draw the line between making concrete analyses of
given historical circumstances--as Marx and Engels clearly favored*--and tearing the very heart right out of a political theory?[28]

---

*Chiding those who use the materialist conception of history
"as an excuse for not studying history," Engels stated that "our
conception of history is above all a guide to study, not a lever
for construction. . . . All history must be studied afresh, the
conditions of existence of the different formations of society
must be examined individually. . . . " And furthermore, "the
practical application of the principles [of the Communist Mani-
festo] will depend . . . everywhere and at all times, on the
historical conditions for the time being existing. . . ." Marx
and Engels, "Preface to the Communist Manifesto," SW, Vol. 1, p. 98
and Engels, "Engels to C. Schmidt," SW, Vol.III, p. 484.

This becomes even more problematical when the theory in question has not been systematically and rigorously laid out by its founding fathers.

Yet, it is clear that Trotsky's theory of revolution is of marxist inspiration. Indeed, the very name of his theory of revolution, itself, was borrowed directly from Marx and Engels. Did they not say that the "battle cry" of the proletariat should be "the revolution in permanence?"[29] Germany is put forward as an example of this process in the Communist Manifesto.

> The communists turn their attention chiefly to Germany, because that country is on the eve of a bourgeois revolution that is bound to be carried out under more advanced conditions of European civilization, and with a much more developed proletariat, than that of England's was in the 17th, and of France in the 18th century, and because the bourgeois revolution in Germany will be but the prelude to an immediately following proletarian revolution.[30]

Unlike the great French bourgeoisie of 1789--which at the head of a mass movement had victoriously taken on both feudalism and absolutism--the "flabby" and "listless" German bourgeoise of 1848 was more afraid of the emerging proletarian movement than it was of German absolutism and feudalism.* However, there are two points concerning Marx's attitude towards Germany that should be noted: 1) unlike Trotsky, Marx was not opposed to a programmatic alliance with the bourgeoisie, however temporarily, in the interest of the political and economic development of Germany and 2) despite his call for "permanent revolution"--essentially made in the context of the 1848 revolutions--Marx remained convinced that social revolution must be associated with advanced industrial conditions.[31] Trotsky, nevertheless, would attempt to provide theoretical content to these suggestions from Marx and Engels. Moreover, unlike Marx and Engels--whose primary

---

*"The German bourgeoisie had developed so slothfully, cravenly and slowly that at the moment when it menacingly faced feudalism and absolutism it saw itself menacingly faced by the proletariat and all factions of the burghers whose interests and ideas were akin to those of the proletariat." Marx, "The Bourgeoisie and the Counter-Revolution," SW,Vol. I, pp. 139-140 and Engels, "The Role of Force in History," SW, Vol. III, pp. 417-420.

interest was Western Europe--Trotsky's theory would issue from the particularities of tsarist Russia and be subsequently universalized for underdeveloped countries in the course of the 1920s. Drawing upon the marxist tradition, contemporary intellectual sources and the revolutionary conditions of tsarist Russia, Trotsky formulated the essence of his theory of revolution or permanent revolution during the period from 1904 to 1906. Although the theory would undergo occasional adjustments over the years, the main features of the theory of permanent revolution--though the term itself would not be used at this time--can be found in Results and Prospects which was written in 1906 while he was in prison for charges stemming from his involvement in the revolution of 1905.*[32]

The theory of permanent revolution as described by Trotsky is essentially a theoretical expression of the law of uneven and combined development during the period of transition from capitalism to socialism or what Lenin called the epoch of "imperialism." Indeed, Trotsky would state in 1928 that the theory of permanent revolution "rested entirely" upon the law of uneven and combined development. Although he would not outline the main components of this law until the 1930's, a coup d'oeil at Results and Prospects would immediately reveal that it underlies Trotsky's whole theoretical outlook. What is the essence of this law? There are basically two interrelated components of this "law of the historic process": 1) unevenness in developmental processes flows from unequal rates of economic growth in the world which, in turn, result from differing socio-historical and natural conditions and 2) as a result of the "combining" of phenomena from societies of unequal development, the less developed society--under certain historical conditions--is able to break the historical pattern and make at the very least a temporary leap forward.

> A backward country assimilates the material and
> intellectual conquest of the advanced countries. But
> this does not mean that it follows them slavishly, re-
> produces all the stages of their past. Although com-
> pelled to follow after the advanced countries, a back-

---

*"In this brochure of eighty pages was the sum and substance of the man. For the rest of his days, as leader of the revolution, as founder and head of an army, as protagonist of a new international and then as hunted exile, he would defend and elaborate the ideas he had put in a nutshell in 1906." Isaac Deutscher, The Prophet Armed, p. 162.

ward country does not take things in the same order.
The development of historically backward nations leads
necessarily to a particular combination of different
stages in the historic process. Unevenness, the most
general law of the historic process, reveals itself
most sharply and complexly in the destiny of the backward countries. Under the whip of external necessity
their backward culture is compelled to make leaps.
From the universal law of unevenness thus derives another
law which, for the lack of combined development--by
which we mean a drawing together of the different
stages of the journey, a combining of separate steps,
an amalgam of archaic with more contemporary forms.
Without this law, to be taken of course in its whole
material content, it is impossible to understand the
history of Russia, and indeed of any country of the
second, third or tenth cultural class.[33]

Though not yet formulated in 1906, Trotsky, in analyzing
the "peculiarities" of Russia's social and economic development
was, in effect,applying this general "law of the historic process" to contemporary Russian and European history. "The
Russian revolution has quite a peculiar character, which is the
result of the peculiar trend of our entire social and historical
development, and which in its turn opens up before us quite new
historical prospects." What are the "peculiarities" of Russia's
social and economic development and what new "prospects" do they
entail for Russian society? Trotsky noted that Russian society--
unlike the "heroic period" of the West European bourgeoisies--
was unable to produce an independent, strong and forward looking
middle class which was both willing and able to take the lead of
the armed masses in the struggle against absolutism and the
survivals of serfdom. As he put it, "it was not the village
craftsman, nor even the rich merchant, but the state itself which
finally came face to face with the necessity of creating a large-
scale industry." Thus, it was the tsarist state--a peculiar combination of Asian and European absolutism--which, under the impact
of the military and economic encroachments from the West, began
the process of introducing large-scale industry in Russia.* As

---

*But Trotsky does not argue that this whole process was
purely the result of the action of the state because "if the
general course of the internal economy of this enormous country
had not been moving in this same direction, if the development of
economic conditions had not created the demand for general and
applied science, all the efforts of the state would have been
fruitless." What he observed in Russia's social and economic
development was a certain "primitiveness" and "slowness" but not

18

a result, whereas the bourgeoisies in the West were industrialists and bankers--having"organically" developed in the pores of the old absolutist society--the Russian bourgeoisie would consist essentially of professionals and state officials. The proletariat, however, is rapidly created as a result of the "grafting" of some of the most advanced techniques upon Russian soil. "The proletariat immediately found itself concentrated in tremendous masses, while between these masses and the autocracy there stood a capitalist bourgeoisie, very small in numbers, isolated from the 'people,' half-foreign, without historical traditions, and inspired only by the greed for gain."[34] Though a small minority of the population, it is increasingly concentrated in the towns and displays a "readiness to fight" which is uncharacteristic of the bourgeoisie.

As backward Russia was still awaiting its bourgeois revolution in the absence of a "national" bourgeoisie, Trotsky advanced his central thesis which stated that the historic tasks of the bourgeoisie--land reform, the establishing of democracy, industrialization, etc.--in 20th century Russia could be accomplished only in the framework of a proletarian revolution. Indeed, said Trotsky, "it is possible for the workers to come to power in an economically backward country sooner than in an advanced country." This, of course, represented a fundamental departure from the marxist theory of revolution. Yet it was introduced in an effort to concretely apply "marxism" to Russian conditions. Rejecting all "historical cliches," we would say marxism, Trotsky said that "the day and the hour when power will pass into the hands of the working class depends directly not upon the level attained by the productive forces but upon the international situation, and, finally, upon a number of subjective factors: the traditions, the initiative and the readiness to fight of workers."* To emphasize the need for the development

---

an inability for internally stimulated development. Trotsky, "Results," PR, pp. 36-37 and 42 and 1905, pp. 3-23.

*"There is no doubt that the numbers, the concentration, the culture and the political imporatnce of the industrial proletariat depend on the extent to which capitalist industry is developed. But this dependence is not direct. Between the productive forces of a country and the political strength of its classes there cut across at any given moment various social and political factors of a national and international character, and these displace and even sometimes completely alter the political expression of economic relations." Trotsky, "Results," PR, pp. 62-65.

of the productive forces as a prerequisite for social revolution
is to flirt with the "absurd." For Trotsky, therefore, political
factors and the state of international relations were much more
important as determining factors for a social revolution than the
level of economic development of a particular country.

Since Russia received its "capitalist baptism" late in the
19th century, the proletariat would be obliged to accomplish both
bourgeois and socialist tasks in the coming Russian revolution.
Would the proletariat--a tiny fraction of the population--need
allies in order to successfully complete its historic tasks?
There was no hesitation on Trotsky's part in recognizing the
necessity of forging an alliance between the working class and
the peasantry. What was in question was the nature and implications of the alliance. Who must lead? Who must follow? What
would be the composition of the new government? Trotsky emphasized again and again that the distinguishing features of this
alliance are that the working class must take the lead and that
"hegemony" in the new government must belong to the working class.
All of this flows from his conception of the role of the town in
modern society and the place of the proletariat in the town:

> While the peasantry is scattered over the entire
> countryside, the proletariat is concentrated in large
> masses in the factories and industrial centers. It
> forms the nucleous of the population of every town
> of any economic or political importance, and all the
> advantages of the town in a capitalist country--con-
> centration of the productive forces, the means of
> production, the most active elements of the popula-
> tion, and the greatest cultural benefits--are natural-
> ly transformed into class advantages for the prole-
> tariat.*

Therefore, steeled and consciously prepared as a result of its
daily struggles against both the bourgeoisie and the state power,
the proletariat--leading and in alliance with the peasant masses--
could win political power in backward Russia before this took
place in the advanced West. This was Trotsky's starting point in
1906.[35] But the international side--both political and economic--
of Trotsky's theory of revolution is as important as its national
side. The salvation of the "socialist dictatorship" does not
spring from an alliance with the peasantry. The alliance with
the peasantry is essential for the winning of political power in

---

*Indeed, for Trotsky, the peasantry is "absolutely incapable
of taking up an independent political role." Thus, he concluded
that "if we are forced to admit that the social contradictions

20

backward Russia. However, for the proletariat to remain in power
it must have political and economic support from the Western proletariat. "Without the direct state support of the European proletariat the working class of Russia cannot remain in power and
convert its temporary domination into a lasting socialist dictatorship." The Russian working class will need political support
from the European working class because its socialist dictatorship will meet determined opposition from two hostile forces:
world reaction and the peasantry. If it is understandable why
the Western bourgeoisie would want to crush the coming Russian
proletarian revolution, why is it also true that the peasantry
would want to bring down that government from which it received
its "emancipation?" The answer, said Trotsky, lies both in the
nature of the peasantry and in the nature of the tasks that the
proletariat in power must perform. "The proletariat [in power]
will begin with those reforms which figure in what is known as
the minimum program [bourgeois-democratic measures]; and directly from these the very logic of its position will compel it to
pass over to collectivist measures." A negative reaction begins
to set in among the peasant population once the working class
government begins to make "deep inroads" into bourgeois property.
As long as the struggle is being directed against the ancien
régime, the working class has the support of the entire peasantry
but once the old social order has been liquidated the individualism and the provincialism of the peasantry inevitably begins to
clash with the collectivism and internationalism of the proletarian state. For the peasantry the revolution stops at the
bourgeois phase but for the proletariat the revolution becomes
permanent.* The Russian working class will also need economic

----

between the proletariat and the peasant masses will not allow the
proletariat to become the leader of the peasantry, and that the
proletariat itself is not strong enough for victory, then we
must reach the conclusion that our revolution is not destined to
win at all." Trotsky, "Results," PR, pp. 70-73 and 1905, pp. 44,
50 and 279.

*"The primitiveness and petty bourgeois character of the
peasantry, its limited rural outlook, its isolation from world
political ties and allegiances, will create terrible difficulties
for the consolidation of the revolutionary policy of the proletariat in power." However, while emphasizing the proletariat in
power is in duty bound to "emancipate the peasantry," he curiously noted that the proletarian regime doesn't even consider the
"expropriation of small holdings" because to do so would be a
"very big blunder" and "at once set the mass of the peasantry
against the town proletariat." But are not the pesant masses inevitably obliged to turn against the proletariat? Is Trotsky
merely seeking to gain time while awaiting "direct support" from

support from the European working class. Although the proletariat, by the "very logic" of its rule, "places collectivism on the order of the day" Trotsky noted that "it would be absurd to suppose that it is only necessary for the proletariat to take power and then by passing a few decrees to substitute socialism for capitalism." While the law of uneven and combined development provides the framework for the possibility of the workers in backward Russia to win political power before the workers of the developed West, it is precisely this very law which compels the victorious working class government to recognize both the low level of economic development of backward Russia and the world-wide economic relations spawned by capitalism. "Binding all countries together with its mode of production and its commerce, capitalism has converted the whole world into a single economic and political organism." As such, if socialism is to be victorious in backward Russia, the working class—for both political and economic reasons—must "carry the revolution on to European soil."*36

III. Summary

The marxist and trotskyist theories of revolution are poles apart. Whereas the former concedes a preeminently economic dimension to revolution, the latter relies primarily on politics. For Marx there are three basic components to the revolutionary process: 1) the existence of modern large-scale industry, 2) a large working class movement independently and self-consciously organized as a result of its economic struggles against the capitalist class and 3) the existence of an economic crisis which springs from the "fetters" placed upon highly developed productive

---

the Western proletariat? Trotsky, "Results," PR, pp. 76-77 and 102-105.

*"Left to its own resources, the working class of Russia will inevitably be crushed by the counter-revolution the moment the peasantry turns its back on it. It will have no alternative but to link the fate of its political rule, and, hence, the fate of the whole Russian revolution, with the fate of the socialist revolution in Europe." Trotsky, "Results," PR, pp. 100, 108 and 115.

forces. Marx and Engels would sanction a social revolution only
upon the preliminary existence of these material and social conditions. "A radical social revolution is connected with definite
historical conditions of economic development; the latter are its
prerequisites [as we have outlined them above]. Therefore, it is
possible only where, alongside with capitalist production, the
industrial proletariat accounts for at least a considerable
portion of the people" [meaning the proletariat and the peasant-
ry]. How does Trotsky respond to Marx on the theme of social revolution? "It is true that, in Russia, the weakness of capitalist liberalism inevitably means the weakness of the labor movement? Is it true, for Russia, that there cannot be an independent labor movement until the bourgeoisie has conquered power?
It is sufficient merely to put these questions to see what a
hopeless formalism lies concealed beneath the attempt to convert
an historically-relative remark of Marx's into a supra-histori-
cal axiom." Though ostensibly responding to "textual marxists,"
he, in fact, is responding to the theory of revolution advanced
by Marx and Engels. To be sure, Trotsky agrees with Marx and
Engels that the "social conditions of Russia are still not ripe
for a socialist economy" but he does not agree with them that
the proletariat is incapable of establishing a dictatorship of
the proletariat in backward Russia.[37] As Russia is not "ripe"
for socialism, the dictatorship of the proletariat, said Trotsky,
must "give a strong impetus" to the proletarian movement in
Western Europe.[38] What would be the consequences for the Russian
proletarian dictatorship if this "impetus" was not felt in Western Europe? Would it not lead--as Marx and Engels predicted--to
the substitution of one form of exploitative society for another?

[1]Although there were clearly differences of style, emphasis and interests between Marx and Engels, the weight of their writings suggests that they were in basic agreement on most substantive questions. This applied most especially with regard to their theory of revolution. This point must be emphasized because there has been a considerable effort employed--especially in recent years--to separate Marx from Engels. Typical of the onslaught against Engels is a recent book by Norman Levine, The Tragic Deception: Marx contra Engels, p. 288, which has as its single purpose the separation of the two life-long collaborators. "Engelsian subjectivity. . . made of Engels the first revisionist. Engels was really the founder of the view that marxism was predestinarian economic determinism. He originated the school of positivist, dogmatic, necessitarian marxism, which was the dominant school of marxism for the Second International and subsequently for Soviet stalinists. In essence, Engels was the first 'vulgar marxist.'" Can we not say the same thing about Marx? Did he not say that "social relations are closely bound up with productive forces" and that "the hand-mill gives you society with the feudal lord; the steam-mill, society with the industrial capitalist?" Was not Marx, himself, the first "vulgar marxist?" To be sure, Engels did say that "all my life I have done what I was cut out for--namely to play second fiddle [to Marx]--and I think that I have done quite well in that capacity." Yet, in spite of Engels' claim of being merely an "interpreter" of Marx's theories, his contributions--as Marx recognized--were central to the ideas that they identified as "scientific socialism." Gustav Mayer, Frederick Engels, pp. 329-330, Frederic L. Bender, ed., The Betrayal of Marx, pp. 53-110, W.O. Henderson, The Life od Friedrich Engels, Vol. II, p. 657, David Riazanov, Karl Marx and Friedrich Engels, pp. 28-43, Shlomo Avineri, The Social and Political Thought of Karl Marx, pp. 65-66, George Lichtheim, Marxism, pp. 234-243, Marx, The Poverty of Philosophy, p. 95 and Engels, "The Housing Question," Marx and Engels, Selected Works, Vol. II, p. 297.

[2]One writer has aptly summed up the period between the French revolution and the revolutions of 1848 as the period of the "dual revolution." Hobsbawm noted that "the economy of the nineteenth century world was formed mainly under the influence of the British Industrial Revolution, its politics and ideology were formed mainly by the French. Britain provided the model for its railways and factories, the economic explosive which cracked open the traditional economic and social structure of the non-European world; but France made its revolutions and gave them their ideas, to the point where a tricolor of some kind became the emblem of virtually every emerging nation. . ." And Bloom correctly stated

that "if Marx appealed to the experience of England in order to
justify his theory of the development of capitalism, he was wont
to turn to the history of France to illustrate his views on the
growth of the modern state machinery, the political forms of the
class struggle, and the tactics of revolution." But it was perhaps Hegel, outstanding German philosopher, who had the single
most important impact on Marx's ideas. This can clearly be seen
on the question of the "dialectical method" of analysis. Both he
and Engels were always prepared to recognize that the "greatest
merit" of Hegel was his "restoration" of the dialectical method--
Engels, "Socialism: Utopian and Scientific," SW, Vol. III, p.
126--while at the same time setting themselves apart from Hegel.
"My dialectic method is not only different from the Hegelian,
but is its direct opposite"--Marx, Capital, Vol. I, p. 25.
Whether Marx actually dispensed with "the mystifying side of [the]
Hegelian dialectic" with its emphasis on the "Idea" as he claimed
--or remained "rooted in Hegel" (A.J. Gregor, A Survey of Marxism,
p. 151 and Max Eastman, Marxism: Is It Science, pp. 43-50)
continues to be a debated issue. Nevertheless, it seems clear
that Marx and Engels regarded the employment of dialectical method
as central to the analysis of social reality. But what is actually meant by the dialectical method? Is it as "scientific" as
Marx and Engels believed or does it not contain "an element
of mysticism" as Bober maintained? At the heart of the marxist
dialectic, Engels tells us, is the idea that "the world is not to
be comprehended as a complex of ready-made things, but as a complex of processes, in which the things apparently stable no less
than their mind images in our heads, the concepts, go through an
uninterrupted process of coming into being and passing away, in
which, in spite of all accidentality and of all temporary retro-
gression, a progressive development asserts itself in the end..."
The key is to find out what is progressive in a particular "contradiction" and promote its further development. But if "progressive" phenomena ultimately "assert itself in the end," why
bother? Furthermore, who is to decide what is and what is not
progressive? The marxist dialectic finds itself in the very "in-
curable contradiction" that it attributed to the hegelian dialectic. M.M. Bober, Karl Marx's Interpretation of History, pp.
44-45, E.J. Hobsbawm, The Age of Revolution, p. 53, Solomon F.
Bloom, The World of Nation, p. 115, Saul K. Padover, ed., Karl
Marx: On Revolution, p. 18, Engels, Anti-Duhring, pp. 31-35 and
"Ludwig Feuerback and the End of Classical German Philosophy," SW,
Vol. III, pp. 362-263 and Edmund Wilson, To the Finland Section,
pp. 210-233.

[3]Engels, "Socialism: Utopian and Scientific," SW, Vol. III,
p. 133. Marx and Engels considered history as ". . . nothing but
the succession of the separate generations, each of which exploits
the materials, the capital funds, the productive forces handed
down to it by all preceding generations, and thus, on the one hand,

continues the traditional activity in completely changed circumstances and, on the other hand, modifies the old circumstances with a completely changed activity." Marx and Engels, "The German Ideology," SW, Vol. I, p. 38.

[4]Engels would later say that all "written history" has been a history of class struggle. Engels, "Preface to Manifesto of 1883," SW, Vol. I, p. 101.

[5]"We set out from real, active men, and on the basis of their real-life process we demonstrate the development of the ideological reflexes and echoes of this life-process." Hunt rightly notes that Marx "never clearly worked out" what the real relationship is between the economic base and the superstructure. If Marx had, continues Hunt, "he would have had to abandon his theory" of history. One does not have to agree entirely with Hunt in order to recognize that Marx's theory of history is seriously flawed. Marx and Engels, "The German Ideology," SW, Vol. I, p. 25, Robert C. Tucker, ed. The Marx-Engels Reader, pp. 640-650, R.N. Carew Hunt, The Theory and Practice of Communism, p. 46, and A.J. Gregor, The Fascist Persuasion in Radical Politics, pp. 86-138.

[6]Marx and Engels did not always distinguish very clearly between the concepts of "productive forces" and "relations of production" though they tended to treat productive forces as instruments of labor and relations of production as the actual relations entered into the process of production. Both concepts represent the economic base which, in turn, is counterposed more or less to the ideological superstructure. Since the productive forces are treated as progressive and the relations of production as conservative in this contradictory relationship, one could conclude from some statements of the founders of "modern socialism" that humanity is but the plaything of historical and economic forces. While this is often said of Engels, it could just as easily be said of Marx. For example, in the work that, according to Marx, was designed to give a "theoretical blow" to the bourgeoisie he pointed out that "technology discloses man's mode of dealing with nature, the process of production by which he sustains his life, and thereby also lays bare the mode of formation of his social relations, and of the mental conceptions that flow from them." This statement (and others like it) poses problems when one realizes that Marx and Engels also emphasized that history is above all "the activity of man pursuing his aims." Marx, Capital, Vol. I, pp. 200 and 406, Engels, "Ludwig Feuerbach," SW, Vol. III, p. 366, Marx and Engels, "German Ideology," SW, Vol. I, p. 25 and "The Holy Family," Collected Works, Vol. IV, p. 93.

[7]Marx and Engels, Correspondence, p. 307 and Marx, Contribution to the Critique of Political Economy, pp. 210-211.

[8]"The bourgeois mode of production is the last antagonistic form of the social process of production. . . but the productive forces developing within bourgeois society create also the material conditions for a solution of this antagonism." Marx, Contribution, p. 21 and Engels, "Preface to Manifesto," SW, Vol. I, p. 101.

[9]Although Marx and Engels never developed a "systematic theory of class" (T.B. Bottomore, Classes in Modern Society, p. 13), it seems clear that they saw "class" in terms of production. One's class is defined not on the basis of income but primarily on one's place in the process of production. Thus, Engels says that "by bourgeoisie is meant the class of modern capitalists, owners of the means of social production and employers of wage-labor. By proletariat, the class of modern wage-laborers who, having no means of production of their own, are reduced to selling their labor-power in order to live." Marx, "Wage Labor and Capital," SW, Vol. I, pp. 159-160 and Engels, "Introduction to Class Struggles in France," and "Communist Manifesto," SW, Vol. I, pp. 180 and 190.

[10]Engels, "Socialism: Utopian and Scientific," SW, Vol. III, p. 134 and Marx and Engels, "Communist Manifesto," SW, Vol. I, pp. 113-114. Apart from the emergence of an independent merchant class, Marx cites the appearance of two key phenomena which were central to the rise of the capitalist system. On the one hand, there was the process of separating the producer from the land so that he "could only dispose of his own person after he had ceased to be the slave, serf, or bondsman of another" and on the other hand the process of accumulating wealth on a world scale so as to develop the nascent bourgeois industries. "The discovery of gold and silver in America, the extirpation, enslavement and entombment in mines of the aboriginal population, the beginning of the conquest and looting of the East Indies, the turning of Africa into a warren for the commercial hunting of black skins, signalized the rosy dawn of the era of capitalist production." Marx, Capital, Vol. I, pp. 786, 823 and 834 and Eric Williams, Capitalism and Slavery, pp. 98-107.

[11]Marx and Engels believed that with the advance of industry the proletariat not only would be strengthened numerically--partly through the "sinking" of other social classes into its rank--and organizationally but also consciously as a result of its increasing "immiseration" (however temporarily lightened) and the relative "openness" of the bourgeois society which provides a clear picture of the exploitative reality of this society. Marx and Engels, "Manifesto," SW, Vol. I, pp. 114-116 and 134, Capital, Vol. I, pp. 838-837 and Engels, "Critique of Draft S.D. Program of 1891," SW, Vol. III, p. 431.

27

[12]In the West, the bourgeoisie has fulfilled its "historic mission." Its task, says Marx, was "the establishment of the world market, at least in outline, and of production based upon that market." Had the bourgeoisie accomplished this task by 1848? Marx and Engels frequently spoke of the "imminence" of revolution during this period. However, by 1870 even the "metropolis of capital" was considered only to have reached a "certain degree of maturity" for social revolution. Engels was to observe a few years later that his and Marx's "youthful ardor" had led them to preach "imminent" social revolution during their barricade days. Engels, "Preface to Condition of the Working Class in England" and "Karl Marx," SW, Vol. III, pp. 85 and 445, Padover, ed., Karl Marx: On Revolution, p. 139, Marx and Engels, Correspondence, p. 223, and Engels, "Principles of Communism," SW, Vol. I, p. 85.

[13]T.B. Bottomore, ed., Karl Marx: Selected Writings in Sociology and Social Philosophy, p. 240 and Engels, The Peasant War in Germany, pp. 135-136 and "On Social Relations in Russia," SW, Vol. II, pp. 387-388. This idea runs like a red thread throughout the works of Marx and Engels. "Only at a certain level of development of the productive forces of society, an even very high level for our modern conditions, does it become possible to raise production to such an extent that the abolition of class distinctions can be a real progress, can be lasting without bringing about stagnation or even decline in the mode of social production." So long as the material conditions for social revolution do not exist "there must always be a dominant class ruling over the productive forces of society and a poor oppressed class." It would be difficult to be more precise on this theme. Marx, "The Future Results of British Rule in India," SW, Vol. I, p. 499 and Engels, "Principles of Communism," SW, Vol. I, p. 88.

[14]We consider marxism, for reasons which we will continue to enumerate throughout this work, as best suited for Western conditions of development. As such, leninism, stalinism, and trotskyism are all treated as essentially non-marxist in this work--except in the vaguest sense of having been inspired by marxism. Indeed, one can only wonder what Marx and Engels, were they alive today, would think of the futile attempts at applying "scientific socialism" (a term they preferred, especially Engels) to an Eastern setting. And this is exactly what leninisim, stalinism, and trotskyism, as will shortly be seen, was all about. As for Marx and Engels, "the great historical justification" for the existence of an exploiting social class is the "insufficiency" of production. We are told that "the last pretext has vanished for a division of mankind into rulers and ruled, exploiters and exploited, at least in the most advanced countries" [our emphasis]. To understand the significance of this point one need only take

a casual glance at those countries which have successfully undergone "marxist" revolutions. In fact, Marx and Engels not only
ruled out social revolution in the East--unless it occurred
simultaneously with revolutions in the West--but even the right
of oppressed nationalities to self-determination. There are three
basic points that ought to be understood when assessing Marx and
Engels' attitude towards the right to self-determination: 1) they
claimed that all forms of oppression, including the oppression of
small states or nations by large ones, would be resolved with the
coming of socialism. So, small states--following their logic--
ought to view the struggle for socialism as the road leading
towards national independence; 2) Marx and Engels tended to favor
large states over small states. After all socialism would be
built within the international framework spawned by capitalism;
3) lastly, they distinguished between "historical and "non-
historical" peoples. The latter--according to Marx and Engels,
especially Engels--were cultures that were "stagnant," "non-
dynamic," and devoid of a "progressive" dimension. Given their
generally racist views concerning people of color and the basic
thrust of their theory of revolution, it is not surprising that
Marx and Engels considered Eastern peoples to be largely outside
of "history." Eastern peoples can be brought into "history"
either through having been swept along following revolutionary
upheavals in the West or through colonial conquest on the part
of the West. Here is how Marx described England's "responsibility"
in the conquest of India: "England has to fulfill a double
mission in India: one destructive, the other regenerating--the
annihilation of the old Asiatic society, and the laying of the
material foundations of Western society in Asia." Even Russia,
that most "barbarous [semi-European] power" and the bete-noire
of Marx and Engels, has a certain "mission" to perform in the
East. "Russian rule, with all its nastiness, with all its
Slavonic filth, is civilizing for the Black and Caspian Seas, for
Bashkirs and [the] Tartars. . . ." While all of the above clearly
apply to the East, what about small states or nations in Europe?
Are they also outside of "history?" Do they have a right to
self-determination? Small states in Europe were considered
"within history" and as having the right to self-determination
if they contributed to the undermining of tsarist Russia--
referred to by Marx and Engels as the principal prop of "reaction"
throughout Europe--and were able to advance the cause of
"civilization." Although mostly out of political expediency, two
notable examples of small European states that Marx and Engels
came to recommend for political independence were Poland and
Ireland. For example, we have seen how important England was to
Marx's theory of revolution. While initially struggling for the
autonomy of Ireland, Marx eventually came to recognize that the
best means for "hastening" the revolution in England was through
struggling "to make Ireland independent" since the exploitation
and plunder of Ireland was "the cardinal means by which the
English aristocracy maintain their domination" in England. As

for their support for Polish independence, Carr correctly observed that "no revolutionary, no liberal of the nineteenth century could have done otherwise." The struggle for the political independence of Poland should be viewed in the context of Marx's anti-Russian and anti-Austrian strategy. Shlomo Avineri, ed., Karl Marx on Colonialism and Modernization, pp. 447 and 473, E.H. Carr, Studies in Revolution, p. 28, Miklos Molnar, Marx, Engels et la Politique Internationale, pp. 72-84, G. Haupt, M. Lowy, C. Weill, ed., Les Marxistes et la Question Nationale, p. 107, Horace B. Davis, Nationalism and Socialism: Marxist and Labor Theories of Nationalism to 1917, pp. 61-68, P.W. Blackstock and B.F. Hoseliz, ed., The Russian Menace to Europe, pp. 71-72 and 119, Marx, "The Future Results of British Rule in India," SW. Vol. I, pp. 494-495, Marx and Engels, Correspondence, pp. 221-223, Engels, "Karl Marx," SW, Vol. III, pp. 85-86 and "The Housing Question," SW, Vol. II, pp. 312-313.

[15]"Only the proletariat created by modern large-scale industry, liberated from all inherited fetters including those which chained it to the land, and herded together in big cities, is in a position to accomplish the great social transformation which will put an end to all class exploitation and all class rule." Engels, "The Housing Question," SW, Vol. II, p. 312. We observe in passing that Marx and Engels rarely used the expression "socialist revolution." They more often spoke of the coming "social revolution," "great social transformation" or the radical "reorganizing of society" and related expressions. The latter expressions were, perhaps, much more sweeping and comprehensive in implication that the expression "socialist revolution."

[16]"For the proletariat to be strong enough to win on the decisive day it must--and Marx and I have advocated this ever since 1847--form a separate party distinct from all others. . . ." Some thirty-eight years earlier, in 1851, Engels had observed that "a revolution is a pure phenomenon of nature that is led more by physical laws than by the rules which in ordinary times determine the development of society" [as cited by Wolfe]. Marx, on the other hand, noted on 1864 that "one element of success they [the working class] possess--numbers; but numbers weigh in the balance only if united by combination and led by knowledge" [our emphasis]. Six years later Marx gave more emphasis to this idea that the working class must be "led by knowledge" while stating that "the English have at their disposal all necessary material preconditions for a social revolution What they lack is the spirit of generalization and revolutionary passion." Marx is recognizing that his theory of revolution was in direct contradiction with British realities. While the material conditions for the social revolution exist, "the English proletariat is actuallv becoming more and more bourgeois" as it "gaily shares the feast"of Britain's

colonial policy. Must "socialist consciousness" now be bestowed
upon the British working class? Marx and Engels would not draw
this conclusion. However, can we not say that the ambiguities and
contradictions surrounding their conception of the role of the
party in the revolutionary process stem partly from their refusal
to treat the problem of "consciousness" in a serious and systematic way? Engels, "Principles of Communism," SW, Vol. I, p. 89
and :Letter to K. Kautsky," SW, Vol. III, p. 480, Marx and Engels,
Correspondence, pp. 103 and 386, Padover, ed., Karl Marx: On the
First International, pp. 11 and 172, Harold J. Laski, On the
Communist Manifesto, p. 61 and Bertram D. Wolfe, Marxism: 100
Years in the Life of a Doctrine, pp. 196-197.

[17]Marx and Engels, "Communist Manifesto," SW, Vol. I, pp.
115-118 and Laski, On the Communist Manifesto, p. 27.

[18]Marx noted that ". . . where the peasant exists in the mass
as a private property owner, where he even forms a more or less
substantial majority, as he does in all the states of the West
European continent, where he has not yet disappeared and been replaced by agricultural day laborers, as in England, the following
alternatives develop: either he prevents or frustrates every
workers' revolution, as he has hitherto done in France; or the
proletariat. . . must take governmental measures directly to improve the peasant's condition, so as to win him over to the revolution. . . ." And Marx hastens to add, "but the government
must not offend the peasant by proclaiming, for example, the
abolition of the right of inheritance or the abolition of his
property." Along similar lines, Engels said that "when we are in
possession of state power we shall not even think of forcibly ex-
propriating the small pesants, as we shall have to do in the case
of the big landowners. . . we shall not interfere in their property relations by force, against their will." Only through the
"dint of example"--via the effectiveness of state-run collectives--
will the peasantry be won over to collectivization. If a worker-
peasant alliance is going to be realized clearly the responsibility for both its initiation and success rest exclusively upon
the working class. Engels, "Critique of Draft S.D. Program of
1891," SW, Vol. III, p. 439 and "Peasant Question in France and
Germany," SW, Vol. III, pp. 470-471, Marx "The Class Struggles in
France," SW, Vol. I, pp. 277 and 288-289 and Padover, ed., Karl
Marx: On the First International, p. xxxvii.

[19]Henderson, The Life of Friedrich Engels, Vol. I, pp. 346-
347, Padover, ed., Karl Marx: On the First International, p. 171
and Marx and Engels, "On Poland," Collected Works, Vol. VI, p.
389.

[20]"The fact that the socialized organization of production within the factory has developed so far that it has become incompatible with the anarchy of production in society, which exists side by side with and dominates it, is brought home to the capitalists themselves by the violent concentration of capital that occurs during crises, through the ruin of many large, and a still greater number of small, capitalists. The whole mechanism of the capitalist mode of production breaks down under the pressure of the productive forces, its own creations." Marx, Capital, Vol. I, pp. 836-837 and "General Rules of the International Working Men's Association," SW, Vol. II, p. 19, Engels, Anti-Dühring, pp. 327-328, "Principles of Communism," SW, Vol. I, p. 88 and "Revolution and Counter-Revolution in Germany," SW, Vol. I, pp. 300-301.

[21]"One can conceive that the old society may develop peacefully into the new one in countries where the representatives of the people concentrate all power in their hands, where, if one has the support of the majority of the people, one can do as one sees fit in a constitutional way: in democratic republics such as France and the U.S.A., in monarchies such as Britain, where the imminent abdication of the dynasty in return for financial compensation is discussed in the press daily and where this dynasty is powerless against the people." For a while Engels opposed advocating such a policy for Germany because to do so would be like removing the "fig-leaf" from the "naked absolutism" that characterized the Bismarck regime. But with the departure of Bismarck and his repressive legislation and the rush of workers' representatives to the parliament, Engels began to change tunes. He now said that "our party [German Social Democrats] is like a great flood which is bursting all the dams that hold it in check and which is flooding both urban and rural districts and penetrating even the most reactionary agrarian regions. Today the growth of the party enables us to predict with almost mathematical certainty the date on which it will achieve power" [our emphasis]. Furthermore, continued Engels, "force of arms can suppress a minor movement operating in a limited area but it cannot wipe out a party supported by two or three million voters spread all over the territories of the German Reich." Old methods of struggle--such as pitched battles at the barricades--are "to a considerable extent" outdated. The bourgeoisie seems to be more afraid of the legal rather than illegal action of the working class. Thus, wherever possible, the weapon to be employed now is the vote. Marxism finally appeared to have penetrated the European continent. But was this the same proletariat described by Marx and Engels in 1848? Why should this "bourgeois proletariat"--partly acknowledged by Marx and Engels--risk its present for an uncertain future. Engels, "Critique of Draft S.D. Program of 1891," SW, Vol. III, p. 434, "Peasant Question in France and Germany," SW, Vol. III, p. 458, "Introduction to the Class Struggles in France," SW, Vol. I, pp. 194-201 and The Condition of the Working-Class

in England, p. 40, Henderson, The Life of Friedrich Engels, Vol. II, pp. 798-800 and Alfred G. Meyer, Communism, pp. 25-26.

[22]"In general, the question is not whether the proletariat when it comes to power will simply seize by force the instruments of production, the raw materials and the means of subsistence, whether it will pay immediate compensation for them or whether it will redeem the property therein by small installment payments. To attempt to answer such a question in advance and for all cases would be utopia-making, and that I leave to others." Engels, "Principles of Communism," SW, Vol. I, p. 90, "Peasant Question in France and Germany," SW, Vol. III, p. 474 and "The Housing Question," SW, Vol. II, p. 370.

[23]". . . the class dictatorship of the proletariat. . . [is] the necessary transit point to the abolition of class distinctions generally. . . ." Marx, "Class Struggles in France," SW, Vol. I, p. 528 and "Critique of the Gotha Program," SW, Vol. III, p. 26.

[24]Since the state is primarily the product of "the split of society into classes," it could be for Marx and Engels "nothing but a machine for the oppression of one class by another, and indeed in the democratic republic no less than in the monarchy." And if necessary, said Marx, the bourgeoisie is prepared to suspend democracy in order "to restore tranquility in the country" so as to "save its purse." Democracy remains, therefore, a weapon to screen the class rule of the bourgeoisie. Having said this, however, neither Marx nor Engels would say that it made no difference to the proletariat whether it lived under a monarchy or a bourgeois democratic republic. "The political freedoms, the right of assembly and association, and the freedom of the press-- those are our weapons. Are we to sit back and abstain while somebody tries to rob us of them?" To pose the question was to answer it. Though the working class party must not be the "tagtail of any bourgeois party," Engels said that it should support all struggles "as regards economic development or political freedom." Central to their "defense" of the democratic republic over other forms of bourgeois political rule is that it "would make easier for the communists the defense, discussion and spread of their principles, and thereby the unification of the proletariat in a compact, combative and well-organized class" in preparation for its capture of political power. Political democracy--even "bourgeois"--must be defended but its best defense is through the establishment of the dictatorship of the proletariat. Engels, "Principles of Communism," SW, Vol. I, pp. 96-97, "Apropos of Working Class Political Action," SW, Vol. II, pp. 245-246, "Introduction to the Civil War in France," SW, Vol. II, p. 189, "Origin of the Family, Private Property and State," SW, Vol. III, p. 330 and "The Role of Force in History," SW, Vol. III, p. 383,

Marx, "The Eighteenth Brumaire of Louis Bonaparte," <u>SW</u>, Vol. I, pp. 436 and 466, Marx and Engels, <u>Correspondence</u>, pp. 386-387 and Meyer, <u>Leninism</u>, pp. 60-61.

[25]Only very rarely did Marx and Engels use the expression, "dictatorship of the proletariat." More often they wrote about the coming "political rule of the proletariat." When the expression dictatorship of the proletariat was used, it was most often used to contrast Marx's concept of proletarian political rule with that of the rule of a revolutionary minority being advocated by the well-known French revolutionary, Auguste Blanqui and his followers. Marx and Engels used the example of the short-lived Paris Commune of 1871 to provide a certain concreteness to their concept of proletarian political rule. Among the essentail political features of the Paris Commune that was born in the context of the Franco-Prussian War of 1870-71 were: a) abolition of the standing army, b) election of all officials on the bais of universal suffrage and right of immediate recall and c) no elected official received wages any higher than that of a skilled worker. On the basis of these and related measures Marx declared that the Commune represented "the political form at last discovered under which to work out the economic emancipation of labor." Marx, in an earlier work, had stressed that all revolutions had "perfected" rather than "smashed" the old state apparatus. The supreme merit of the Communards was that they not only smashed the old state apparatus but introduced the "political form" needed for the elimination of wage slavery. Later, Engels would bluntly refer to this new "political form" as the dictatorship of the proletariat. "Look at the Paris Commune. That was the dictatorship of the proletariat." Curiously, however, Marx's attitude towards the Commune was not altogether consistent. Immediately after the fall of Bonaparte and just prior to the establishment of the Commune, he had cautioned the French workers against the "desperate folly" of "upsetting the new [republican] government." But with the establishment of the Commune he would let it be known that "history has no like example of like greatness." Yet ten years later Marx would say that the Paris Commune was "merely a revolt of a city under exceptional conditions" which perhaps could have accomplished something "useful for the whole mass of the people" if the Communards had had the "common sense" to reach a "compromise" with the central government. Despite these apparent contradictions in their attitude toward the Paris Commune, Marx and Engels would appropriate--as other nineteenth century revolutionary movements would do--the experiences of the Commune as their own. Padover, ed., <u>Karl Marx: On Revolution</u>, p. 66, Marx, "The Civil War in France," <u>SW</u>, Vol. II, pp. 200 and 220-224, "Marx to L. Kugelman," <u>SW</u>, Vol. II, p. 420 and "The Eighteenth Brumaire of Louis Bonaparte," <u>SW</u>, Vol. I, p. 477, Engels, "Introduction to the Civil War in France," <u>SW</u>, Vol. II, p. 189, Richard N. Hunt, <u>The Political Ideas of Marx and</u>

Engels, Vol. I, pp. 337-342, Lichtheim, Marxism, pp. 112-121 and Hal Draper, "Marx and the Dictatorship of the Proletariat," New Politics, Vol. I, No. 4 (Summer, 1962), pp. 91-104.

[26]"All socialists are agreed that the political state, and with it political authority, will disappear as a result of the coming social revolution, that is, that public functions will lose their political character and be transformed into the simple administrative functions of watching over the true interest of society." As soon as proletarian class rule has ended, "the government of persons is replaced by the administration of things." Though Marx and Engels did't emphasize the "repressive" side of the dictatorship of the proletariat, occasionally one finds a few references. ". . . So long as the proletariat still uses the state, it does not use it in the interests of freedom but in order to hold down its adversaries. . . ." Moreover, "if the victorious party does not want to have fought in vain, it must maintain this rule by means of the terror which its arms inspire in the reactionaries." However, Engels' remarks, though contradictory, should be seen in the broader context of his and Marx's defense of political democracy--as we have already indicated. The general orientation of their position on the dictatorship of the proletariat was that its primary purpose was to unleash the productive potentialities of modern industry and agriculture inherited from the capitalist era. As Engels put it, "once liberated from the yoke of private ownership, large-scale industry will develop on a scale that will make its present level of development seem as paltry as seems the manufacturing system compared with large-scale industry of our time." Marx and Engels, "Fictitious Splits in the International," SW, Vol. II, p. 285, Engels, "Principles of Communism," SW, Vol. I, p. 92, "On Authority," SW, Vol. II, p. 379, "Introduction to the Civil War in France," SW, Vol. II, p. 189, "Letter to A. Bebel," SW. Vol. III, p. 35, "Introduction to Wage Labor and Capital," SW, Vol. I, p. 149, Anti-Dühring, pp. 332-336, Padover, ed., Karl Marx: On the First International, p. xxxviii, and Kazem Radjavi, La Dictature du Prolétariat et le Dépérissement de l'État de Marx a Lenine, p. 67.

[27]Leon Trotsky, Writings of Leon Trotsky [1939-40], pp. 158-159.

[28]Trotsky, "Results and Prospects," The Permanent Revolution, p. 64.

[29]"While the democratic petty bourgeois wish to bring the revolution to a conclusion as quickly as possible. . . it is our interest and our task to make the revolution permanent, until all more or less possessing classes have been forced out of their

position of dominance, until the proletariat has conquered state power, and the association of proletarians, not only in one country but in all the dominant countries of the world, has advanced so far that the competition among the proletarians of these countries has ceased and that at least the decisive productive forces are concentrated in the hands of the proletarians." Marx and Engels, "Address of the C.C. to the Communist League," SW, Vol. I, pp. 178-179 and 184-185 and Marx, "The Class Struggles in France," SW, Vol. I, p. 282.

[30]Marx and Engels, "Manifesto," SW, Vol. I, p. 137.

[31]It is interesting, also, to contrast Trotsky's appreciation of 1848 with that of Marx and Engels. Commenting on the bourgeoisie, Trotsky said that "it not only failed to lead the masses in storming the old order, but placed its back against this order so as to repulse the masses who were pressing it forward." Engels, however, came from another angle. He said that "the state of economic development on the Continent at that time was not, by a long way, ripe for the elimination of capitalist production; it has proved this by the economic revolution which, since 1848, has seized the whole of the Continent, and has caused big industry to take real root in France, Austria, Hungary, Poland and recently, in Russia, while it has made Germany positively an industrial country of the first rank--all on a capitalist basis, which in the year 1848, therefore, still had great capacity for expansion." As a result of the absence of material conditions, "the fruits of the revolution [of 1848] were reaped by the capitalist class." Trotsky, to be sure, acknowledged that capitalism in 1848 had not "sufficiently" developed to allow the weakly organized and inexperienced proletariat to supplant the cowardly bourgeoisie. But, unlike Marx and Engels, he does not give supreme attention to the economic dimensions of a social revolution. Trotsky, "Results," PR, pp. 55-57, Engels, "Introduction to the Class Struggles in France," SW, Vol. I, pp. 191-192, "Preface to the Manifesto," SW, Vol. I, p. 106 and Padover, ed., Karl Marx: On Revolution, p. 59.

[32]Like Marx and Engels before him, Trotsky freely acknowledged his intellectual debt to some of the outstanding 19th and 20th century thinkers. Apart from Marx and Engels, there are at least three of them that should be briefly mentioned: 1) Antonio Labriola, Italian socialist philosopher and author of the well-known Essays on the Materialist Conception of History, 2) Ferdinand Lassalle, a key figure in the German working class movement and founder of the first independent national labor organization and 3) Alexander I. Helphand (Parvus), Russian émigré and an influential leader of the left-wing of the German social democratic party. Reflecting on the "delight" he had in reading Labriola's writings on the materialist conception of history Trotsky noted that "un-

like most Latin writers, Labriola had mastered the materialist
dialectics, if not in politics. . . at least in the philosophy of
history. . . . He made short work. . . of the theory of multiple
factors which were supposed to dwell on the Olympus of history
and rule our fates from there. . . . After Labriola, all the
Russian proponents of the multiplicity of factors. . . seemed
utterly ineffectual to me." He increasingly came to reject the
"textual marxists" after having read Labriola. What impressed
Trotsky about Lassalle was that he had recognized the frailty of
seeking an alliance with the liberal bourgeoisie and had thus
called for and organized a strong, independent, working class
movement in Germany. Lassalle, himself, said that "it is in the
greatest interest of political freedom to mobilize a class interest, a social interest and, in particular, the interest of the
propertyless classes which predominate in sheer numbers and
[potential] power. . . . I am turning against the sleepy and
feeble movement which the bourgeoisie promotes as a class and can
only promote as a class, the liberal-progressive movement." However, it was Parvus who had the greatest influence upon Trotsky
in the shaping of the theory of permanent revolution. Trotsky
was quick to observe that "there is no doubt that he [Parvus]
exerted considerable influence on my personal development, especially with respect to the social-revolutionary [marxist] understanding of our epoch." There are three specific areas in which
Parvus' influence prevailed upon Trotsky: 1) on the reasons for
the impotence of the Russian bourgeoisie and why the proletariat
would play the leading role in the coming Russian revolution,
2) on the nature of the global unity of the world market and its
significance for world revolution and 3) on the vanguard role of
the Russian proletariat in the coming world revolution. Though it
is clear that Trotsky borrowed considerably from Parvus, they,
however, disagreed on two basic points: 1) Parvus' negative appreciation of the necessity for an alliance between the working class
and the peasantry and 2) his conception that the coming Russian
revolution--though accomplished by the working class--would confine itself to bourgeois tasks. In any event, the "intellectual
partnership" between Parvus and Trotsky would begin to progressively deteriorate from 1906 until the ultimate break in 1914 when
Parvus supported the war faction in the German parliament during
the First World War. Trotsky, My Life, p. 119, Stalin, pp. 429-
Deutscher, The Prophet Armed, pp. 103-104, Guenther Roth, The
Social Democrats in Imperial Germany, pp. 42-44, G.D.H. Cole,
Socialist Thought: Marxism and Anarchism, pp. 71-87, Alain Brossat,
Aux Origine de la Révolution Permanent, pp. 94-95 and Z.A.B. Zeman,
and W.B. Scharlau, The Merchant of Revolution: The Life of A.I.
Helphand (Parvus), pp. 110-111.

[33]Trotsky, History of the Russian Revolution, Vol. I, p. 5
and The Permanent Revolution, pp. 149 and 241. Although Marx and
Engels--unlike Trotsky--did not formulate a specific law of un-

even development, it is not true--as Stalin would later claim--
that they were unaware of the significance of unevenness in the
historic process and especially under capitalist conditions. "It
is evident that big industry does not reach the same level of development in all districts of a country. This does not, however,
retard the class movement of the proletariat, because the proletarians created by big industry assume leadership of this movement and carry the whole mass along with them, and because the
workers excluded from big industry are placed by it in a still
worse situation than than the workers in big industry itself. The
countries in which big industry is developed act in a similar
manner upon the more or less non-industrial countries, insofar
as the latter are swept by universal commerce into the universal
competitive struggle." Marx and Engels, "The German Ideology,"
SW, Vol. I, p. 62 and Engels, Anti-Dühring, pp. 321-322.

[34]"Only 15 percent of the total number of the existing
Russian industrial enterprises were created before 1861. Between
1861 and 1880, 23.5 per cent were created, and more than 61
percent between 1881 and 1900, 40 per cent of all existing enterprises having been created during the last decade of the nineteenth century alone." Trotsky, 1905, pp. 18-20 and "Results,"
PR, p. 51.

[35]It should be noted that Trotsky's conception of the revolutionary political party and its role in the struggle for the
dictatorship of the proletariat will be discussed in the next
chapter. However, during the period from 1904 to 1906--when he
formulated the essence of his theory of revolution--he would
sharply counterpose leninist "substitutionism" with the "self-
activity" of the working class (which he clearly favored at this
time). What is sufficient to point out at this time is that,
for Trotsky, socialist consciousness would develop "on the basis
of unceasing class struggle." There is no conception of the
necessity for a vanguard party to bestow socialist consciousness
upon an unenlightened working class. Trotsky, Nos Tâches Politiques, p. 128 and "Results," PR, pp. 88-90 and 98.

[36]Years later he would point out that "from the world-wide
division of labor, from the uneveness of development of different
countries, from their mutual economic dependence, from the uneveness of different aspects of culture in the different countries,
from the dynamic of the contemporary productive forces, it
follows that the socialist structure can be built only by a system of economic spiral, only by taking the inner discords of a
separate country out into a whole group of countries, only by a
mutual service between different countries, and a mutual supplementation of the different branches of their industry and cul-
ture--that is, in the last analysis, only on the world arena."

Trotsky, <u>History of the Russian Revolution</u>, Vol. III, p. 413.

[37]Marx, "From Comments on Bakunin's Book," <u>SW</u>, Vol. II, pp. 411-412 and Trotsky, "Results," <u>PR</u>, pp. 64 and 67.

[38]Trotsky, "Results," <u>PR</u>, pp. 105, 108 and 115.

CHAPTER II

THE BOLSHEVIK REVOLUTION:

MARXISM TURNED INSIDE OUT

I. Bolshevism and Marxism

The leninist theory of revolution represents a fundamental departure from the theory of revolution of Marx and Engels. Indeed, Lenin--like Trotsky--introduced a new doctrinal system. This theory of revolution began to take shape right at the beginning of this century but would crystallize only in the course of Russia's 1905 revolution. There are three basic components in the leninist theory of revolution: 1) the necessity of a vanguard political party as the agency of socialist consciousness which directs the working class movement both organizationally and ideologically, 2) the conception that Russia's belated bourgeois revolution would be accomplished by the democratic dictatorship of the proletariat and peasantry which, in turn, resulted from a revolutionary alliance between the proletariat and pesantry under the leadership of the proletariat and its vanguard political party, and 3) the idea that the objective basis for revolution--whether bourgeois or socialist*--springs from the existence of a revolutionary situation. Lenin will make certain adjustments to this theory beginning with the period of the First World War--particularly in 1917--and again around 1920.

Before examining the basic components of this theory of revolution, we should point out that prior to 1905 Lenin--with the notable exception of his idea of a vanguard political party-- held the position that the Russian bourgeoisie not only had a leading role to play in the coming bourgeois revolution but that it would exercise political power after the completion of that revolution. The proletariat would begin its bid for political power only when it emerged from the womb of bourgeois society. This, of course, was the standard marxist argument. Yet, Marx and Engels, themselves, seemed to have progressively

---

*Lenin--unlike Marx and Engels--often referred to the coming "socialist revolution." We suggested in Chapter I that the expressions used by Marx and Engels concerning the coming revolution--"the great social transformation," "social revolution," "reorganizing society," etc.--were much more sweeping than the seemingly narrow political expression of the coming "socialist revolution."

moved away from this rigid position on the coming Russian revolution. They stated that the Russian Mir (village commune)--
under the impact of the world revolution--could conceivably serve
as the starting point for an advancement towards socialism without Russia's having undergone the agony of capitalist development.
To be sure Marx and Engels didn't agree with the kind of "peasant
socialism" preached by the narodniks or populists.* But why this
"quasi-narodnik deviation?" Baron suggests that Marx might have
deliberately "refrained from attacking the theoretical position

----

*The Russian populist movement was born in the 1870's. Basing
themselves upon the village commune and the virtually "instinctively" rebellious peasantry, the populists stated that Russian
"exceptionalism" would prevail over traditional Western developmental processes towards socialism. Described by Venturi as "one
of the most precise accounts we have of the populists' view of
the revolution for which they are fighting," the following statement by Peter Lavrov, a leading populist, clearly highlights the
basic disagreements between the populist and marxist theories of
revolution: "A local disturbance on a big enough scale is supported by risings which break out simultaneously in other parts of
the country. . . . [The defeat of the army] leads to the fire
spreading quickly over a vast area. Under the leadership of organized members of the Social-Revolutionary Union made up mostly
of peasants, groups of people who want a social revolution appear in the villages with instructions to turn all private estates into 'communal, undivided land' and to merge all property
'into a single property of all the workers.' This call, backed by
the news of the successes of the revolution in other villages,
arouses over a vast area the unemployed, the poorest members of
the families, destitute peasants, those who now, despite hard
work, have no means of feeding themselves every day of the year;
and, finally, the majority of workmen and small townsfolk" [our
emphasis]. Furthermore, Peter Tkachov, another populist, said
that a revolutionary "must regard himself as right to summon the
people to an uprising; what distinguishes him from the philistine
philosopher is just this, that without waiting until the current
of historical events itself indicates the moment, he selects it
himself." Cole observed that there is no wonder that "these
views have laid Lavrov [and other populists] open to strong attack from every generation of marxists." G.D.H. Cole, Socialist
Thought: Marxism and Anarchism, p. 55, Franco Venturi, Roots of
Revolution: A History of the Populist and Socialist Movements in
Nineteenth Century Russia, p. 463, Oliver H. Radkey, The Agrarian
Foes of Bolshevism, pp. 3-23 and F.I. Dan, The Origins of Bolshevism, p. 89.

of the narodniks in order not to demoralize a group that was
striving actively to overthrow the Russian depotism he so des-
pised."[1] Whatever the real reason, Marx and Engels would cling
to their basic views on the coming Russian revolution. Lenin--
basing himself on the work of Plekhanov*--was likewise convinced
in his assessment of the economic characteristics of the Russian
countryside and on the meaning that this would have for revolutionary developments in Russia. As far as he was concerned capitalism was forging ahead in Russia. "One can 'greet' the capitalism developing in Russia only in two ways: one can regard it
either as progressive, or as retrogressive; either as a step forward on the right road, or as a deviation from the true path. . ."
For Lenin it was progressive and a step forward. And contrary to
the ideas of the populists, not only was the market already
[1893] the "regulator of social production' in the countryside
but it was "inevitable" that the peasantry be exploited under
this new economic orientation. "The wider and more deeply capi-
talim developed, the more distinctly did the countryside display
the contradictions common to every commodity-capitalist society,
the more and more glaringly did the antithesis stand out between
the narodniks' honeyed talk about the peasants' 'community spirit'
. . . [as opposed to] the actual division of the peasantry into
a rural bourgeoisie and a rural proletariat. . . ."[2] Indeed,
argued Lenin, the most important task confronting Russain social
democracy--as the marxist movement was then identified--was to
bring the bourgeoisie to power and thus deepen the class divi-
sions both in the countryside and towns so as to prepare the proletariat for its future showdown with the bourgeoisie. He wrote
in 1895 that "the main obstacle in the struggle of the Russian
working class for its emancipation is the absolutely autocratic
government" which is retarding the "development of capitalism
and consequently the development of the working class." It
would be "advantageous to the workers for the bourgeoisie to openly influence policy. . . ." Therefore, social democrats "support

---

*Plekhanov, who "laid the foundations of Russian marxism"
pointed out in one of his major works, Our Differences, that
"dear Peter Lavrov" and other populists were off base in their
idealization of the village commune. Indeed, capitalism is
favored "by the whole dynamic of our social life." This trend
"cannot be stopped" but it can be channeled towards the future
proletarian revolution. G. Plekhanov, Selected Philosophical
Works, Vol. I, pp. 238-275 and Baron, Plekhanov, p. 89.

the progressive social classes against the reactionary classes, the bourgoisie against the representatives of privileged land-owning estate and the bureaucracy, <u>the big bourgeoisie against the reactionary strivings of the petty bourgeoisie</u>" [our emphasis].* After making this statement, Lenin hastens to add that "this solidarity [with the bourgeoisie] is temporary and conditional" and notes that in the final analysis only the proletariat can be "a consistently democratic, determined enemy of absolutism, incapable of making any concessions or compromises."** Despite these qualifications it seems clear that it is with the bourgeoisie and not the petty bourgeoisie (including the peasantry) that the working class would look for sure allies in it struggle for political liberty and the elimination of the "survivals of serfdom." Lenin, to be sure, did say that "the working class party should inscribe on its banner support for the peasantry" and argued for "carrying the class struggle into the country-side." But he tells us that "it would be senseless to make the peasantry the vehicle of the revolutionary movement [and that]. . . a party would be insane to condition the revolutionary character of its movement upon the revolutionary mood of the peasantry." In truth he seemed more concerned at this time with merely winning over the "revolutionary elements" among the peasantry than would be the case after 1905.[3]

During this period Lenin also advanced the main features of his conception of the working class political party. Although his ideas on the organizational question were increasingly in circulation within the social democratic movement before the convening of the party congress in 1903--especially as a result of the publication of <u>What Is To Be Done</u> in 1902--it was during this congress in the context of a fight over the overhauling of

---

*"The petty bourgeoisie is two-faced by its very nature, and while it gravitates, on the one hand, towards the proletariat and democracy, on the other, it gravitates towards the reaction-ary classes, tries to hold up the march of history, is apt to be seduced by the experiments and blandishments of the autocracy." Though he cautions the proletariat that the bourgeoisie might "at any moment" enter into an alliance with the autocracy he nevertheless would state that "the proletariat must support the constitutional movement of the bourgeoisie."

**"While rendering support to all representatives of the bourgeoisie in the fight for political freedom, the workers should remember that the propertied classes can only be their allies for a time, that the interest of the workers and the capitalists cannot be reconciled, that the workers need the abolition of the government's absolute rule only in order to wage an open and extensive struggle against the capitalist class." Lenin, "Draft

the leadership and the nature of the party statutes that, for all
practical purposes, irrevocably split the Russian social democratic organization into two warring factions. Yet, as we shall
presently see, organizational differences were only the visible
side of a much deeper split over strategy and tactics in the
coming Russian revolution. For now, Lenin and the bolsheviks--
who ultimately won a "majority" at the party congress on the
issues at stake--insisted that the "concept party member must be
narrowed so as to separate those who worked from those who merely
talked." Martov, representing the mensheviks--or "minority"--
insisted that "the wider the title of party member is spread, the
better. We could but rejoice if every striker or demonstrator. . .
could declare himself a party member." Lenin favored a "narrow"
political party and Martov favored a "broad" political party.*
But it should be remembered that this dispute centered around

---

and Explanation of Program of the S.D. Party," Vol. II, pp. 96
and 118-120, "The Tasks of the Russian Social Democrats," Vol. II,
pp. 334-337 and "The Autocracy and the Proletariat," Vol. VIII,
pp. 24-27.

*"It is better that ten workmen should be unable to call
themselves party members--what do ranks and titles mean to a
genuine working man?--than that one chatterbox should have the
right to call himself a member. . . . What we have to do is to
preserve the purity, strength and consistency of our party. We
must aim to raise higher and even higher the importance and
dignity of party membership--and that is why I am against Martov's
formula." But Lenin made it clear that he was not opposed to
"broad" organizations as such. "We need the most diverse organizations of all types, ranks and shades, beginning with extremely
limited and secret and ending with very broad, free, loose
organizations." As an example he noted that it was not in "our
interest" to insist that "only social democrats should be eligible
for membership in the 'trade' unions since that would only narrow
the scope of our influence upon the masses." Martov, on the
other hand, was not inherently opposed to the kind of narrowly
based organization proposed by Lenin. How could he be in
autocratic Russia? "To my mind, a clandestine organization only
makes sense in so far as it is the nucleous of a large social
democratic workers' party. . . . I agree with Lenin that in
addition to organizations of professional revolutionaries we need
'loose organizations' of various types. But our formula is the
only one to reflect our aim to have the organization of professional revolutionaries linked with the masses by a series of
other organizations" [our emphasis]. Lenin, "What Is To Be
Done," Vol. V, p. 54, "Second Congress of the R.S.D.L.P.,"
Vol. VI, pp. 489-502 and "Account of the Second Congress of the
R.S.D.L.P.," Vol. VII, p. 27, Abraham Ascher, ed., The Mensheviks

the kind of organization to be employed and not on that of organization versus no organization. Lenin insisted that the political conditions of Russia and the tasks of the prletarian party did not auger well for the kind of open ended organization proposed by the mensheviks. "Disunited by the rule of anarchic competition in the bourgeois world, ground down by forced labor of capital, constantly thrust back to the 'lower depths' of utter destitution, savagery and degeneration, the proletariat can, and inevitably will, become an invincible force only through its ideological unification on the principles of marxism. . . ." But this "grounded down" proletariat can reach these marxist principles "only from without, that is, only from outside the economic struggle, from outside the sphere of relations between workers and employers."* And only a small, secret and disciplined organization of professional revolutionaries--armed with the "most advanced theory"--is capable of bestowing this socialist consciousness upon the working class.** Whereas Marx and Engels had said that socialist consciousness would be merely an "outgrowth" of the economic struggles of the working class, Lenin now argues that this consciousness must be brought to the working class "from without" by a vanguard party "which directs its struggle both ideologically and practically."[4] This idea of a vanguard party is the central thesis in the leninist theory of revolution. Indeed the essence of leninism is expressed in his famous battle-cry, "give us an organization of revolutionaries and we will overturn Russia."[5] With the approach of 1905, therefore,

---

in the Russian Revolution, pp. 46-47, Israel Getzler, Martov, p. 79, Allan K. Wildman, The Making of a Workers' Revolution, pp. 98-102 and Pierre Broué, Le Parti Bolchevique, pp. 29-43.

*"We have said that there could not have been social democratic consciousness among the workers. It would have to be brought to them from without. The history of all countries shows that the working class, exclusively by its own effort, is able to develop only trade union consciousness, i.e., the conviction that it is necessary to combine in unions, fight the employers, and strive to compel the government to pass necessary labor legislation, etc." Lenin, "What Is To Be Done," Vol. V, p. 375 and "One Step Forward, Two Steps Back," Vol. VII, p. 412.

**Lenin would later define the "iron discipline" of the bolshevik party as "democratic centralism." This expression, which has become somewhat of a leninist shibboleth, implies full freedom of criticism and discussion within the party but "rules out all criticism which disrupts or makes difficult the unity of an action decided on by the party." Lenin, "Freedom to Criticize and Unity of Action," Vol. X, p. 443.

Lenin's conception of the coming Russian revolution does not differ in essentials from that generally accepted within the social democratic movement. The real difference--as we have indicated--between Lenin and the mensheviks (as his opponents would be designated) centered on the question as to whether or not a vanguard party was needed as the historical agency of socialist consciousness. 1905, however, would reveal more important differences on their conceptions of the coming bourgeois revolution.

The Russian 1905 revolution took place against the background of an unsuccessful war against Japan and continuing social and economic difficulties. And although there was considerable mass participation in the revolution--mainly in the towns--there was a "lack of clearly defined leadership." The revolution proved to be as spontaneous as that of February 1917 would be.[6] Neither of the two warring factions of the social democratic party--mensheviks nor bolsheviks, especially the latter--could claim the leadership of the struggle. Indeed, it was the workers, themselves, who introduced an institution that would subsequently have "world-historic significance." The creation of soviets--councils of workers deputies, and later peasants and soldiers--said Carr, "seems to have been the result of spontaneous action by groups of workers on strike." It was through these soviets, above all in St. Petersburg, that the working class--occasionally supported by peasant rebellions--was able to temporarily force the tsar's hand during the fall of 1905. Most importantly, during the decisive "October" days of this bourgeois revolution the bourgeoisie recoiled in fright. Could it be that it feared the working class more than it did the tsar? The "tentative achievements [of the revolution]--the granting of a constitution, the Duma [parliament], the formation of political parties--had been bourgeois." But the revolution proved abortive, said Carr, "because the bourgeoisie had been incapable not merely of making a revolution, but of garnering the fruits of a revolution made for them by others."[7]

As a result of his observations of the 1905 revolution, what conclusions did Lenin reach? The aim of any revolution in Russia must be bourgeois. He stated that "the degree of Russia's economic development (an objective condition), and the degree of class consciousness and organization of the broad masses of the proletariat (a subjective condition inseparably bound up with the objective condition) make the immediate and complete emancipation of the working class impossible." Indeed, "in countries like Russia the working class suffers not so much from capitalism as from the insufficient development of capitalism." Those who would seek the "salvation" of the Russian working class other than through the further development of capitalism are

...right "reactionary."*[8] However the crucial elements in
...nin's observations of 1905 lie elsewhere. They center on the
questions concerning what social forces would carry out the revolution and what would be the relation of the Russian bourgeois revolution to the European socialist revolution. Unlike
much of his earlier writing in which he seemed to have as much--
if not more--confidence in the bourgeoisie than in the "two faced"
petty bourgeoisie, 1905 taught him that the working class must
seek its surest allies outside the ranks of the bourgeoisie.
After cautioning the workers "not to allow the leadership of the
revolution to be assumed by the bourgeoisie," he flings the
bourgeoisie about as an "inconsistent, self-seeking and cowardly"
class. "The bourgeoisie," we are now told, "will inevitably
turn towards counter-revolution, toward autocracy, against the
revolution and against the people as soon as its narrow, selfish
interests are met. . . ." And since the bourgeoisie is "inevitably" counter-revolutionary, the proletariat must seeks its
surest ally in the peasantry.** "Without. . . becoming socialist,
or ceasing to be petty bourgeois, the peasantry is capable of
becoming a wholehearted and most radical adherent of the democratic revolution." Though the peasant is not anti-capitalist,
he is at least anti-landlord. And on this basis a worker-
peasant alliance can be forged. Yet, Lenin's increasing over-

---

* Following this bourgeois revolution, said Lenin, "the entire economy of society will still remain under the domination
of the market, of money, even when there is the broadest freedom
and the peasants have won a complete victory in their struggle
for the land." Lenin, "Agrarian Question and the Forces of
Revolution," Vol. XII, p. 334.

**"The bourgeois revolution under the leadership of the
bourgeoisie can only be an unconsummated revolution (i.e., strictly speaking, not revolution but reform). It can be a real revolution only under the leadership of the proletariat and the
peasantry." Lenin, "Two Tactics," Vol. IX, pp. 52 and 97-98,
"Attitudes of Parties to Duma Elections," Vol. XI, p. 417 and
"Strength and Weakness of the Russian Revolution," Vol. XII,
p. 357. This, of course, was not Lenin's final word on the
bourgeoisie--either in its Russian or Asian version. He would
later acknowledge "collaborating" with the "revolutionary bourgeoisie" in Russia. Lenin, "When You Hear the Judgement of a
Fool," Vol. XI, pp. 458 and 471.

tures toward the peasantry should not be misconstrued. While the peasantry is the surest ally of the working class in the bourgeois revolution it "cannot be the vehicle for socialism" because the peasantry "will inevitably turn against the proletarians when they pass from freedom [the bourgeois revolution] to socialism."* Thus, if the peasantry is only interested in removing the "survivals of serfdom" and the liberal bourgeoisie is outright "counterrevolutionary," how can a working class minority progress from the bourgeois revolution (during which it has the support fo the peasantry) to the socialist revolution-- at which time the peasantry (bulk of the population) "inevitably turns against the proletarians?" Lenin left no room for any serious doubt with his response. "To be able to retain its victory, to be able to prevent restoration, the Russian [socialist] revolution will need non-Russian reserves, will need outside assistance. Are there such reserves? Yes, there are: the socialist proletariat in the West."**

-----

* The bolsheviks have asserted, and still do, that the only firm and reliable ally the proletariat can have <u>in the epoch of the bourgeois-democratic revolution (until the revolution wins)</u> is the peasantry." But he also said that "the petty bourgeois will <u>certainly and inevitably</u> serve as the bulwark of restoration against the proletariat, no matter whether the land is nationalized, municipalized or divided" [our emphasis]. Lenin, "Report on the Unity Congress of the R.S.D.L.P.," Vol. X, pp. 333-335, 411 and 462-463, "Socialist-Revolutionary Mensheviks," Vol. XI, pp. 202-203 and "Agrarian Program of Social Democracy," Vol. XIII, p. 421.

**Writing in early 1905 Lenin said that "we will make the Russian political revolution [bourgeois] the prelude to the socialist revolution in Europe." And during the "October days" of the same year he noted that the Russian revolution would "serve as a signal" for the socialist revolution in Europe. Though Lenin does not consistently link Russia's bourgeois and socialist revolutions in the period prior to the First World War, he does do it occasionally. He said in 1905 that "from the democratic revolution we shall at once. . . begin to pass to the socialist revolution. We stand for uninterrupted revolution." And later in the same year he said that "the sooner this [bourgeois] victory is achieved. . .the faster and more profoundly will fresh contradictions and a fresh class struggle develop within the fully democratized bourgeois system." We maintain-- despite his assertion in <u>Two Tactics</u> that during Russia's socialist revolution the proletariat must ally itself with "the mass of semi-proletarian elements" or poor peasantry--that until it became clear to Lenin that revolution was not imminent in the West (around 1920), he saw the "salvation" of Russia's October

As we have indicated, however, Lenin was less concerned now with socialism than he was with the further development of Russian capitalism. And it would be the responsibility of the "revolutionary democratic dictatorship of the proletariat and peasantry" to carry out the bourgeois content of this bourgeois revolution.[9] "At best, it [this dictatorship] may bring about a radical redistribution of landed property in favor of the peasantry, establish consistent and full democracy, including the formation of a republic, eradicate all the oppressive features of Asiatic bondage, not only in rural but factory life, lay the foundation for a thorough improvement in the condition of the workers and for a rise in their standard of living. . . ." And he says "last but not least"--as is characteristic of the leninist theory of revolution--the democratic dictatorship of the proletariat and peasantry must "carry the revolutionary conflagration into Europe."[10] But what would happen if the democratic dictatorship (governmental alliance of the working class and peasantry) made little or no effort to accomplish these and other bourgeois tasks? Would responsibility then fall exclusively upon the proletariat to accomplish both bourgeois and socialist tasks? Furthermore, what should be the actual relationship of strength between cne proletariat and peasantry in the democratic dictatorship? If "without the initiative and guidance of the proletariat the peasantry counts for nothing," [our emphasis] how is it possible that peasant representatives could even have a "predominance" in the democratic dictatorship?[11] Lenin would not seriously attempt to answer these questions until 1917.*

1917 revolution essentially in terms of an alliance between the Russian working class and the European working class. This will become especially apparent during the period from 1917 to roughly 1920. However, Lenin is now (1905-1914) primarily concerned with achieving and consolidating Russia's bourgeois revolution. Lenin, "Revolutionary-Democratic Dictatorship," Vol. VIII, p. 303, "Two Tactics," Vol. IX, p. 100, "S.-D.'s Attitude Towards Peasant Movement," Vol. IX, pp. 236-237, "Socialism and Peasantry," Vol. IX, p. 308 and "First Victory of Revolution," Vol. IX, p. 434.

*We indicated earlier that the other major current in the Russian social democratic movement, menshevism, would draw conclusions from the 1905 revolution that were sharply different from those of Lenin. Indeed, they became more convinced than ever that the working class must remain "involuntary political servants of the bourgeoisie." Pavel Axelrod, a leading menshevik, stated bluntly that "instead of taking advantage of the nation-wide movement against the old regime so as to raise the proletariat to the status of an independent organized force

During the dark days of the tsars reaction to the 1905 revolution
he would be content with fuming at "semi-anarchist thinking" and
the "betrayers of the revolution."

Having advanced two of the three components of the leninist
theory of revolution--the conceptions of the vanguard party and
the democratic dictatorship--we will now introduce the third.
This concerns the objective basis for revolution--whether bourgeois or socialist--or what Lenin often referred to as the "revolutionary situation." It comprises three interrelated elements:

> [A revolutionary situation exists] when it is im-
> possible for the ruling classes to maintain their rule
> without any change; when there is a crisi, in one form
> or another, among the 'upper classes,' a crisis in the
> policy of the ruling, leading to a fissure through which
> the discontent and indignation of the oppressed classes
> burst forth. For a revolution to take place, it it
> usually insufficient for the 'lower classes not to want'
> to live in the old way; (2) when the suffering and want
> of the oppressed classes have grown more acute than
> usual; (3) when, as a consequence of the above causes,
> there is a considerable increase in the activity of the
> masses, who uncomplainingly allow themselves to be rob-
> bed in 'peace time,' but, in turbulent times, are drawn
> both by all the circumstances of the crisis and by the
> 'upper classes' themselves into independent historical action.

---

within that movement, we should have helped to place the proletariat under the hegemony of the democratic bourgeoisie, to
serve as cannon-fodder and a mere instrument of the revolution
directed by the latter." And in contrast to Lenin's democratic
dictatorship of the proletariat and peasantry, the mensheviks
argued that "the [proletarian] party should not aim to seize
power or share it within a Provisional Government, but should
remain a party of the extreme revolutionary opposition." For
them, there could only be a bourgeois dictatorship or a proletarian dictatorship. The peasantry is not the surest ally
of the proletariat in the bourgeois revolution. Was it not a
peasant army that ultimately beat back the revolutionary tide?
Therefore, they reasoned, Lenin was not only violating a cardinal principle of marxism--never join a non-proletarian govern-
ment--but was making it exceptionally difficult for the proletariat to go through the "preparatory school" of   "unfettered"
bourgeois rule. Ascher, ed., The Mensheviks in the Russian Revolution, pp. 53-64, Haimson, ed., The Mensheviks, p. 368, J.L.H.
Keep, The Rise of Social Democracy in Russia, pp. 293-296, S.M.

And he said "without these objective changes, which are independent of the will, not only of individual groups and parties but
even of individual classes, a revolution, as a general rule, is
impossible."[12] While this approach to revolution does not iden-
tify Lenin with Blanqui--at least in theory--it is far removed
from the ideas on revolution advanced by Marx and Engels.[13] Yet
Lenin's concept of the "revolutionary situation" seems to flow
from his "internationalizing" of Marx's Capital; that is, his
concept of imperialism provides the "economic" framework--that
would otherwise be wanting--for revolution throughout the world.
But he emphasized that since "highly developed large-scale industry" was required for socialism itself, revolution in the
semi-colonial world could only serve as a "signal" for proletarian or socialist revolution in the West.*[14]

With the coming of the First World War--or the war for the
"redivision of the booty"-Lenin became convinced that "we are
undoubtedly on the eve of a socialist revolution." And most
importantly that in "all the advanced countries the war has
placed on the order of the day the slogan of socialist revolution. . . ."[15] Yet, the "revolutionary conflagration" would
occur in Russia rather than in Western Europe.** And it was
from this unexpected development--in the sense that Lenin didn't

---

Schwarz, The Russian Revolution of 1905, p. 8 and Carr, The
Bolshevik Revolution, Vol. I, p. 64.

*Without large factories, such as capitalism has created,
without highly developed large-scale industry, socialism is
impossible anywhere; still less in a peasant country. . . ."
Lenin, "Tenth All Russia Conference of the R.C.P. (B)," Vol.
XXXII, p. 408. He accepted the position of Marx and Engels
that socialism could only exist on the basis of large-scale industry but he rejected the idea that any revolution not founded
on this basis must of necessity lead to the replacing of one
form of exploitative domination by another.

**Lenin, however, during the war years just prior to 1917,
would continue to point out that "since Russia is most backward
and has not yet completed its bourgeois revolution" it was in-
cumbent upon social democrats to continue to organize for this
central task. He would not place the slogan of socialist revolution on the order of the day in Russia until 1917. Lenin,
"The War and Russian Social Democracy," Vol. XXI, p. 33.

think his generation would live to see it--and its relationship to revolutionary possibilities in Western Europe that compelled him to undertake a certain modification of his theory of revolution.[16] Lenin now says that because of the default of the democratic dictatorship it was now the responsibility of the Russian working class--in alliance with the West European working classes--to accomplish both bourgeois and socialist tasks of revolution. To be sure, he does acknowledge that the "mass of semi-proletarian elements" or poor peasantry is an ally of the working class. But the flow of his statements--especially up to around 1920-- makes it clear that the peasantry is only a "temporary ally" and that genuine support for the prletarian dictatorship can only come from the Western proletariat. It is to this adjustment in Lenin's theory that we now turn.

There were two revolutions--or major phases of the same re-volutionary process--that occurred in Russia in February and October (using the old Russian calendar) of 1917. The February revolution took place in much the same manner as the revolution of 1905. It was both spontaneous and leaderless. And with the fall of the tsar--due primarily to repercussions from the war, economic stagnation, scandals, etc.--power fell not to a single source but to a dual source.[17] "One is the main, the real, the actual government of the bourgeoisie, the 'Provisional Govern-ment' of Lvov and Co., which holds in its hands all the organs of power; the other is a supplementary and parallel government, a 'controlling' government in the shape of the Petrograd Soviet of Workers' and Soldiers' Deputies, which holds no organ of state power, but directly rests on the support of an obvious and in-disputable majority of the people, on the armed workers and soldiers." Lenin went on to say that this "dual power merely expresses a transitional phase in the revolution's development, when it has gone farther than the ordinary bourgeois-democratic revolution, but has not yet reached a 'pure' dictatorship of the proletariat and peasantry." However, the existence of this dual power stemmed from the "immaturity" of the political conscious-ness of the working class and the predominance of the menshevik and peasant oriented social revolutionary parties in the Petro-grad Soviet. But unlike these Soviet leaders (including some members of his bolshevik party) who reached revolutionary Petro-grad before he did, Lenin, recognizing the failure of the "demo-cratic dictatorship" to accomplish the much advertised bourgeois revolution and sensing revolutionary winds in Western Europe, began to advance the slogan of "all power to the soviets." Immediately upon arriving from exile in April 1971--less than two months after the revolution began--he said that "the specific feature of the present situation in Russia is that the country is passing from the first stage of the revolution-- which owing to the insufficient class-consciousness and organiza-tion of the proletariat, placed power in the hands of the bour-

geoisie--to its second stage, which must place power in the hands
of the proletariat and the poorest sections of the peasants."*
The point to note here, however, is that the revolution was now
passing from its first to its second phase without ever having
resolved the central question in the bourgeois revolution--the
problem of land. Henceforth, the proletarian dictatorship would
be responsible for fulfilling both bourgeois and socialist tasks.
Lenin stated that this "new bolshevism"--as he called it-- was
absolutely necessary because the "democratic dictatorship" was
"surrendering power to the bourgeoisie." The old formula of the
democratic dictatorship "is obsolete. It is no good at all. It
is dead. And it is no use trying to revive it."** But he insisted
again and again--wanting to distinguish himself from Blanqui--
that the political preparation for the proletarian dictatorship
was not the same as its technical preparation. "As

----

   *Indeed, in his well-known "Farewell Letter to Swiss Workers,"
Lenin had already suggested the direction that he felt the
Russian revolution would take. "The objective circumstances of
the imperialist war make it certain that the revolution will not
be limited to the first stage of the Russian revolution, that the
revolution will not be limited to Russia." Lenin, "Farewell
Letter to Swiss Workers," Vol. XXIII, p.373.

   **Lenin had considerable difficulty convincing some of his
closest collaborators that they should "not cling to a theory of
yesterday." In fact, he would even be charged by some of his
followers, especially Kamenev, with adopting Trotsky's heretical
theory of permanent revolution. In the end, however, the "old
bolsheviks" surrendered to Lenin's new orthodoxy. Even the
anarchists--who would occasionally march with bolsheviks until
the October revolution--came to "rejoice" at Lenin's call for the
replacement of the Provisional Government by the Soviet system.
Carr, The Bolshevik Revolution, Vol. I, pp. 70-101, Victor
Chernov, The Great Russian Revolution, p. 418, N.N. Sukhanov,
The Russian Revolution: 1917, pp. 285-287, Paul Avrich, ed., The
Anarchists in the Russian Revolution, pp. 14-17 and 89-91 and
Lenin, "The Tasks of the Preletariat in the Present Revolution,"
Vol. XXIV, pp. 22, 23 and 60-61, and "Letters on Tactics," Vol.
XXIV, pp. 42-54.

long as we are in the minority [and the bolsheviks would remain a minority party in the soviets until September] we carry on the work of criticizing and exposing errors and at the same time we preach the necessity of transferring the entire state power to the Soviets of Workers' Deputies, so that the people may over- come their mistakes by experience."*

After several months of political preparations--both inside and outside the party--Lenin's bolshevik party in the name of the workers and poor peasants in October 1917 assumed political power in an almost bloodless revolution. But how could this dictatorship of the proletariat--albeit "supported by the poor peasants"--survive for long in a country in which the property inclined peasantry constituted the overwhelming majority of the population?[18] Was the dictatorship of the proletariat--as had been the case of the <u>ancien regime</u>-- ultimately bound to be over- thrown? The fact is that Lenin, however mistakenly, saw the Soviet state as merely "a contingent of the world army of socialism." As he put it:

------

*"To become a power the class-conscious workers must win the majority to their side. As long as no violence is used against the people there is no other road to power. We are not blanquists, we do not stand for the seizure of power by a minority. We are marxists, we stand for proletarian class strug- gle. . . ." Years earlier, however, Lenin had said that "history does not know any cases of the ruling and oppressing classes voluntarily relinquishing their right to rule and to oppress, their right to huge incomes from enslaved peasants and workers." But in April 1917 he could consider "the possibility of a peace- ful and gradual transition to socialism." Just three months later he would tell us that "all hopes for a peaceful develop- ment of the Russian revolution <u>have vanished for good</u>" [our emphasis]. The difference between April and July, he tells us, is that the "objective situation" has changed. With the van- ishing of the "unstable condition of state power" which existed in April and the determined rightist reaction to the premature and ill-fated anarchist inspired workers' rising during the "July Days," the only course now open for the victorious conclu- sion of the revolutionary process was a violent overturning of the Provisional Government. Lenin, "Draft Speech on the Agra- rian Question in the Duma," Vol. XII, p. 277, "Tasks of the Proletariat in the Present Revolution," "Dual Power," "A Part- nership of Lies," Vol. XXIV, pp. 24, 40 and 120 and "The Poli- tical Situation," "On Slogans," Vol. XXV, pp. 177 and 183-190 and Avrich, ed., <u>The Anarchists in the Russian Revolution</u>, pp. 16-17.

> To the Russian proletariat has fallen the great
> honor of beginning the series of revolutions which the
> imperialist war has made an objective inevitability.
> But the idea that the Russian proletariat is the
> chosen revolutionary proletariat among the workers of
> the world is absolutely alien to us. . . . It is not
> its special qualities, but rather the special con-
> juncture of historical circumstances that <u>for a certain,
> perhaps very short, time</u> has made the proletariat of
> Russia the vanguard of the revolutionary proletariat
> of the whole world [emphasis in the original].

And again he said that "our backwardness has put us in the fore-
front and we shall perish unless we are capable of holding out
until we receive powerful suport from workers who have risen in
revolt in other countries." While "holding out" for the decisive battles" in the West, Lenin insisted time and again that
the working class must come to an "agreement" with the peasant
masses. [19] This agreement consisted essentially in satisfying
the demand of the peasantry for land. In fact, in the famous
"Decree on Land" of the new Soviet Government, Lenin stated that

---

*". . . if the German revolution does not come, we are
doomed." It is true that most of these statements were made
in the period from 1917 to 1920--a period of civil war, foreign
intervention and severe economic difficulties--but it is also
true that they evidence that Lenin, as we have often indicated,
felt that the Western proletariat and not the Russian poor
peasantry was the "most trustworthy and most reliable" ally of
the Russian working class. Even from 1920--when he increasingly
began to look Eastward and towards Russia's internal resources
in order to sustain the dictatorship of the proletariat--he
would say that "so long as there is no revolution in other
countries [meaning the West], only agreement with the peasantry
can save the Socialist revolution in Russia." Thus the alliance
with the peasantry, however important it is, remains "temporary"
pending the outcome of the much awaited "decisive battles" in
the West. Lenin, "Seventh Congress of the R.C.P. (B),"
Vol. XXVII, p. 98, "The Chief Task of Our Day," Vol. XXVII, p.
163, "Speech in the Moscow Soviet," Vol. XXVII, p. 232, "The
Russian Revolution and Civil War," Vol. XXVI, pp. 40-41, "Farewell Letter to Swiss Workers," Vol. XXIII, pp. 371-373 and
"Tenth Congress of the R.C.P. (B)," Vol. XXXII, pp. 214-216.

"landed proprietorship is abolished forthwith without any compensation. . . [and that] the landed estates. . . shall be placed at the disposal of the Volost land committees. . . ." Obviously proud of this accomplishment, he would observe four years later that "we solved the problems of the bourgeois-democratic revolution in passing, as a 'by-product' of our main and genuinely proletarian-revolutionary, socialist activites" which was made all the easier because "we adopted the agrarian program of the [peasant oriented] social revolutionaries instead of our own, and put it into effect" [our emphasis].[20]

For Lenin, therefore, the Russian socialist revolution--despite the necessity of having to establish and maintain a working alliance with the peasant masses--could be victorious* only on the basis of the world-wide socialist revolution.

II. Trotsky and Bolshevism

We will now examine the two main areas in which Lenin and Trotsky were in disagreement from 1903 to approximately the February revolution. This will be done against the background of their captious polemical debate but with the expressed aim of assessing the evolution of Trotsky's theory of revolution. The two areas in question centered on their differing conceptions

---

*Lenin often used the word "victory" to describe the transition from the dictatorship of the proletariat to the future classless society. For example, he said that "we have been telling the workers again and again that the cardinal task, and the fundamental condition of our victory is to spread the revolution to, at least, a few of the most advanced countries." And a year later, in 1922, he said that "we have always urged and reiterated the elementary truth of marxism--that the joint efforts of the workers of several advanced countries are needed for the victory of socialism." However, it has been argued and to a certain extent can be supported that Lenin believed--or had no choice but to believe--that socialism could be established in Russia in the absence of socialist revolutions in the industrialized West. There is, to be sure, a certain ambiguity in his theory of revolution. But, as we have shown and will further elucidate in the context of the Trotsky-Stalin debate, when considered in its entirety, Lenin's theory of revolution squarely placed the "salvation" of the Russian revolution on the shoulders of the Western proletariat. Lenin, "Speech at Fourth Congress of Garment Workers," Vol. XXXII, p. 113 and "Notes of a Publicist," Vol. XXXIII, p. 206.

of the roles to be played by the party and the peasantry in the revolutionary process. And clearly the most important difference between the leninist and trotskyist theories of revolution prior to 1917 was the organizational question. The essence of leninism was symbolized by the famous battle-cry, "give us an organization of revolutionaries and we will overturn Russia." Did Trotsky agree with what this statement meant for Lenin? There is some indication that while in Siberian exile in 1901 he was independently developing a position on centralism similar to that then being developed by Lenin in What Is To Be Done.* But this position would not be systematically explored.

The differences between Lenin and Trotsky have their origins at the 1903 social democratic party congress. As we have seen, two basic camps emerged at this congress on the question of party organization. One centered around Lenin and the other around Martov. As Lenin put it:

> We argued that the concept party member must be narrowed so as to separate those who worked from those who merely talked, to eliminate organizational chaos, to eliminate the monstrous and absurd possibility of there being organizations which consisted of party members but which were not party organizations, and so on. Martov stood for broadening the party and spoke of a broad class movement needing a broad--i.e.--diffuse-- organization, and so forth.

Lenin simply did not want to "fling open the doors" of the party to anyone who might want to join.[21] But it should be remembered that the differences between Martov and Lenin--and menshevism and bolshevism in general--were not on the question of organiza-

---

*Trotsky argued that the revolutionary movement--if it is to be successful--must come under the control of a strong Central Committee which has the power to disband or expel any undisciplined organization or individual. "The Central Committee will cut off its relations with [the undisciplined organization] and it will thereby cut off that organization from the entire world of revolution. The Central Committee will stop the flow of literature and of wherewithal to that organization. It will send into the field. . . its own detachment, and, having endowed it with the necessary resources, the Central Committee will proclaim that this detachment is the local committee." As cited by Deutscher, The Prophet Armed, p. 45 and Trotsky, My Life, p. 132.

tion versus no organization but on the nature and role of the revolutionary organization in the working class movement. In opposition to Martov's "autonomously formed and secure collectivity" which simply gives direction to the "initiative" of the working class itself, Lenin argues vigorously that under tsarist conditions and in an effort to "bring social democratic consciousness" to the working class, "the only serious organizational principle for the active workers of our movement should be the strictest secrecy, the strictest selection of members, and the training of professional revolutionaries."[22]

Where and how did Trotsky enter the picture at the 1903 party congress. After flailing the "bundists" and "economists" during the early sessions of the congress--and even defending leninist centralism--Trotsky abruptly and openly denounced Lenin's organziational plans as merely an attempt by Lenin to establish his "hegemony over social democracy."[23] In opposition to the "state of seige" that Lenin's formula would impose on the party he pointed out that "the formula of comrade Martov [for a broadly based party]. . . can become an admirable tool in the hands of the central committee."*[24] With these statements--as a member of the Siberian delegation at the congress-Trotsky inaugurated the process which would within a year or two effectively place him outside the two warring factions of Russian social

---

*Trotsky would later say that "in 1903 the whole point at issue was nothing more than Lenin's desire to get Axelrod and Zasulitch off the editorial board [of the party's journal]. My attitude towards them was full of respect and there was an element of personal affection as well." And then goes on to say that "my whole being seemed to protest against this merciless cutting off of the older ones when they were at last on the threshold of an organized party. It was my indignation at his attitude that really led to my parting with him at the second congress. His behavior seemed unpardonable to me, both horrible and outrageous." Whether Lenin was merely seeking to remove the "least effective" individuals from the editorial board--as Deutscher maintains--or scheming to remove some of Trotsky's close friends--as Trotsky thought--is of no major concern to us here. What is important is that Trotsky considered Lenin's behavior "sacrilegious" and thereby decided to march to a different tune. Trotsky, My Life, pp. 160-165 and "Le Rapport De La Délégation De Siberie," Politique de Trotsky, pp. 186-187, Deutscher, The Prophet Armed, p. 79, Carr, The Bolshevik Revolution, Vol. I, pp. 29-32 and Max Eastman, Leon Trotsky: The Portrait of a Youth, pp. 163-165.

democracy until the coming of the First World War begins to propel him in another direction. While organizationally at ease with menshevism, he was repelled by its inclination towards liberalism. Thinking that the positive sides of both social democratic wings should merge in the course of concrete revolutionary conditions--as was partly the case in 1905--he felt that his central task was to struggle for the unification of the movement.[25] Be that as it may, some of his most pointed salvoes were directed against Lenin. In his violently anti-Lenin tract Our Political Tasks--written in 1904 and which Lenin refers to as "a pack of brazen lies"--Trotsky firmly establishes his anti-vanguardist perspective. "The Russian revolutionary movement must. . . be transformed without further delay into a process for proletarian political self-determination; otherwise, Russian social democracy--as such--is an historical error." And he further states that

> The system of political substitutionism [i.e., leninism]. . . results--consciously or unconsciously--from a false and sophistic conception of the links between the objective interest of the proletariat and its consciousness. Marxism teaches that the interests of the proletariat are determined by the objective conditions of its existence. There interests are so powerful and inevitable that, in the final analysis, the consciousness of the proletariat is obliged to take them into account; that is, the subjective interests of the proletariat result from its objective interest.

Trotsky's organizational battle-cry was, "down with political substitutionism" and "long live the self-activity of the proletariat." To Lenin's assertion that bolshevism "proceeds from the top downward and upholds an extension of the rights and powers of the center in relation to the parts," Trotsky retorts that ultimately out of this kind of situation "the party organization is substituted for the party, the central committee for the party organization and finally the dictator takes the place of the central committee."[26]

Throughout this polemical work Trotsky fulminates against the "reactionary wing of our party" and its leader "Maximilien Lenin" who is trying to establish his "dictatorship over the proletariat." This allusion to the French revolution relates to charges and countercharges initially made at the party congress in 1903. When charged with "jacobinism" at the congress Lenin--and even Trotsky during the earlier sessions--did not retreat in fright. Indeed, Lenin would now say that "a jacobin who wholly identifies himself with the organization of the proletariat--a proletariat conscious of its class interests--is a revolutionary social democrat."[27] Trotsky, on the other hand, argued that one could not be both a social democrat and a jacobin. The reason, he said, is that the methods and practices of the jacobins--even though representing the "maximum" of bourgeois radicalism--belong to another epoch and class. Moreover, he suggested that Lenin's "distrust" of the working class might lead him-- as it had led Robespierre--to seek a "mechanical" solution when confronted with a serious challenge from his left.* At the root of the differences between Lenin and Trotsky on the organizational question was the role that Lenin assigned the intellectual in the revolutionary process. He wrote in What Is To Be Done that Russian socialist thought emerged not as the spontaneous product of the working class movement but as the "natural and inevitable outcome of the development of thought among the revolutionary socialist intelligentsia." And then cited approvingly the "profoundly true and important words" of the future "renegade" Karl Kautsky who said that "the vehicle of science is not the proletariat but the bourgeois intelligentsia. . . it was in the minds of individual members of this stratum that modern socialism originated and it was they who communicated it to the more intellectually developed proletarians who, in their turn, introduce it into the proletarian class struggle where conditions allow that to be done." Trotsky charged in 1903 that the idea that socialist consciousness had to be brought to the

---

*"They [the jacobins] were utopians; we want to be the representatives of objective tendencies. They were idealists from foot to head; we are materialists from head to foot. They were rationalists; we are dialecticians. They believed in the redemptive strength of the Truth--located above classes and before which all were supposed to bow. We believe only in the class strength of the revolutionary proletariat. Their theoretical and intrinsically contradictory idealism drove them on the way towards political distrust and ruthless suspicion. Our theoretical materialism arms us with an unyielding confidence in the historic 'will' of the proletariat. Their method was to guillotine the least deviations, ours is to politically and theoretically go beyond differences. They cut off heads, we inspire them with class consciousness." And he concludes interestingly and with an eye towards Lenin that "there is no doubt that the whole international movement of the proletariat in its entirety would have been charged with moderantisme by the revolutionary tribunal [of Robespierre] and Marx's lion head would have been the first to fall under the guillotine's blade." Some thirty years later Trotsky would refer to his "immature and erroneous" criticism of Lenin in this 1904 pamphlet. His point is well-taken. But were they "immature and erroneous" after the October revolution? Trotsky, Nos Tâches Politiques, pp. 187-192 and Stalin, p. 62.

working class "from without" would make it "more difficult for workers to join the party than for the intelligentsia" and he would later herald the coming of the 1905 revolution as marking the end of intellectual "substitutionism" in the working class movement.*[28]

Trotsky, who "thought of the split [between menshevism and bolshevism] as an outstanding episode but nothing more," would hold these positions on Lenin's organizational principles until the war years convinced him that menshevism was the revolution's dead end. "I was still hoping that the new revolution would force the mensheviks--as had that of 1905--to follow a revolutionary path. But I underestimated the importance of preparatory ideological selection and of political case-hardening. In questions of the inner development of the party I was guilty of a sort of social-revolutionary fatalism." Trotsky finally acknowledged in July 1917--after an initial and perhaps prideful hesitation following his arrival in Petrograd in May 1917--that he was in agreement "with the main thesis of Lenin" and the bolsheviks.[29] All talk of unity with menshevism had now become "sacrilegious." With this acknowledgement, the organizational differences with Lenin officially died. After 1917 his emphasis would no longer be on the "self-activity" of the working class but instead on the fact that "the fundamental instrument of the proletarian revolution is the party."[30]

The other major difference between Lenin and Trotsky before 1917 centered on the role to be played by the peasantry in the coming Russian revolution. Although they both agreed on the necessity for an alliance between the working class and peasantry

---

*Lenin, however, responded to Trotsky, Luxemburg and other critics in his One Step Forward, Two Steps Back by saying that bourgeois intellectuals imbued with "individualism" and lacking in "discipline" would--contrary to Trotsky's assertion--be more likely to join the open-ended organization proposed by Martov. "In a word, comrade Martov's formulation will either remain a dead letter, an empty phrase, or it will be of benefit mainly and almost exclusively to 'intellectuals who are thoroughly imbued with bourgeois individualism' and do not wish to join an organization. In words, Martov's formulation defends the interests of the broad strata of the proletariat, but in fact it serves the interests of the bourgeois intellectuals, who fight shy of proletarian discipline and organization." Thus, Lenin turns the cards on his critics. Only revolutionary intellectuals would be willing to join his organization of professional revolutionaries. Lenin, "One Step Forward, Two Steps Back," Vol, VII, p. 267 and Trotsky, The Intelligentsia and Socialism, pp. 14-16.

in the coming revolution,* they arrived at different conclusions
as to the outcome of this revolutionary alliance owing to a certain openness and flexibility in Lenin's formula of the democratic dictatorship. Lenin would not rule out the possibility
that the peasantry, under revolutionary conditions, might create
its own independent revolutionary political party which could then
participate on equal terms (or possibly even predominate) in the
future revolutionary government. He wrote in 1909 that "the proletariat cannot count on the ignorance and prejudices of the
peasantry as the powers that be under a bourgeois regime count
and depend on them, nor can it assume that in time of revolution
the peasantry will remain in their usual state of political ignorance and passivity. The history of the Russian revolution shows
that the very first wave of the upsurge at the end of 1905, at
once stimulated the peasantry to form a political organization
(the All-Russian Peasant Union) which was undoubtedly the embryo
of a distinct peasant party."[31] Moreover, the revolutionary democratic dictatorship of the proletariat and peasantry would confine
itself to bourgeois tasks--and on this latter point Lenin was one
with menshevism. Trotsky, of course, took exception with all of
this. He argued that "historical experience shows that the pea-

---

*Trotsky wrote on the eve of the 1905 revolution--when he was
just beginning to develop his theory of revolution--that a "political strike, as a single combat of the city proletariat with the
police and the army, and the remaining population being hostile or
even indifferent, is doomed to failure" [our emphasis]. And
shortly after the massacre of men, women and children in a peaceful demonstration by the tsar's troops on January 9, 1905, Trotsky
made a ringing appeal to the peasantry: "hearken, hearken peasants!
Let every word engrave itself on your heart. . . . Tell all and
sundry in what way the tsar has dealt with the toilers of St.
Petersburg!. . .Remember, Russian peasants, how every Russian tsar
has repeated with pride: 'In my country, I am the first courtier
and the first landlord.' . . . Russian tsars have made the
peasants into an Estate of serfs; they have made of them, like of
dogs, presents to their faithful servants. . . . Peasants, at your
meetings tell the soldiers, the people's sons who live on the
people's money, that they dare not shoot at the people. . . .
Peasants, let this fire burst all over Russia at one and the same
time, and no force will put it out. Such a nation-wide fire is
called Revolution," The Age of Permanent Revolution: A Trotsky
Anthology, p. 45 and Deutscher, The Prophet Armed, pp. 122-123.

santry are absolutely incapable of taking up an independent political role"* and furthermore that

> while the antirevolutionary aspects of menshevism have already become fully apparent, those of bolshevism are likely to become a serious threat only in the event of victory. . . . 'Self-limitation' by a workers' government would mean nothing other than the betrayal of the interests of the unemployed and strikers--more, of the whole proletariat--in the name of the establishment of a republic. The revolutionary authorities will be confronted with the objective problems of socialism, but the solution of these problems will, at a certain stage, be prevented by the country's economic backwardness. There is no way out from this contradiction within the framework of a national revolution. The workers' government will from the start be faced with the task of uniting its forces with those of the socialist proletariat of Western Europe. Only in this way will its temporary revolutionary hegemony become the prologue to a socialist dictatorship. Thus permanent revolution will become, for the Russian proletariat, a matter of class self-preservation.

Thus, Lenin's "naive" and "metaphysical" construct of the democratic dictatorship of the proletariat and peasantry as a preliminary governmental form to the dictatorship of the proletariat would end "either in the repression of the workers by the peasant

---

*In July 1905 he wrote that "the class which is capable of winning this battle will have to fight it, and will then have to assume the role of a leading class--if Russia is to be truly reborn as a democratic state. These conditions, then, lead to the hegemony of the 'fourth estate.' It goes without saying that the proletariat must fulfil its mission, just as the bourgeoisie did in its own time, with the help of the peasantry and the petty bourgeoisie. It must lead the countryside, draw it into the movement, make it vitally interested in the success of its plans. But, inevitably, the proletariat remains the leader. This is not the 'dictatorship of the proletariat and the peasantry' [Lenin's formula], it is the <u>dictatorship of the proletariat supported by the peasantry</u> [our emphasis]. And the proletariat's work will not, of course, be confined within the limits of a single state. The very logic of its position [as a minority in an overwhelmingly peasant and backward country] will immediately throw it into the world arena." Trotsky, "Results and Prospects," <u>PR</u>, p. 72 and <u>1905</u>, pp. 277, 279 and 309-310.

party or in the removal of that party [the peasant party] from power."[32]* Lenin would then tax the "wind bag" Trotsky with "muddled thinking" for having underestimated the potential role of the peasantry in the revolutionary process. "Trotsky is in fact helping the liberal-labor politicians in Russia, who by 'repudiation' of the role of the peasantry understand a refusal to raise up the peasants for the revolution."**[33]

However, the expected revolutionary possibilities in the West introduced by the "imperialist" war and the refusal of the Russian democratic dictatorship of the proletariat and peasantry-- albeit incompletely formed--to seriously commit itself to carrying out the long awaited bourgeois revolution would impress upon Lenin the necessity of abandoning this "obsolete" formula. He would say four years after the October revolution--as Trotsky had

---

*Apart from the very nature of the peasantry, Trotsky was also probably considering the role the peasantry had played in the 1905 revolution. Though the peasantry was ultimately "awakened from a long sleep" in 1905, was it not a peasant army that finally crushed the workers' revolution? "The Russian proletariat in December 1905 foundered, not on its own mistakes, but on a more real force: the bayonets of the peasant army." Yet, we repeat, the differences between Lenin and Trotsky were not on the question of the need for a worker-peasant alliance but on the implica- tions--or "political mechanics," to use Trotsky's later expres- sion--of this alliance. Trotsky, 1905, pp. 187, 263 and 296 and The Permanent Revolution, p. 189.

**Let's, however, remember that while Lenin was sharply critical of Trotsky, he had no illusions about the nature of the support that the proletariat could expect from the peasantry. "The Russian revolution is strong enough to achieve victory by its own efforts; but it is not strong enough to retain the fruits of victory. It can achieve victory because the proletariat jointly with the revolutionary peasantry can constitute an invincible force. But it cannot retain its victory, because in a country where small production is vastly developed, the small commodity producers (including the peasants) will inevitably turn against the proletarians when they pass from freedom [the bourgeois democratic revolution] to socialism." The only salvation then for the workers' government would come from the Western pro- letariat. Lenin, "Report on the Unity Congress of the R.S.D.L.P.," Vol. X, pp. 334-335.

been insisting would be the case since 1905--that it was the
dictatorship of the proletariat which "in passing" accomplished
Russia's bourgeois revolution.*

III. Summary

We have seen that there are three basic components to the
Leninist theory of revolution: 1) the necessity of a vanguard
party as the instrument of socialist consciousness which
directs the working class movement both organizationally and
ideologically, 2) the conception that Russia's belated bourgeois
revolution would be accomplished by the democratic dictatorship of
the proletariat and peasantry under the leadership of the proletariat and its vanguard political party, and 3) the idea that the
objective basis for revolution springs from the existence of a
revolutionary situation. The modifications that he began to
introduce from the First World War--allying the proletariat with
the poor peasantry and especially the Western proletariat in
order to introduce Russia's dictatorship of the proletariat--were
not specifically leninist. After all, it was Trotsky who first
said that "it was possible for the workers to come to power in an
economically backward country sooner than in an advanced country."[34] Moreover, Lenin's increasing inclinations toward the
East around 1920 didn't introduce any fundamental modifications
of his theory since revolutions in the East could only serve to
"kindle" the necessary revolutionary flames in the West. We
remain, therefore, with the already assessed three basic components.
On the other hand while Lenin and Trotsky were in basic disagreement prior to 1917 on the question of the working class political
party, they were much closer on the theme of the revolutionary
process itself than their captious polemics would lead one to
believe. Following the 1905 revolution, this could be seen in
three areas: 1) their hostility towards the liberal bourgeoisie,
2) their "distrust" of the peasant allies of the working class,
though less pronounced in Lenin prior to the First World War and

---

*"The bourgeois-democratic content of the revolution means
that the social relations. . . of the country are purged of
medievalism, serfdom, feudalism. . . . In a matter of ten weeks.
. . we accomplished a thousand times more in this respect than was
accomplished by the bourgeois democrats and liberals. . . and by
the petty-bourgeois democrats (the mensheviks and the socialist-
revolutionaries) during the eight months they were in power. . . .
We solved the problems of the bourgeois democratic revolution in
passing, as a 'by-product' of our main and genuinely proletarian-
revolutionary, socialist activities." Lenin, "Fourth Anniversary
of the October Revolution," Vol. XXXIII, pp. 51-54.

3) especially Lenin's conception that the democratic dictatorship must "carry the revolutionary conflagration into Europe." This latter development serving to close the gap separating the demo-cratic dictatorship from the proletarian dictatorship.[35]

Still, the leninist theory of revolution--as we have seen in the case of Trotsky--represents a fundamental departure from the theory of revolution advanced by Marx and Engels. Indeed it re-presents a new doctrinal system. Politics have replaced economics as the motor of revolution. As Meyer put it, "political action determines economic development; consciousness is stronger than social relations. Causes turn into effects, and effects into causes."[36] We now turn to the consequences of this turning of marxism inside out.

IV. Notes to Chapter II

[1] C.H. Carr, _Studies in Revolution_, p. 34 and Samuel H. Baron, _Plekhanov: The Father of Russian Marxism_, p. 67. Engels stated in 1873 that "no revolution in Western Europe can be definitely and finally victorious as long as the present Russian state exists at its side. Germany is its nearest neighbor. Germany must sustain the first shock from the armies of Russian reaction. The overthrow of the Russian empire is therefore one of the first conditions for the final victory of the German proletariat. This revolution need not be brought about from the outside, although a foreign war could hasten it greatly. Within the Russian empire itself are forces which contribute powerfully to its decline." McLellan has suggested that Marx left an "ambivalent" legacy on Russia; that is, he could not decide whether "this nightmare that hovers all over Europe" would be brought down by external or internal forces. But McLellan nevertheless concludes that "after the failure of the Turkish war [of 1877] to shake the tsarist system, Marx pinned his hopes more and more on the possibilities of some revolutionary movement inside Russia." It seems clear to us that Marx and Engels' flirtation with the Russian Mir had more to do with their obsessional concern with tsarist absolutism than it did with any modification of their theory of revolution. Lowy, Haupt and Weill, _Les Marxistes et la Question Nationale_, p. 18, David McLellan, _Karl Marx: His Life and Thought_, p. 439 and P.W. Blackstock and B.F. Hoselitz, ed., _The Russian Menace to Europe_, pp. 203-204.

[2] V.I. Lenin, "New Economic Developments in Peasant Life," _Collected Works_, Vol. I, p. 73, "The Heritage We Renounce," Vol. II, pp. 518 and 532, "The Development of Capitalism in Russia," Vol. III, p. 172 and Donald W. Treadgold, _Lenin and His Rivals_, p. 96. Lenin's analysis of the development of Russian capitalism differs slightly from that of Trotsky. The latter's analysis gave more attention to the foreign impact on Russia's capitalist development than Lenin. Can this difference be attributed to a differing appreciation of the "law of uneven and combined development?" Denise Avenas, _La Pensée de Leon Trotsky_, pp. 23-24.

[3] "The role of the peasantry as a class that provides fighters against the autocracy and against the survivals of serfdom is by now played out in the West, but not yet in Russia." Lenin then asserted that "the small peasantry [the overwhelming majority] can free itself from the yoke of capital only by associating itself with the working class movement, by helping the workers in their struggle for the socialist system, for transforming the land, as well as the other means of production (factories, works, machines, etc.) into social property." Lenin undoubtedly saw a role for

68

the peasantry in his revolutionary strategy at this time but it
would be insignificant when placed beside that assigned to the
peasantry after 1905. Lenin, "The Workers' Party and the Peasantry " Vol. IV, pp. 422-423, "A Draft Program of Our Party," Vol.
IV, pp. 242-243.

[4]Lenin, to be sure, did not always argue that consciousness
must be brought to the working class "from without." In 1894
he wrote that the "social movement" is a "process of natural
history [which is] governed by laws not only independent of human
will, consciousness and intentions, but, rather, on the contrary,
determining the will, consciousness and intentions of man" [our
emphasis]. He later wrote that "every strike brings thoughts of
socialism very forcibly to the worker's mind, thoughts of the
struggle of the entire working class for emancipation from the
oppression of capital." By 1901, however, Lenin was already
singling out the "worthy ideologist" as one who "points out the
road" to consciousness. Lenin, "What the 'Friends of the People'
Are," Vol. I, p. 166, "On Strikes," Vol. IV, p. 315, "A Talk with
Defenders of Economism," Vol. V, p. 316, and "The Third Congress
of the R.S.D.L.P.," Vol. VIII, p. 373.

[5]Carr observed that "the notion of a centralized and disciplined party as the instrument of revolution was cardinal to
Lenin's thought." E.H. Carr, The Bolshevik Revolution, Vol. I,
p. 35 and Lenin, "What Is To Be Done," Vol. V, p. 467.

[6]W.H. Chamberlin, The Russian Revolution, Vol. I, pp. 46 and
50.

[7]Carr, The Bolshevik Revolution, Vol. I, pp. 47-51. Dan observed that "the menshevik conception of the 'pressure' of the
working class on the bourgeoisie with the aim of 'revolutionizing'
it and pushing it into power, while simultaneously strengthening
and organizationally reinforcing the class positions of the proletariat, proved to be unfeasible--primarily because the presumed
object of the 'pressure' [the bourgeoisie] was not there." Yet,
both Dan--himself a longtime menshevik--and Schapiro excuse away
the irresoluteness and cowardliness of the bourgeoisie during the
critical October phase of the revolution because the bourgeoisie,
they claim, was not "sufficiently organized to be ready to take
over the reins of government from the crumbling autocracy." Dan,
Origins of Bolshevism, p. 340, Leonard Schapiro, The Communist
Party of the Soviet Union, p. 69, Oskar Anweiler, The Soviets:
The Russian Workers, Peasants, and Soldiers Councils, p. 46 and
Sidney Harcave, First Blood: The Russian Revolution of 1905,
p. 137.

[8]"Marxists are absolutely convinced of the bourgeois character of the Russian revolution. What does that mean? It means
that the democratic reforms in the political system, and the social and economic reforms that have become a necessity for
Russia, do not in themselves imply the undermining of capitalism,
the undermining of bourgeois rule; on the contrary, they will, for
the first time, really clear the ground for a wide and rapid,
European, and not Asiatic, development of capitalism; they will,
for the first time, make it possible for the bourgeoisie to rule
as a class." Lenin, "Two Tactics of the S.D. in the Democratic
Revolution," Vol. IX, pp. 28 and 48-50.

[9]Lenin began to distinguish between the "socialist dictatorship of the proletariat" and the "democratic dictatorship of the
proletariat and peasantry" as early as March 1905. "More will be
accomplished in the months of the revolutionary dictatorship of
the proletariat and peasantry than in decades of the peaceful,
stupefying atmosphere of political stagnation. . . . " Lenin,
"Social-Democracy and the Provisional Revolutionary Government,"
Vol. VIII, p. 303.

[10]Lenin, "Two Tactics," Vol. IX, pp. 56-57.

[11]"There is no salvation for the peasant except by joining
in the activities of the proletariat. . . ." Lenin, "The
Assessment of the Russian Revolution," Vol. XV, p. 59, "Social-
Democracy and the Provisional Revolutionary Government," Vol. VIII,
p. 291 and "A Draft Program of Our Party," Vol. IV, p. 243.

[12]Five years later (1920) he would again define the objective
basis for revolution in exactly the same manner and say that it
has been "confirmed by all revolutions." Lenin, "The Collapse
of the Second International," Vol. XXI, pp. 213-214 and "Left-
Wing Communism--An Infantile Disorder," Vol. XXXI, pp. 84-85.

[13]Auguste Blanqui was a well-known French revolutionary leader
of the nineteenth century. He argued that a small conscious revolutionary minority ought to seize power--as he and his followers
unsuccessfully attempted to do while seeking to establish on
several occasions la dictature Parisienne--and then seek to win
over the popular masses to the idea of introducing a communist
social system. In this connection Lenin observed that a successful insurrection "must rely not upon conspiracy and not upon a
party, but upon the advanced class. That is the first point.
Insurrection must rely upon a revolutionary upsurge of the people.
That is the second point. Insurrection must rely upon that turning point in the history of the growing revolution when the acti-

vity of the advanced rank of the people is at its height, and when
the vacillations in the ranks of the enemy and in the ranks of the
weak, half-hearted and irresolute friends of the revolution are
strongest. That is the third point. And these three conditions
for raising the question of insurrection distinguish marxism from
blanquism" [our emphasis]. Thus, Lenin clearly does not emphasize the mere technical side of insurrection. But is it not also
true that the "advanced class" or proletariat--however representative Lenin might have been--had to win the battle for the
overwhelming majority of the Russian population after the capture
of political power by a small conscious revolutionary minority?
Blanqui, Textes Choisis, pp. 7-47, Maurice Dommanget, Les Idées
Politiques et Sociales d'Auguste Blanqui, pp. 170-195, Cole,
Socialist Thought, Vol. I, p. 164, Robert C. Tucker, ed., The
Lenin Anthology, pp. 407-412 and O.H. Radkey, The Sickle Under
the Hammer, pp. 203-279.

[14]While Marx and Engels were certainly aware of the changing
nature of British capitalism and the effect that this was having
both on the world scene and the domestic front--as was seen in
Chapter I --there is no coherent theory of imperialism, as such,
to be found in their works. Lenin, however, aided by the works
of 19th and 20th century liberal and "marxist" economists, did
advance such a theory. Imperialism, he said, is the "monopoly
stage of capitalism." All of the contradictions of "national"
capitalism--such as uneven development, competition for markets
and sources of investment, etc.--with their revolutionary implications are now transferred to the colonial and semi-colonial world.
"Imperialism is capitalism at that stage of development at which
the dominance of monopolies and finance capital is established;
in which the export of capital has acquired pronounced importance;
in which the division of the world among the international trusts
has begun, in which the division of all territories of the globe
among the biggest capitalist powers has been completed." And,
said Lenin, out of the "enormous superprofits [obtained in the
colonial and semi-colonial world]. . . it is possible to bribe
the labor leaders and the upper stratum of the labor aristocracy"
in the West. But what the capitalists take as a final settling
of the "national" contradictions is merely a deepening and internationalizing of these contradictions because the "labor lieute-
nants of the capitalist class" and the "superprofits" will be able
to contain the working class movement in the West for a short
period of time. Lenin adduced two basic reasons for his optimism:
1) the coming Russian revolution (or presumably another "weak
link" in the imerialist chain--thus, in part, his support for the
right of self-determination for oppressed nationalities) could
serve to "kindle" socialist revolution in the West, and 2) because
the unavoidably uneven development spawned by imperialism
"inevitably" leads to wars for a "redivision of the booty." As a
result of this, all the contradictions of the imperialist wars--
which lead to a general attack upon the living standards of the

Western workers, the weakening of their illusions about "bourgeois democracy," etc.--convince the Western working class of the
necessity to struggle for socialism where "all the objective conditions " exist for its realization. Lenin, "Imperialism, the
Highest Stage of Capitalism," Vol. XXII, pp. 190-191 and 265-276,
"The Socialist Revolution and the Right of Nations to Self-Determination," Vol. XXII, pp. 143-144 and On Britain, pp. 42 and
64.

[15]Writing from his Swiss exile in 1916 Lenin said that "without ceasing its fight to improve the position of the wage-slaves,
the [Swiss social democratic] party calls upon the working class
and its representatives to put on the order of the day propaganda
for an immediate socialist revolution in Switzerland." Indeed
all of Europe was now "pregnant with revolution." Why was this
so? As Cliff correctly put it, "Lenin's prediction that the
imperialist war, by exacerbating the internal contradictions
of capitalism, would lead to civil war, was largely based on
the experience of 1904-1905. Then the military defeat of tsarism
by Japan had led directly to the first Russian revolution. Now
the imperialist war was on a much wider scale. The revolutionary
repercussions must therefore be greater." Lenin, "Kautsky, Axelrod, Martov--True Internationalist," Vol. XXI, p. 399, "The War
and Russian Social Democracy," Vol. XXI, p. 37, "Theses on the
Attitude of the Swiss Social Democratic Party Towards the War,"
Vol. XXIII, pp. 150-151, "Lecture on the 1905 Revolution," Vol.
XXIII, pp. 252-253 and Tony Cliff, Lenin, Vol. II, p. 62.

[16]He wrote in January 1917 that "we of the older generation
may not live to see the decisive battles of this coming revolution. But I can, I believe, express the confident hope that the
youth which is working so splendidly in the socialist movement of
Switzerland, and of the whole world, will be fortunate enough not
only to fight, but also to win, in the coming proletarian revolution." Lenin, "Lecture on the 1905 Revolution," Vol. XXIII, p.
253.

[17]"It is often said that the February revolution was spontaneous, and in fact it was not organized by any party or by any
political leader." Marcel Liebman, The Russian Revolution, pp.
98 and 175. Moreover, the bolsheviks were in an especially difficult situation as they had been--from the beginning of the war--
sent into exile, jailed, etc. Their initial participation in the
revolution would therefore be of necessity somewhat limited.

[18]Lenin regarded the "dictatorship of the proletariat" as
the "touchstone" of marxism. "A marxist is solely someone who
extends the recognition of the class struggle to the recognition

of the dictatorship of the proletariat. This is what constitutes
the most profound distinction between the marxist and the ordinary petty (as well as big) bourgeois. This is the touchstone
on which the real understanding and recognition of marxism should
be tested." And whereas Marx and Engels--who rarely used the ex-
pression--considered the period of the dictatorship of the proletariat as a "short transitional" period towards the classless
society, Lenin now tells us that it consists of "an entire historical epoch." And lest we be mistaken about what this "epoch"
will be all about, Lenin assures us that "the word dictatorship
is a cruel, stern, bloody and painful one; it is not a word to
play with." But, if the working class and its peasant allies
constitute the overwhelming majority of the population under the
dictatorship of the proletariat, why must there be another epoch
of stern, painful and bloody rule? Lenin tells us that "it is
precisely after the bourgeoisie is overthrown that the class
struggle assumes its acutest forms." And this is so because
the bourgeoisie "still have an international base in the form of
international capital, of which they are a branch." Thus, the
"mercilessly severe rule" of the dictatorship of the proletariat--
lasting a whole "epoch"--is directed only against a tiny fraction
of the population--the local "bourgeoisie"--which is backed by the
system of international finance capital. We have traversed quite
a distance from the ideas of Marx and Engels. To be sure, Lenin
gives a more "international" flavor to this "intensified" class
struggle than would Stalin--as we shall see in the next chapter--
but is not the die already cast? Lenin, "Economics and Politics,"
Vol. XXX, pp. 108-115, "First All-Russia Congress on Adult Education," Vol. XXIX, pp. 355-356 and 381, "The State and Revolution," Vol. XXV, pp. 411-412 and Alliance of the Working Class
and the Peasantry, p. 216.

[19]As we have seen Lenin never had any illusions about what
he called the petty bourgeois nature of the peasantry. "Owing
to their economic status in bourgeois society the peasants must
follow either the workers or the bourgeoisie. There is no middle
way." The only "salvation" for the peasants is to follow the
lead of the proletariat. But Lenin said that in the struggle
with the bourgeoisie for leadership of the peasant masses no force
must be used in order to reach an "agreement" with them. "We
must render every support to the working peasant, treat him as an
equal, without the slightest attempt to impose anything on him by
force--that is our first task." And he said further that "the
middle peasants [the majority of the population and the result
of the October revolution] do not exploit others and are not exploited themselves; they earn their livelihood on their small
farms by their own labor. Not a single socialist in the world
ever proposed that the small farmer should be deprived of his
property. The small farmer will exist for many years to come.
No decrees will have any effect here; we must wait until the

peasants have learned to be guided by experience. When they see
that collective farming is far better, they will come over to our
side. We must win their confidence." As there was "no question
of forcibly imposing socialism on anyone," Lenin--though for
practical reasons--likewise sought to win the confidence of the
intellectual community. "Communism cannot be built without knowledge, technique, and culture, and this knowledge is in possession
of bourgeois specialists. Most of them do not sympathize with
Soviet power, yet without them we cannot build communism. They
must be surrounded with an atmosphere of comradeship, a spirit of
communist work, and won over to the side of the workers' and
peasants' government." But Lenin's appeal for an "agreement" with
the peasantry (and even the intellectual community) will increasingly seem to take on the flavor of being much more than a mere
temporary pact pending the outcome of the world revolution. Lenin,
"Plenerary Meeting of Moscow Soviet," Vol. XXIX, pp. 265-266,
"First All-Russia Congress on Adult Education," Vol. XXIX, pp.
365-370, "Left Narodniks Whitewash Bourgeoisie," Vol. XX, p. 216,
"1st Conference on Party Work in the Countryside," Vol. XXX, pp.
145-150, "Elections and the Dictatorhsip of the Proletariat,"
Vol. XXX, p. 257 and "Moscow Party Workers' Meeting," Vol. XXVIII,
p. 203.

[20]It should be noted that having won political power the
bolshevik party--partly flowing from Lenin's conception of the
imminence of world revolution--had no clearly defined economic
program for industry or agriculture. Economic policy tended to be
dictated by events. For example, immediately after the revolution
ithere was a certain flirtation with "workers' control" of industry
that swiftly gave way in the course of the Civil War to the
nationalization of "the great bulk of the means of production."
Furthermore, why did the bolsheviks endorse in October what
amounted to a dividing up of the land among the peasantry? Lenin,
of course, felt that he had covered his tracks while saying that
the land, however divided, was now "the property of the whole
nation." Be that as it may, Lenin probably had no other choice--
less he risk open warfare with the countryside--but to adopt the
agrarian program of the social revolutionary party. He would
answer all his critics in the following manner: "As a democratic
government, we cannot ignore the decision of the masses of people
[the peasants were then seizing the landed estates and dividing
them up among themselves], even though we may disagree with it."
He, however, was convinced that "in the fire of experience. . .
the peasants will themselves realize where the truth lies."
And there was no doubt--as far as Lenin was concerned--that the
"truth" was the advantages of large-scale farming over individual
farming. Lenin's "agreement" with the peasantry would receive
its firmest sanctification with the introduction of the New
Economic Policy in 1921--to which we shall turn in the context of
the Trotsky-Stalin debate. It is sufficient for us to point out

here that from around 1920, Lenin's "firm conviction" of 1918 that "happy time is not far away" had soberly vanished. Instead of so much talk about world socialism being just around the corner, his primary concern now was in finding a way to stabilize the Soviet Government. Thus, his concessions to the peasantry took on that much more importance. Lenin, "Congress of Peasants' Deputies," Vol. XXIV, p. 169, "First Congress of Soviets of Peasants' Deputies," Vol. XXVI, pp. 324-326, "The Third Congress of the Communist International," Vol. XXXII, p. 475, "Fourth Anniversary of the October Revolution," Vol. XXXIII, p. 54 and "Ninth All-Russia Congress of Soviets," Vol. XXXIII, p. 160.

[21] Lenin, "Account of Second Congress of R.S.D.L.P.," Vol. VII, p. 27, Dan, The Origins of Bolshevism, pp. 254-255, and Getaler, Martov, p. 79.

[22] In this connection Martov pointed out that "in our eyes, the labor party is not limited to an organization of professional revolutionaries. It consists of them plus the entire combination of the active, leading elements of the proletariat. . . . " As cited by Leopold H. Haimson, The Russian Marxists and the Origins of Bolshevism, pp. 176 and 186 and Lenin, "What Is To Be Done," Vol. V, p. 480.

[23] Trotsky's sharp attacks on economism and bundism during the early sessions of the congress earned him the title of Lenin's "big stick." The economistic current in Russian social democracy asserted that there was a basic distinction between economic and political questions in the working class movement. As politics was of no concern to the workers, the struggle around existing "petty needs" in the factory would impel the workers toward more "serious struggle." They stated that "the masses are really enlightened only by the experience of their own struggle, which initially must necessarily be economic in character. . . the economic struggle constitutes the first form of the mass movement, the beginning of the class awakening of the proletariat, the school of its political training. . . . From this follows the well-known gradualness of our agitational activity. The latter constitutes a pedagogical method for the purpose of attracting the masses to the movement and developing their class consciousness." However, in 1901 (less than a year after this statement was written), the political line of the economists--under the impact of the unexpected political demands of the worker-student demonstrations of that year--began to shift "with dramatic suddenness" towards a hastening of the political struggle against tsarism. Haimson, The Russian Marxists and the Origins of Bolshevism, pp. 121-123. Can it be said then--as Lenin and Trotsky charged at the party congress--that economism represented a "bowing to spontaneity?" On the other hand, the bund or Jewish workers' organi-

zation was not only demanding autonomy within the social democratic party but the exclusive right to represent the Jewish
proletariat. Trotsky put it this way, "should the bund be the
only representative of the interests of the Jewish proletariat
in the party and before the party, or should the bund be a
special organization of the party for agitation and propaganda
among the Jewish proletariat? This is how the problem can be
posed. And in recognizing the necessity of the independent
existence of the bund in the second sense, it can be brought
into the party as a subordinate organization, exercising independence in certain spheres on a limited number of given problems.
In such a case, there can be no talk about special guarantees for
the bund against encroachments on the part of the party."
Neither the economists nor bundists had it their way at the 1903
congress. Dan, The Origins of Bolshevism, pp. 207-216, Carr,
The Bolshevik Revolution, Vol. I, pp. 10-13, Richard Pipes,
Social Democracy and the St. Petersburg Labor Movement, 1885-
1897, pp. 124-125, Joseph Nedava, Trotsky and the Jews, pp. 84-
99, Henry J. Tobias, The Jewish Bund in Russia, pp. 207-220 and
and Lenin, "What Is To Be Done," Vol. V, p. 378.

[24]According to Lenin, however, "the root of the mistake made
by those who stand for Martov's formulation is that they not only
ignore one of the main evils of our party life, but even sanctify
it. The evil is that, at a time when political discontent is
almost universal, when conditions require our work to be carried
on in complete secrecy, and when most of our activities have to
be confined to limited, secret circles and even to private meetings, it is extremely difficult, almost impossible in fact, for
us to distinguish those who only talk from those who do the work.
There is hardly another country in the world where the jumbling
of these two categories is as common and as productive of such
boundless confusion and harm as in Russia." Lenin, Second Congress of the R.S.D.L.P.," Vol. VI, p. 501.

[25]Trotsky, the leader of the Petersburg Soviet during its
heroic "fifty days," would grudgingly acknowledge years later that
"under the pressure of the masses, the mensheviks in the soviets
[in 1905] during its first period did their utmost to keep in line
with the left flank." Yet, a menshevik resolution--perhaps under
a certain Parvus-Trotsky influence--as late as November stated
that "although we are bound to go through a democratic revolution
as a prelude to the socialist one, the two may not be separated,
as in the West, by a long period of peaceful development. It is
quite possible that, if the civil war were prolonged for any length
of time, what began as a democratic revolution in our country
might turn into a socialist one. At all events we must never lose
sight of this possibility." To be sure, the mensheviks would
"lose sight" of this perspective in a very short while. But this

temporary "revolutionizing" of menshevism under revolutionary conditions in 1905 is exactly what Trotsky hoped would happen during the next phase of the revolutionary process to both wings of the social democratic party. Trotsky, My Life, p. 182, Ascher, ed., The Mensheviks in the Russian Revolution, pp. 58-59 and Haimson, ed., The Mensheviks, p. 368.

[26]Trotsky, Nos Tâches Politiques, pp. 122 and 128 and Lenin, "One Step Forward, Two Steps Back," Vol. Vii, p. 394. We note also that Rosa Luxemburg, a leader of the German social democratic party, was similarly attacking Lenin's "ultra-centralism" in 1904. In her "Organizational Question of Social Democracy" she said that "the ultracentralism asked by Lenin is full of the sterile spirit of the overseer. It is not a positive and creative spirit. Lenin's concern is not so much to make the activity of the party more fruitful as to control the party--to narrow the movement rather than to develop it, to bind it rather than to unify it." After charging Lenin with being victimized by the "same subjectivism that has already played more than one trick on socialist thinking in Russia," she goes on to say that "nothing will more surely enslave a young labor movement to an intellectual elite hungry for power than this bureaucratic straitjacket, which will immobilize the movement and turn it into an automaton manipulated by a Central Committee. On the other hand, there is no more effective guaranteee against opportunist intrigue and personal ambition than the independent revolutionary action of the proletariat, as a result of which the workers acquire a sense of political responsibility and self-reliance. What is today only a phantom haunting Lenin's imagination may become reality tomorrow" [our emphasis]. Mary-Alice Waters, ed., Rosa Luxemburg Speaks, pp. 122, 126-127 and 129-130 and Lenin "To Yelena Stasova,F.V. Lengnik, and Others," Vol. XLIII, p. 129.

[27]Lenin, "One Step Forward, Two Steps Back," Vol. VII, p. 381.

[28]Luxemburg likewise questioned the role that Lenin assigned the intellectual in the revolutionary process. She said that "the milieu where intellectuals are recruited for socialism in Russia is much more declassed and by far less bourgeois than in Western Europe. Added to the immaturity of the Russian proletarian movement, this circumstance is an influence for wide theoretical wandering, which ranges from the complete negation of the political aspects of the labor movement to the unqualified belief in the effectiveness of isolated terrorist acts, or even total political indifference sought in the swamps of liberalism and Kantian idealism. . . [and] it is by extreme centralization that a young, uneducated proletarian movement can be most completely handed over to the intellectual leaders staffing a Central Committee." Waters, ed., Rosa Luxemburg Speaks, pp. 125-126, Alain Brossat,

Aux Origines De La Révolution Permanente, pp. 70-84, Joel Carmichael, Trotsky, pp. 91-92, Deutscher, The Prophet Armed, pp.
187-190, Haimson, The Russian Marxists and the Origins of Bolshevism, p. 177, Pierre Fervacque, La Vie Orgueilleuse De Trotsky,
pp. 14-33 and Lenin, "What Is To Be Done," Vol. V, pp. 375-376
and 383-384.

[29]"After 1904 I stood outside of both the social democratic
factions. I . . . hoped . . . that the mensheviks would move
farther to the left and I made several attempts to bring about a
union in the party. It was not until the war that I became finally convinced of the utter hopelessness of the mensheviks." One
of these "attempts" was the so-called "August Bloc" (a coalition
of mensheviks, splinter bolshevik groups, trotskyists, etc.) which
officially existed from August 1912 until 1914. It represented
Tortsky's last attempt at seeking "unity at all cost." Lenin,
however, soundly denounced "Judas Trotsky" who "beats his breasts
and loudly professes his loyalty to the party" while in league
with "conciliators," "splitters" and other such anti-party elements. And with the bankruptcy of Trotsky's last ditch effort,
Lenin would officially declare the bolsheviks as the Party of
Russian social democracy in 1912. We might add here that during
the early years of their feud, it was Trotsky who wielded the
fiercer epithets. But with the approach of the war years, it was
Lenin. Trotsky, My Life, pp. 165, 224 and 329 and The Permanent
Revolution, p. 173, Lenin "Judas Trotsky's Blush of Shame," Vol.
XVII, p. 45, "Historical Meaning of Inner-Party Struggle in
Russia," Vol. XVI, p. 391, "Unity," Vol. XX, pp. 230-232, "Dis-
ruption of Unity Under Cover of Outcires for Unity," Vol. XX, pp.
325-247 and Trotsky, "Statement of Solidarity with the Bolshevik
Leaders," The Age of Permanent Revolution, p. 98.

[30]"Without a party, apart from a party, over the head of a
party, or with a substitute for a party, the proletarian revolution cannot conquer." This is clearly not the Trotsky who wrote
years earlier that consciousness is born "as a consequence of the
inexorable laws of the dependence of human psychology upon the
conditions of social life and labor. . . ." Yet, Trotsky--even
after the October revolution--occasionally gives the impression
of not having fully absorbed the significance of the leninist
party in the revolutionary process. For instance, in his chef-
d'oeuvre The History of the Russian Revolution--though he clearly
sees the need for a "revolutionary organization capable of rising
to the height of its historic task"--he appears to give greater
weight in the revolutionary process to the "swift, intense and
passionate changes in the psychology of classes." This has led
some of his critics to charge him with "sociologism." And some
have gone so far as to say that this is the original sin of
trotskyism. According to Nicholas Krasso, "economism naturally

leads to passivity and tailism; sociologism, on the contrary, tends
to lead to voluntarism. . . . In his [Trotsky's] writings mass
forces are presented as constantly dominant in society, without
any political organizations or institutions intervening as necessary and permanent levels of the social formation. Lenin's marxism,
by contrast, is defined by the notion of a complex totality, in
which all levels-economic, social, political, and ideological--
are always operational, and there is a permutation of the main
locus of contradictions between them. Trotsky's extrapolation
of mass forces from this complex tier of levels was the ultimate
source of his theoretical mistakes, both before and after the
revolution." We believe that as an assessment of Trotsky's pre-
1917 positions this statement is essentially correct. But more
importantly--despite the assertions of Krasso and others--and on
a more general level, Trotsky, Lenin, Marx, Engels and Stalin
(whom we shall meet presently) can all be indicted for having
"extrapolated" from the "complex totality" of human society.
Trotsky, "Problems of War" and "The Lessons of October," Challenge
of the Left Opposition, pp. 185, 205 and 252-253, The History of
the Russian Revolution, Vol. I, p. XVIII and Vol. III, p. 173,
"Results and Prospects," PR, p. 98 and Nicolas Krasso, ed.,
Trotsky: The Great Debate Renewed, pp. 18-22.

[31]Lenin, "The Aim of Proletarian Struggle in Our Revolution,"
Vol. XV, p. 374.

[32]But it should be remembered that while Trotsky said that
the coming Russian revolution would be proletarian, he never
failed to underline that its immediate tasks would be bourgeois.
"So far as its direct and indirect tasks are concerned, the
Russian revolution is a 'bourgeois' revolution because it sets
out to liberate bourgeois society from the chains and fetters of
absolutism and feudal ownership. But the principal driving force
of the Russian revolution is the proletariat, and that is why, so
far as its method is concerned, it is a proletarian revolution."
Trotsky, "Results and Prospects," PR, pp. 66-67, 1905, pp. 49 and
316-217 and Denise Avenas, La Pensée de Leon Trotsky, p. 19.

[33]Lenin would also charge that "Trotsky's major mistake is
that he ignores the bourgeois character of the revolution and has
no clear conception of the transition from this revolution to the
socialist revolution." But as we have seen, Trotsky quite specifically considered the coming Russian revolution as bourgeois in
its immediate objective tasks. These and similar statements by
Lenin evidence either a misreading or lack of reading of what
Trotsky was actually saying at the time. It is not for nothing
that Trotsky would later say that Lenin never read his basic
work. "Never," he said, "did Lenin anywhere analyze or quote, even
in passing, Results and Prospects, and certain objections of

Lenin to the permanent revolution, which obviously have no reference to me, directly prove that he did not read this work." And Carr said that "Trotsky was probably right in holding that Lenin had never read Results and Prospects." Lenin, "The Aim of Proletarian Struggle in Our Revolution," Vol. XV, pp. 371-374 and "On the Two Lines in the Revolution," Vol. XXI, pp. 419-420, Trotsky, The Permanent Revolution, p. 166, Carr, The Bolshevik Revolution, Vol. I, p. 60 and Deutscher, The Prophet Armed, p. 162.

[34]Trotsky, "Results and Prospects," PR, p. 63.

[35]Lenin, "Two Tactics," Vol. IX, pp. 57 and 130, Meyer, Leninism, p. 144, Carr, The Bolshevik Revolution, Vol. I, pp. 99-100, Anweiler, The Soviets, p. 87 and Deutscher, The Prophet Armed, pp. 255-259.

[36]Meyer, Leninism, pp. 271-272.

CHAPTER III

THE STRUGGLE FOR SOCIALISM AND DEMOCRACY

IN THE WORKERS' STATE

I. Stalin and Socialism in One Country

Although Stalin is not usually thought of as a theoretician, the ideas on socialism that he began to advance in 1924 assume considerable importance because of the supreme position of leadership that he would subsequently exercise and the impact of the Soviet Union on the further development of "marxist" thought.[1] And while Stalin liked to emphasize that he was a "creative" rather than a "dogmatic" marxist, it seems clear the the theory of socialism in one country--at least in its more polished sense-- was as much the product of Bukharin as Stalin. But it was Stalin who transformed it into an article of faith in "marxist" thought.[2] The general background for the emergence of this new doctrine in 1924 was the apparent exhaustion of the revolutionary process both in Russia and Western Europe.* However, the immediate stimulus

---

*The new conditions of life facing the Soviet Government in 1924 flowed essentially from powerful events that began to take shape both internally and internationally as early as 1920: 1) on the international front the most important event was the realization by Lenin and his government that the long awaited supportive revolutions in the West were not immediately forthcoming. This was dramatically symbolized in 1920 by Lenin's decision following the defeat of the Polish Army in the Ukrainian region during the Civil War to march the Red Army on Warsaw as liberators in the hopes of arousing the Polish peasants and workers to the side of the Russian revolution. In fact, the Red Army was "received" as an invading force and bitterly opposed. Lenin would later say of this Napoleonic effort that "our offensive. . . was undoubtedly a mistake." Indeed, he was now convinced that a sort of "relative equilibrium" now temporarily existed on the revolutionary fronts. The new international situation called for "winning the majority of the workers" rather than organizing the insurrection; 2) and as was indicated in Chapter II, the new internal reality was symbolized by the urgency of Lenin's new "agreement with the peasantry" or New Economic Policy. This "reverting to capitalism to a considerable extent"--as Lenin described the NEP--was fraught with difficulties for Soviet economic development. Though Lenin made it clear that "we shall carry out this policy in earnest and for a long time, but, of course. . .

for the unfolding of Stalin's ideas on socialism was the challenge
of the largely trotskyist inspired 1923 Opposition and its after-
math, the so-called literary debate. This Opposition--to which we
will shortly turn--brought into question what it saw as a bureaucratic and economic disaster which was rapidly consuming the party,
country, and the revolution. It challenged Stalin and the Majority to reintroduce within the party and country the leninist
approach to revolutionary organization and development. But the
problem here is that both groups within the party hierarchy--the
Majority and the Opposition--advanced their arguments from the
standpoint of leninism. And as we have seen, leninism is so ambiguous on many points that both sides--through selectively
quoting and emphasizing--could justifiably claim that heritage as
its own. With this in mind, would not the "less revolutionary
side" of leninism find firmer roots in a Russia that was neither
capable nor willing to be what it thought it would be in 1917?
And would not the struggle between Stalin and Trotsky be inherently unequal?

It was against this background and in the context of a debate
with Trotsky[3] that Stalin began to advance his ideas on socialism:

> Formerly, the victory of the revolution in
> one country was considered impossible, on the
> assumption that it would require the combined
> action of the proletarians of all or at least of
> a majority of the advanced countries to achieve
> victory over the bourgeoisie. Now this point of
> view no longer fits in with the facts.

But what exactly did Stalin mean by "the victory of the revolution
in one country?" A few passages later in the same work he states

---
ll

not for ever," he left several grey areas of contention for his
followers. At what point would a conflict between town and countryside make it necessary to progressively (or abruptly) abandon the
NEP? How much weight should be accorded to the inevitable development of a differentiation of wealth among the peasantry?
With the death of Lenin in 1924 and facing these "new realities,"
the stage was set for the introduction of Stalin's new ideas on
the nature and meaning of socialism. Lenin, "Tenth Congress of
the R.C.P. (B.)," Vol. XXXII, p. 173 and "Ninth All-Russia Congress of Soviets," Vol. XXXIII, p. 160.

that "after consolidating its power and leading the peasantry in
its wake the proletariat of the victorious country can and must
build a socialist society." This is so because "we possess all
that is needed" in order to build a "complete socialist society."*
This appears to be a clear abandoning of the international character of the socialist revolution. Stalin, however, edged away from
this very implicit reference by distinguishing between the "victory" in one country and the "final" and necessary victory on the
international plane. He tells us that the victory in one country
means the possibility of building "a complete socialist society in
our country, with the sympathy and the support of the proletarians
of other countries, but without the preliminary victory of the
proletarian revolution in other countries." But the idea of the
final victory "means the impossibility of having a full guarantee
against intervention, and consequently against the restoration of
the bourgeois order, without the victory of the revolution in at
least a number of countries."[4]

And the "law of uneven development"--over which Trotsky and
Stalin would later clash--provides the theoretical basis for the
theory of socialism in one country. Thus Marx and Engels' "old
formula"--which declared that the joint activity of workers of
several, if not all, advanced countries was needed for the victory
of socialism--should be understood as an essentially 19th century
outlook on the prospects for socialist revolution. Stalin, however, would argue that during the "pre-imperialist" phase of
capitalism there was historical justification in accepting the
"old formula":

> In the old period. . . when the globe had not yet
> been divided up among financial groups, when the forcible
> redivision of an already divided world was not yet a matter
> of life or death for capitalism, when unevenness of

---

*It should be noted that the views that Stalin is now (1924)
beginning to expound were not always his. "It is there, in the
West, that the chains of imperialism. . . must first of all be
smashed. It is there, first of all in the West, that the new,
socialist life must vigorously develop." To be sure, Stalin had
frequently commented on the "subterranean forces" of the revolution or that the Russian revolution would spring "from the depth"
of the laboring people without in the same context giving any
attention--unlike Lenin--to the primarily international framework
of the forthcoming socialist revolution in Russia. But, on the
whole, Stalin--until late 1924--tended to place the Russian revolution within the framework of the international revolution;
namely, the non-acceptance of the idea that socialism in Russia
could be built "by our own efforts." Stalin, "To All the Toilers,"

economic development was not, and could not be, as
sharply marked as it became later, when the contradictions of capitalism had not yet reached that degree
of development at which they convert flourishing capitalism into moribund capitalism thus opening up the
possibility of the victory of socialism in individual
countries--in that old period the formula of Engels
[and Marx] was undeniably correct.

During the period of "imperialism," however, it is incorrect not
to recognize the significance of unevenness in the historical
process and its revolutionary implications:

The law of uneven development in the period of
imperialism means the spasmodic development of some
countries relative to others, the rapid ousting from
the world market of some countries by others, periodic
redivisions of the already divided world through military conflicts and catastrophic wars, the increasing
profundity and acuteness of the conflicts in the imperialist camp, the weakening of the capitalist world
front, the possibility of this front being breached
by the proletariat of individual countries, and the
possibility of the victory of socialism in individual
countries.*

Vol. III, p. 150, "Don't Forget the East," and "One Immediate
Task," Vol. IV, pp. 76 and 174, "The Foundations of Leninism,"
Vol. VI, pp. 109-111 and "The Results of the Work of the Fourteen-
th Conference of the R.C.P.(B.)," Vol. VII, pp. 117-118.

*Stalin's charge that since the "law of uneven development
of capitalism had not yet been discovered and could not have been
discovered" in the 19th century "the old formula of Marx and
Engels no longer corresponds to the new historical conditions" is
incorrect. We noted earlier that although Marx and Engels were
not as precise in their definition of this "law"--as for example,
Trotsky--that they were aware of the significance and implications of unevenness in the revolutionary process cannot seriously
be brought into question. Stalin, "The Social Democratic Deviation in Our Party," Vol. VIII, pp. 259-261, "The Seventh Enlarged Plenum of the E.C.C.I.," Vol. IX, p. 111 and Marxism and
Linguistics, pp. 42-43 and Marx and Engels, "The German Ideology"
and "The Communist Manifesto," Selected Works, Vol. I, pp. 37,
62 and 127.

And lest we be misled, Stalin tells us immediately that it was
Lenin--and not he--who first advanced both the law of uneven development and the conception of "building socialism" in one
country. "Lenin's greatness as the continuer of the work of Marx
and Engels consists precisely in the fact that he was never a
slave to the letter of marxism." Dismissing the "textualists and
Talmudists" Lenin "raised the question of the necessity for a
new formula about the possibility of the victory of the proleta-
rain revolution in individual countries" in our party "as early
as 1915."[5] But what is the nature of this socialism which is now
possible in a single country as a result of Lenin's "discovery"
of the law of uneven development?

In 1927 Stalin outlines a perspective on communist society
that does justice to that provided by Marx and Engels:

> It is a society in which: a) there will be no private
> ownership of the instruments and means of production,
> but social collective ownership; b) there will be no
> classes or state power, but there will be working people
> in industry and agriculture who manage economic affairs as
> a free association of working people; c) the national
> economy, organized according to plan, will be based on the
> highest level of technique, both in industry and agri-
> culture; d) there will be no antithesis between town and
> country, between industry and agriculture.*

The essential point here is that "there will be no classes or
state power" within the future communist society as described
by Stalin in 1927. Things, we are told, must be entirely different under socialism. Confronted with the internal "remnants" of

---

*Note that Stalin--in the tradition of Lenin--makes a care-
ful distinction between socialist and communist society. Thus,
when Stalin decreed in 1936 that "we have already achieved the
first phase of communism, socialism" he said nothing about the non-
existence of classes nor the "withering away" of the state. He
merely said that the capitalist and landlord classes have been
"eliminated." As such, the remaining classes (workers and peasants) are non-antagonistic since the "exploitation of man by man
has been abolished" in the Soviet Union. Stalin, "Interview with
the First American Labor Delegation," Vol. X, pp. 139-140 and
"Report on Constitution," Selected Writings, pp. 382 and 386 and
Lenin, "Speech Before Metal Workers," Vol. XXXII, p. 109.

the now defeated exploiting classes and the external danger of
the "capitalist encirclement" the state--under the leadership of
the communist party[6]--must be strengthened to the utmost if it is
to survive in a hostile environment:

> Some comrades have interpreted the thesis about the
> abolition of classes, the creation of a classless society,
> and the withering away of the state as a justification of
> laziness and complacency, a justification of the counter-
> revolutionary theory of the extinction of the class
> struggle and the weakening of the state power. . . . The
> abolition of classes is not achieved by the extinction of
> the class struggle, but by its intensification. The
> state will wither away, not as a result of weakening
> the state power, but as a result of strengthening it to
> the utmost, which is necessary for finally crushing the
> remnants of the dying classes and for organizing defense
> against the capitalist encirclement, which is far from
> having been done away with as yet, and will not soon be
> done away with.*

Under socialism, therefore--and perhaps even communism--the continued existence of the state seems assured in Stalin's conception of the new society. Moreover, we are not certain as to
what he means by either socialism or communism except as he de-
fines them at a given moment.[7]

----

*This was written in 1933 in the midst of the crash collecti-
vization and industrialization campains in the Soviet Union. Yet,
even after the official proclamation of having reached socialism
in 1936 Stalin would continue to rail that "we must smash and throw
out the rotten theory that with each forward movement we make the
class struggle will die down more and more. . . . This is not
only a rotten theory but a dangerous theory for it lulls our
people to sleep. . . and makes it possible for the class enemy to
rally for the struggle against Soviet power." It would not be
until 1939--at the close of his massive blood purges--that Stalin
would officially declare that the "remnants of the exploiting
classes have been completely eliminated" in the Soviet Union.
Thus, we see that the conception of the intensification of the
class struggle after the victory of socialism in one country and
the existence of a "capitalist encirclement" are the major props
for Stalin's argument that the state must be "strengthened to
the utmost" so that it will be able to "wither away." Engels,
"old formula" on the "withering away of the state," said Stalin,
"is inapplicable to the case when socialism triumphs in one particular country while capitalism rules in all other countries."
Indeed, contrary to his position in 1927, Stalin would go so far
as to say that the state possibly could even exist under communism

When all is said and done, however, the ideas on socialism that can more or less be defined as Stalin's--only the germs of which can be found in Lenin's writings--are the following: 1) the conception that after the proletarian revolution not only can the process of constructing socialism in one country begin but that it can be completed in the absence of several revolutions occurring in the "advanced" countries; and 2) the idea that the workers' state--under the leadership of the communist party-- facing the intensification of the class struggle after the victory of socialism in one country and the dangers posed by the capitalist encirclement must be strengthened "to the utmost" before it ultimately "withers away."

II. Trotsky and the World Socialist System

We have seen that Stalin considered the law of uneven development as the very foundation for his theory of socialism in one country. In this section we will present Trotsky's response to that argument and his conceptions of socialism and the workers' state. Let's recall here that the starting point for Trotsky's theory of revolution or permanent revolution is the law of uneven or combined development. "Unevenness. . . reveals itself most sharply and complexly in the destiny of the backward countries. . .   From the universal law of unevenness. . . derives another law which, for the lack of a better name, we may call the law of combined development. . ." The important point here is that "backward" nations forming "a peculiar combination of different stages in the historic process" can--under certain historical conditions--temporarily leap ahead of the more "advanced" nations in the revolutionary process. But he emphasized that even though "the prediction that historically backward Russia could arrive at the proletarian revolution sooner than advanced Britain rests

---

proper. "Will our state remain in the period of communism also? Yes, it will, unless the capitalist encirclement is liquidated, and unless the danger of foreign military attack has disappeared." Nowhere in the works of Marx, Engels and Lenin could Stalin find support for such a claim. But since he prided himself at being a "creative" rather than a "dogmatic" marxist, why should he have sought such support? Stalin, "The Result of the First Five-Year Plan," Vol. XIII, p. 215, "Report to the 18th Party Congress," SW, pp. 445 and 474 and Marxism and Lingusitics, p. 43, R.V. Daniels, ed., A Documentary History of Communism, Vol. II, p. 57, Robert Conquest, The Great Terror, pp. 699-713 and Lenin, "Economics and Politics," Vol. XXX, pp. 114-115 and "Speech at Transport Workers Congress," Vol. XXXII, p. 272.

entirely upon the law of uneven development,"* this was only
the national side of the revolutionary process. "The Workers'
state can be preserved from mortal dangers, not only military
but also economic, only by the victorious development of the proletarian revolution in the West." Only timely assistance from the
West can carry the revolutionary process towards a socialist conclusion.** This is not so merely because of the military threat
posed by the advanced West but more importantly because the law
of uneven development, itself, is subordinated to the processes
of the world economy. Therefore, Trotsky argued, even if a
victorious proletarian revolution in a backward country were able
to beat back a military assault from the West, it still--contrary
to Stalin--would not be able to build a "complete" socialist society. At best, the victorious proletarian revolution could only
begin the process of socialist construction. Yet, the very dependence of the law of uneven development upon economic categories makes it impossible for advanced no less than backward
countries to reach socialism independently of a world socialist

---

*"We have attributed the October revolution in the last
analysis not to the fact of Russia's backwardness, but the law
of combined development." Trotsky, The History of the Russian
Revolution, Vol. I, pp. 5-6 and Vol. III, p. 379 and The Permanent Revolution, p. 241. Note that he seprately refers to "uneven" and then "combined" development. There is, however, no real
distinction between the two aspects of the same "law."

**We should point out that when Trotsky, in the late 1920s,
undertook to debate Stalin on the theory of socialism in one
country he began to stress--unlike earlier years both before and
after the bolshevik victory--the "economic" threat to the revolution. With the threat of foreign invasion less and less a real
factor after the first years of the revolution, he increasingly
tended to de-emphasize the "military" side of the threat facing
the Soviet Union--though this would change in the period just
prior to the Second World War. For now, "a Ford tractor is just
as dangerous as a Creusot gun, with the sole difference that
while the gun can only function from time to time, the tractor
brings its pressure to bear upon us constantly. Besides the
tractor knows that a gun stands behind it, as a last resort."
Trotsky, The Third International After Lenin, p. 48, The Permanent Revolution, pp. 262-264 and La Guerre Et La Revolution,
Vol. II, p. 325.

system. "From the uneven, sporadic development of capitalism flows the non-simultaneous, uneven, and sporadic character of the socialist revolution; from the extreme intensity of the interdependence of the various countries upon each other flows not only the political but also the economic impossibility of building socialism in one country."[8]

There are, therefore, two crucial sides to Trotsky's conception of the law of uneven development. On the one hand, while this "law" allows for the possibility of a backward country to begin the process of socialist construction, the very existence of "uneven development" proves to be an insurmountable obstacle in the path of any attempt to build a complete socialist society with the resources of any single backward country. On the other hand, however, because of the interdependence of the world economy this same "law" makes it impossible for any advanced country to realize socialism outside of the international arena. Citing Britain as an example of this latter point Trotsky observed that precisely "because of the excessive development of her productive forces which require almost the whole world to furnish the necessary raw materials and to dispose of her products" even Britain has "no chance for successful socialist construction" within her own borders. The question of building socialism is not settled by the industrial maturity or immaturity of a particular country, he said, but is instead primarily a problem of international economics.*[9]

But what is the nature of Trotsky's socialism? Most importantly he clearly distinguishes between socialism and communism proper on the one hand and a victorious proletarian revolution or the creation of a workers' state on the other hand. In fact, his conception of a socialist or communist society is much in the manner of Marx and Engels. It would be a soicety

---

*"From the world-wide division of labor, from the unevenness of development of different countries, from their mutual economic dependence, from the unevenness of different aspects of culture in the different countries, from the dynamic of the contemporary productive forces, it follows that the socialist structure can be built only by a system of economic spiral, only by taking the inner discords of a separate country out into a whole group of countries, only by a mutual service between different countries, and a mutual supplementation of the different branches of their industry and culture--that is, in the last analysis, only on the world arena." This is important because "internationalism is not an abstract principle but the expression of an economic fact." Trotsky, The History of the Russian Revolution, Vol. III, pp. 380-381 and 413 and The Third International After Lenin, pp. 56-58.

possessing neither classes nor state power and above all one of
material abundance. As he put it, "the material premise of communism should be so high a development of the economic powers of man
that productive labor, having ceased to be a burden, will not
require any goad, and the distribution of life's good, existing
in continuing abundance, will not demand. . . any control except
that of education, habit and social opinion." And since Trotsky
is here referring to the more developed phase of the future
classless society, he immediately insists that even at its lower
phase--sometimes called the socialist phase--this classless and
stateless society "from the very beginning stands higher in its
economic development than the most advanced capitalism." Again
and again emphasis is put on the need for the existence of an
abundance of goods. "The contemporaries of Marx knew nothing of
automobiles, radios, moving pictures, aeroplanes. A socialist
society, however, is unthinkable without free enjoyment of these
goods."*

Furthermore, the flow of Trotsky's perspective on socialism--
depsite its clear international dynamic--increasingly suggests
that a victorious socialist revolution in the principal Western
capitalist center (which was more and more the United States)
with its advanced technique and "international connections" would
have the effect of introducing the world socialist era almost
overnight. To be sure, he insists that even in America a socialist revolution would not "immediately" provide everyone with as
much as he needs, but unlike a regime springing from a proletarian revolution in an underdeveloped region of the world--which
he says might last "a whole historic epoch"--at least the material
foundations for socialist development exist in America prior to

------
*"The historical ascent of mankind consists in just this, that
a regime which assures a higher productivity of labor supersedes
regimes with a lower productivity. If capitalism supplanted
ancient feudal society it was only because human labor is more
productive under the rule of capital. And the main and sole reason why socialism will vanquish capitalism completely and definitely is because it will assure a far greater volume of products
per each unit of human labor power." Trotsky, The First Five
Years of the Communist International, Vol. II, p. 246, Problems
of Everyday Life, pp. 146-147, Literature and Revolution, pp.
254-256, The Age of Permanent Revolution: A Trotsky Anthology,
p. 212, Writings of Leon Trotsky [1932-33], pp. 215-216 and The
Revolution Betrayed, pp. 45-47, 57, 61 and 260.

the socialist revolution.* As socialism is closely bound up with
the destiny of the West, it seems clear that Trotsky, practically
speaking, was primarily concerned with characterizing that society
which he considered to be a "workers' state." In this connection,
he defined the Soviet state as a "transitional regime" situated
somewhere between capitalism and socialism. "The nationalization
of the land, the means of industrial production, transport and
exchange, together with the monopoly of foreign trade, constitute
the basis of the soviet social structure. Through these relations,
established by the proletarian revolution, the nature of the soviet
union as a proletarian state is for us basically defined." And he
tells us that the fundamental tasks of this workers' state should
be the "construction of a society without classes and without
material contradictions." Yet, the state, as both "stimulator"
of the productive forces and regulator of scarce resources--in
the context of international isolation and material and cultural
backwardness--might conceivably emerge as an obstacle in the path
of furthering the process of socialist development.[10] Here we
approach the hub of the problem confronting Trotsky's conception
of a workers' state in an underdeveloped country. Can it not be
said that a "workers' state" in such a situation can not be much
more than a regime of policemen?** It is with this in mind that
we will now examine Trotsky's views on the nature of the Soviet
state.

_____

*"Soviet forms of property [planning and social ownership] on
a basis of the most modern achievements of American technique
transplanted into all branches of economic life--that would indeed
be the first stage of socialism." He would also say that "Japan,
Great Britain and the other capitalist countries which intervened
in Russia couldn't do anything but take American communism lying
down. As a matter of fact that victory of communism in America--
the stronghold of capitalism--will cause communism to spread to
other countries." Just as Marx referred to Britain as the
"metropolis of capital," Trotsky came to refer to the United
States as the "stronghold of capitalism." And both drew the same
conclusions for the future of the world socialist system. Trotsky,
The Age of Permanent Revolution, pp. 215-216 and The Revolution
Betrayed, p. 61.

**"The basis of bureaucratic rule is the poverty of society
in objects of consumption, with the resulting struggle of each
against all. When there is enough goods in a store, the purchasers can come whenever they want to. When there is little
goods, the purchasers are compelled to stand in line. When the
lines are very long, it is necessary to appoint a policeman to
keep order." Trotsky, The Revolution Betrayed, p. 112. Thus,
Trotsky, himself, seems to confirm our standpoint. But he quick-

III. Trotsky's Struggle for Democracy in the Workers' State

Trotsky's concept of political revolution emerged against the background of his struggle for democracy in the Soviet Union. His "democratic" opposition to Stalin took place in two distinct phases.* We date the first from the fall of 1923 until his expulsion from the communist party in the fall of 1927 and the second from the fall of 1933 until his assassination in 1940. The introduction of the NEP and the banning of oppositional currents—both inside and outside of the communist party—in a war weary, exhausted and isolated Russia provided the setting for the first phase of Trotsky's struggle for democracy. Thus, we must initially turn our attention to the NEP and the problems of democracy in the Soviet state. The NEP was introduced by Lenin at the 10th party congress as a transitional measure away from the rigorous and extremely centralist policies of War Communism which existed from 1918 to 1920. "Under this peculiar War Communism we actually took from the peasant all his surpluses—and sometimes even a part of his necessaries—to meet the requirements of the army and sustain the workers." But, said Lenin, although this policy was very "crude and imperfect," it was a necessary policy flowing from conditions of war and ruin. However, facing the absence of revolutions in the West and the complete alienation of the peasantry and broad sections of the working class, Lenin was forced to introduce the NEP or "tax in kind" as a substitute for the policy of "requisitioning" that characterized War Communism. Lenin now

---

ly added that the absence of "workers' democracy" and a revolutionary foreign policy equally contributed to the rise of a regime of policemen in the Soviet Union. Is he not trying to have it both ways? Can it not be argued that backwardness led to a conservative foreign policy and authoritarian rule? For Trotsky to have drawn this conclusion would have meant a bringing into question of his theory of permanent revolution.

*Although he introduced the concept of the political revolution after having universalized the theory of permanent revolution, we will examine the former first. Our reasoning is that the two phases of his "democratic" opposition were so closely bound up with the introduction of the concept of political revolution that we have decided to treat them in unison. While the overall chronological flow of the work will be maintained, we have opted—in this special case—for theoretical clarity and continuity.

said that "the correct policy of the proletariat exercising its dictatorship in a small-peasant country is to obtain grain in exchange for the manufactured goods the peasant needs. . . . The tax in kind is a transition to this policy. . . . We shall take the minimum of grain we require (for the army and the workers) in the form of a tax and obtain the rest in exchange for manufactured goods." All of this, he said, was being done in order to give the peasant an "incentive" to grow his crops which, in turn, would contribute to the revival of general economic activity in the country and the consolidation of the alliance between the peasantry and the working class.* Yet, Lenin was not unaware that these "concessions" to private trading would lead to a sharp differentiation within the peasantry which ultimately could have serious implications for the worker-peasant alliance and the transition to socialism. He said that "we must not shut our eyes to the fact that the replacement of requisitioning by the tax means that the kulak [rich peasant] element under this system will grow far more than hitherto. It will grow in places where it could not grow before." Lenin nevertheless maintained that the survival of the workers' state necessitated paying this price. What's more, he insisted that "we shall carry out this policy [the NEP] in earnest and for a long time, but of course. . . not for ever." But when would the maintenance of this policy be inconsistent with the transition towards socialism? Indeed, is NEP to be the basis for a socialist Russia? On these and similar questions, Lenin, it seems, left enough ammunition for both the Majority and the Opposition in his party.[11]

Apart from the introduction of the New Economic Policy or NEP, the other major event at the 10th party congress in 1921 was the banning of "factions" within the communist party and effectively throughout the country. Lenin argued that with the reintroduction of private trading--an economic "retreat"--which occurred on the heels of the rebellion of the Kronstadt sailors**and the bitter

---

*The implications of the foreign component of the NEP will be examined in the next chapter. Lenin, "Tenth Congress of the R.C.P.(B.)," "The Tax in Kind," and "The Third Congress of the Communist International," Vol. XXXII, pp. 224-226, 342-343, 457-458 and 490-491.

**The importance of Kronstadt--a naval garrison near Petrograd--stems from the fact that it had long been both a symbol and stronghold of bolshevism. Rebelling against the abandonment of bolshevik ideals and reflecting the general dissatisfaction of both peasants and workers with Lenin's government, the Kronstadters--for approximately two weeks before being mercilessly crushed in the name of the October revolution by Tukhachevsky's troops--assailed

debates over trade union policy, it was imperative that isolated
and backward Russia put a lid on "factional" quarrels inside the
communist party. And although this ban did not technically apply
to other political parties, it, nevertheless, would be interpreted and applied as a formal banning of all other political formations. But it should be said that from the first days after the
October revolution until 1921, Lenin's government can be said to
have at best "officially tolerated" the legal opposition--meaning
those formations that did not actively engage in open rebellion
against the workers' state. For example, the menshevik press--
reflecting the inconsistencies and dissensions within the menshevik party--was on several occasions banned and then permitted
to appear again until the fateful decision of the 10th party
congress.[12] Feeling hemmed in on all sides in 1921--as a result
of the Kronstadters, internal party quarrels, revolutionary isolation, the restiveness of the working people, etc.--Lenin greeted
the congress with a determined appeal for unity and discipline.
"Comrades," he said, "let's not have an opposition just now! I
think the party congress will have to draw the conclusion that
the opposition's time has run out and that the lid's on it. We
want no more oppositions." And not surprisingly this would be
the exact position of the congress. "The congress. . . hereby declares dissolved and orders the immediate dissolution of all
groups without exception formed on the basis of one platform or
another. . . . Non-observance of this decision of the congress
shall entail unconditional and instant expulsion from the party."
When one is in "retreat"--and this was Lenin's general character-
ization of the period ushered in by the 10th party congres--what
is needed is discipline and not opposition.*[13]

---

the "new form of slavery" being imposed on the workers and peasants
by Lenin's party and government. "Here in Kronstadt has been laid
the first stone of the third revolution, striking the last fetters
from the laboring masses and opening a broad new road for socialist creativity." What rankled Lenin and Trotsky most--both of
whom declared the rebels to be under "counterrevolutionary" in-
fluence--was that the Kronstadters considered themselves to be to
the left of the communist party. Paul Avrich, Kronstadt 1921, pp.
157-192 and 241-243, Daniels, The Conscience of the Revolution, pp.
143-146, W.H. Chamberlin, The Russian Revolution, Vol. II, pp. 439-
440, Trotsky, The Revolution Betrayed, p. 96 and Writings of Leon
Trotsky [1937-38], pp. 134-145 and 376-378 and Lenin, "Tenth Congress of the R.C.P.(B.)," Vol. XXXII, pp. 183-184.

*"If, during an incredibly difficult retreat, when everything
depends on preserving proper order, anyone spreads panic--even
from the best of motives--the slightest breach of discipline must
be punished severely, sternly, ruthlessly. . . . When an army is
in retreat a hundred times more discipline is required than when

It was the implications of these two decisions--the introduction of the NEP and the banning of all organized opposition within the communist party--which were adopted in a setting of exhaustion, isolation and backwardness that provided the fuel for the struggle between the stalinist Majority and the trotskyist inspired Opposition over the direction of Soviet policy throughout the 1920s. What were the political and economic implications of these 1921 decisions? On the political side, the banning of all organized opposition within the communist party and effectively throughout the country contributed to furthering the consolidation of the political monopoly of Lenin's party over the Soviet Union. This development, as we shall see, was not contested by Trotsky. What provoked his ire from late 1922 and with it a crisis among the party leadership was the fact that a section of this leadership--described by him as "the" bureaucracy--under the growing influence of Stalin was rapidly seizing the levels of power within the party and laying exclusive claim to the mantle of leninism.[14] And on the economic side, by 1923 the NEP had resulted into a spectacular recovery of agricultural production to approximately its 1914 level. This development, however, was not reflected in industry which barely approached a third of its 1914 output. The result of this unevenness was that by 1923 there was a widening gap--or "scissors crisis" as defined by Trotsky--between the high prices of industrial products and the low prices of agricultural products. As Sherman put it, "during 1923 the price ratio moved three to one in favor of industry and against agriculture. This situation was of grave portent. The farmer was able to buy less and less with the meager returns he received from the sale of his products. What incentive would he have to produce for the market if the goods he desired were priced far out of his reach."[15] This was the context in which Trotsky came forward.

---

it is advancing, because during an advance everybody presses forward. If everybody started rushing back now, it would spell immediate and inevitable disaster." Can the political "retreat" away from at least the semblance of democratic procedures be likened to the economic "retreat" involving the NEP? If yes, then the political "retreat" just as the economic "retreat" cannot last "forever." Lenin does not say so but he carefully implies it. Yet at the 11th party congress he would call for a "halt" to the economic retreat to begin "regrouping our forces" for the transition to socialism without saying anything about the political retreat. Lenin, "Tenth Congress of the R.C.P. (B.)," Vol. XXXII, pp. 200 and 244 and "Eleventh Congress of the R.C.P. (B.), Vol. XXXIII, pp. 280-282 and Marcel Liebman, Leninism Under Lenin, p. 303.

Thus, his response to the crisis which arose from Lenin's 1921 decisions, which he supported, must be both political and economic. What was Trotsky's economic program for the development of the Soviet Union? How did it relate to the theory of permanent revolution?

The mainspring of Trotsky's economic program centered on the need for a rapid but balanced industrialization of Soviet Russia within the framework of the NEP. And the first step in this direction must be, he said, the introduction of a "single" or comprehensive economic plan.[16] Still, he recognized the impossibility of building a "complete socialist society" solely with Russia's human and material resources. What his program aimed at above all was the maintenance and strengthening of the bond between the working class and the peasantry while at the same time advancing the construction of socialism in Russia in the context of a revolutionary foreign policy; that is, a foreign policy which acknowledged the impossibility of building a complete socialist society within the borders of any single country. Trotsky began to fully expound his program for Russia's industrialization in 1923. Just prior to the convening of the 12th party congress in April of that year he emphasized that the fundamental task of the Soviet government "is to establish correct economic and political relations between the working class and the peasantry, for to make a mistake in this field means to risk a mortal fall. And this is all the more dangerous because up to the present nobody is as yet ready to support us, nobody in the West will hold us up if we stagger and are about to fall; the proletariat is not yet in power over there." But he insisted that this necessary alliance between the proletariat and peasantry would be "built on sand" if it did not have industry as its "unshakable" foundation:

> The regeneration of state industry, in the general economic structure of our country, will necessarily be closely dependent on the development of agriculture; the necessary means of exchange must be formed in agriculture, by way of the excess of the agricultural product over the consumption of the village before industry can take a decisive step forward. But it is just as important for state industry not to lag behind agriculture; otherwise, on the foundation of the latter private industry would be created, which, in the last analysis, would swallow up state industry or suck it dry.

Thus, Trotsky urged that the State Planning Commission be granted "a more definite position, a firmer organization, clearer and more undisputed rights and (especially) obligations. . . ." But he stressed time and again that the method to be employed by the State Planning Commission must be that of "economic maneuvering"

and "balance" and not "arbitrary administration."[17] Indeed, it
seems that two of his most important economic watchwords were
"balance" and "economic maneuvering." He insisted that "only by
maintaining a certain balance between the material interests of
the workers and peasants can we assure the political stability
of the Soviet state." In the absence of revolutionary assistance
from the West there was no other way to advance the process of
socialist construction:

> The rate of industrial development, the acceleration
> of which is in the interest of both the city and the
> village, does not of course depend on our good will. There
> are objective limitations here: the level of peasant
> economy, the actual equipment of industry, the availa-
> bility of working capital, the cultural level of the
> country, and so forth. Any attempt to leap over these
> limitations would surely take its own bitter revenge,
> striking the proletariat at one end and the peasantry
> at the other. But no less danger would arise if indus-
> try lagged behind the economic upturn of the rest of the
> country.*

---

*Emphasizing that "we must measure our cloth seven times be-
fore we cut it," Trotsky, while considering the contribution that
the peasantry must make in the industrialization campaign, said
in 1923 that "the problem of how much the peasants can contribute
is a very important one, but it is a practical problem, not one
of principle. We need to establish the rule: take from the
peasant so much as will still leave him richer next year than he
is this year. . . . A balance between taxation in kind and in
money must be established in accordance with the special features
of the particulat district and region, in accordance with the
strength or weakness of the peasant." Later in the year he would
say that "during the coming years we must adapt the Soviet state
to the needs and the strength of the peasantry while preserving
its character as a workers' state; we must adapt Soviet industry
to the peasant market, on the one hand, and to the taxable
capacity of the peasantry, on the other, while preserving its
character as a state, that is, socialist industry. Only in this
way, shall we be able to avoid destroying the equilibrium in our
Soviet state until the revolution will have destroyed the equilibrium in the capitalist states." Trotsky, "Our Differences" and
"Toward Capitalism or Socialism," The Challenge of the Left
Opposition [1923-25], pp. 299-302 and 375-276, Tasks Before the
Twelfth Congress of the Russian Communist Party, pp. 12-13 and
The New Congress, pp. 84-85 and 108.

So that the dictatorship of the proletariat is not "emptied of
its socialist content" Trotsky maintained that "one must orient
oneself and feel one's way in the situation by means of constant,
active maneuvering. . . . Our maneuvering, both economic and political, comes down to this--a series of measures, based on the
alliance of workers and peasants, by which the dictatorship of
the proletariat, and consequently the possibility of further
socialist construction, can be ensured."

Trotsky, however, was not always so "balanced" and measured
when presenting his program for Russia's industrialization. For
example, in late 1922 he said that "we have taken over a ruined
country. The proletariat, the ruling class in our state, is compelled to embark upon a phase which may be described as that of
primitive socialist accumulation. We cannot content ourselves with
using our pre-1914 industrial plant. This has been destroyed
and must be reconstructed step by step by way of a colossal ex-
ertion on the part of our labor force." Moreover, he said, the
working class can reach socialism "only through the greatest
sacrifices, by straining all its strength and giving its blood
and nerves. . . ." And a few months later at the 12th party
congress he would say that "the working class, being in power, has
the possibility when class interests require it, of giving
industry a credit at the expense of the worker's wages. In other
words. . . there may be moments when the state does not pay a
full wage or pays only a half, and you, the worker, give a credit
to your state at the expense of your wages." This, of course, was
not the first time that Trotsky had spoken in such terms.* But

_____

*During the period of War Communism and in general right up
to 1922 Trotsky was perhaps the sternest disciplinarian among the
principal Soviet leaders. This was particularly true during the
intense debates in 1920-21 on the role to be played by the trade
unions in the Soviet state. Before having "melted away" into
socialism the dictatorship of the proletariat, said Trotsky, will
represent the "highest possible intensification" of the principle
of the state. "Just as a lamp, before going out, shoots up in a
brilliant flame, so the state, before disappearing, assumes the
form of the dictatorship of the proletariat, i.e., the most
ruthless form of state, which embraces the life of the citizens
authoritatively in every direction." Indeed, the worker "is subordinated to the Soviet state, under its orders in every direction
--for it is his state." And as man is "instinctively" lazy, "compulsory labor service" rather than "free labor" which character-
izes bourgeois societies is required or "we cannot even dream of
a transition to socialism." The trade unions, therefore, assume
the function of a state agency. "Without general labor services,
without the right to order and demand fulfilment of orders, the

on balance, however, it was Preobrazhensky, an Oppositionist ally, who best articulated the need for "primitive socialist accumulation" rather than Trotsky who--perhaps under the impact of bukharinist inspired criticism--increasingly toned down his language following the bitter reaction he invited, especially from trade union representatives, when he sought the "blood and nerves" of the working class at the 12th party congress.[18]

Thus, Trotsky--especially during the early years of this debate--presented somewhat of a mixed bag on the theme of Russia's industrialization. On the one hand, there was a call for "balance" and "economic maneuvering" on the part of the Soviet agencies which would be responsible for implementing this process.

---

trade unions will be transformed into a mere form without reality; for the young socialist state requires trade unions, not for a struggle for better conditions of labor--that is the task of the social and state organizations as a whole--but to organize the working class for the ends of production, to educate, discipline, distribute, group, retain certain categories and certain workers at their posts for fixed periods--in a word, hand in hand with the state to exercise their authority in order to lead the workers into the framework of a single economic plan ." But he insisted that although "repression for the attainment of economic ends is a necessary weapon," the chief weapon of the socialist dictatorship must be its "moral influence" because "if compulsory labor came up against the opposition of the majority of the workers it would turn out a broken reed and with it the whole of the Soviet order." Lenin, after initially supporting Trotsky's compulsory labor scheme, would rebuke him for wanting to "shake up" the trade unions. However, with the introduction of the NEP and the concomitant necessity for trade union defense of the interests of the working class, the debate lost its raison d'être. Yet Trotsky's later claim that the issues raised during these 1920 debates were merely "episodic" is not completely true as we shall presently see. Trotsky, The New Course, p. 64, Terrorism and Communism, pp. 140-147 and 168-170 and The Stalin School of Falsification, pp. 28-32, Carr, The Interregnum, p. 32 and The Bolshevik Revolution, Vol. II, p. 379, Deutscher, The Prophet Unarmed, p. 44 and 101-102, Lenin, "On the Trade Unions," Vol. XXXII, pp. 19-26 and 42 and Daniels, The Conscience of the Revolution, pp. 122-123.

But, on the other, he emphasized the need for a "colossal exer-
tion" on the part of the labor force and pointed out that the
worker might have to concede half his wages in the interest of
industrializing "your state." The point is that Trotsky does not
seem to consistently distinguish between the different layers of
the Soviet population until 1926-27. And in fact, unlike earlier
years, he would, from 1926, consistently emphasize the need for a
heavy taxation of the rich peasants. "The existing system of
universal agricultural tax ought to be changed in the direction
of freeing altogether from taxation 40 to 50 percent of the
poorest peasant families, without making up for it by any addi-
tional tax upon the fundamental mass of the middle peasants."
And furthermore, he said, "the tax system is not keeping up with
the growth of accumulation among the upper layers of the peasants
and the new bourgeoisie in general." Trotsky's program for the
rapid industrialization of the Soviet Union would be financed--as
in the case of Preobrazhensky--through a progressive tax policy,
the manipulation of the state monopoly of the "commanding heights"
of the economy, a prudent credit policy, etc. But most importantly, Trotsky insisted that in conjunction with these measures there
must be a "renunciation of the theory of an isolated socialist
economy" if the Soviet Union were to successfully and harmonious-
ly make the transition from backwardness to modernization. "No
domestic policy can of itself deliver us from the economic, political, and military danger of the capitalist encirclement. The
domestic problem is, by strengthening ourselves with a proper
class policy, a proper inter-relation of the working class with
the peasant, to move forward as far as possible on the road of
socialist construction" [our emphasis]. And he emphasized that
a proletarian victory "in certain leading countries" was ultimately necessary in order to make the transition to a classless
society.[19]

At what point did the Majority disagree with the Trotsky-
Preobrazhensky economic program? Both the Majority and the
Opposition accepted the idea that socialism must be based upon
modern industry and planning. Furthermore, there was no real
disagreement on the idea that this industrialization must emerge
within the framework of the NEP; that is, there would be no
abrupt abandonment of the NEP. The disagreement, then, between
the two principal blocs in the party on industrialization policy
seems to center on the questions of tempo and method. Bukharin,
who from 1925-28 was the chief spokesman for the stalinist Majority on these questions, put it this way in 1926:

It would be wrong to argue that industry should
grow only on what is produced within the limits of
this industry. But the whole question involves how
much we can take from the peasantry. . . to what extent
we can carry this pumping over [Preobrazhensky em-

ployed this term to signify the transferring of resources from the agrarian to the state sector of the
economy], by what methods, where are the limits of
this pumping over, how . . . to receive the most
favorable result. . . . Here is the difference
between us and the opposition. . . . Comrades of
the opposition stand for pumping over excessively, for
such intense pressure on the peasantry which. . . is
economically irrational and politically inpermissible.
Our position in no way renounces this pumping over;
but we calculate much more soberly. . . .

He would write two years later in his "Notes of an Economist"
that "in their simplicity, the ideologists of Trotskyism assume
that the maximum annual pumping out of resources from the peasant
economy into industry will assure the maximum tempo of the development of industry. But that is clearly not so. The greatest
not temporary but continuous tempo can be attained by such a
coordination in which industry develops on the foundation of a
rapidly growing agricultural economy. . . . What the Trotskyites
fail to comprehend is that the development of industry is dependent
on the development of agriculture." Bukharin's argument was
quite simple. The implementation of the Opposition's program for
the rapid industrialization of Russia which, of necessity, must
be financed primarily on the backs of the peasantry--though he
occasionally, and as we have seen correctly, observed a slight
difference between Preobrazhensky and Trotsky on this question--
would inevitably lead to the dissolution of the alliance between
the peasantry and the working class and thereby bring into question the very existence of the workers' state itself. Thus,
reasoned Bukharin, the only sound alternative to the dangerous
proposals of the Opposition was to impose a moderate tax policy
with the aim of allowing all strata of the rural population to
prosper and become rich. The result of this process would serve
as the basis for the development and modernization of industry.[20]
However, the Opposition charged that Bukharin's peasant policy
would contribute to the widening of the breach between the rich
and the poor peasants and all that that implied for the continued
existence of the workers' state. Moreover, they argued, the
rapid industrialization of the economy would make available to
the peasant the equipment, machinery and the goods he needed
which, in turn, would finally close the dangerous blades of the
"scissors." And so the debate continued. But the debate would
suddenly come to a screeching halt in 1928 when Stalin--whose
attitude towards the peasantry was slightly less conciliatory
than Bukharin's and under the impact of a grain crisis which had
been forecasted by the Opposition--undertook a "left" turn and
adopted in his own way numerous planks from the economic program
of Trotsky and Preobrazhensky in order to rapidly industrialize
the Soviet economy.[21]

Thus, much of Trotsky's economic response to the implications of Lenin's 1921 decisions--the introduction of the NEP and the banning of organizaed opposition within the party--obtained a curious fate in the hands of Stalin at the conclusion of the successional struggle between "the two outstanding leaders" of Lenin's party.[22] But, as was indicated earlier, Trotsky also advanced a political response in order to confront the implications of Lenin's 1921 decisions. And this response occurred during two principal periods. The first occurred from the fall of 1923 until his expulsion from the communist party in the fall of 1927 and the second from the fall of 1933 until his assination in 1940. The first phase of Trotsky's "democratic" opposition to Stalin and the Majority began to unfold as Stalin continued to increase his power over the party and state via the mechanisms of the party's general secretariat. "When acute dissensions broke out once more in the summer and autumn of 1923 they took the new form of an undisguised struggle for power [between Stalin and Trotsky], whose prize was supreme control not merely of the party but of the state."[23] Trotsky opened his attack on the current Soviet leadership with a letter to the central committee of the party in October 1923:[24]

> [The current Soviet regime] is much farther re-
> moved from workers democracy than was the regime during
> the fiercest periods of War Communism. The bureaucrati-
> zation of the party apparatus has reached unheard-of pro-
> portions through the application of the methods of
> secretarial selection. . . . There has been created a
> very broad layer of party workers, belonging to the
> apparatus of the state or the party who have totally
> renounced the idea of holding their own political
> opinions or at least of openly expressing such opinions,
> as if they believe that the secretarial hierarchy is the
> proper apparatus for forming party opinions and making
> party decisions.

He then went on to say that "party democracy must enjoy its right-ful place--at least enough of it to prevent the party from the threat of ossification and degeneration."[25] Trotsky would here-after constantly refer to the "degeneration" of the party and of the workers' state. About a week later and in language simi-lar to that of Trotsky's letter, a group of prominent bolsheviks issued "The Platform of the Forty-Six" in which they noted "the ever increasing, and now scarcely concealed, division of the party between a secretarial hierarchy and 'quiet folk,' between professional party officials recruited from above and the general mass of the party which does not participate in the common life."* A few weeks later the party's ruling triumvirate (an uneasy and shortlived alliance of Stalin, Zinoviev and Kamenev)-- in response to the challenge of the Opposition--issued a call for a "new course" in the life of the party. Its document, in language similar to that of the Opposition, insisted upon the need for "serious change in the party's course in the sense of an active and systematic implementation of the principles of workers democracy." And it defined "workers democracy" as the "liberty of frank discussion of the most important questions of party life by all members and the election of all leading party functionaries and commissions by those bodies immediately under them." Trotsky--without waiting for the realization of this "democracy"-- immediately declared his solidarity with the aims of the ruling triumvirate.[26]

Yet, barely a day after declaring his solidarity with the democratic intentions of the Majority, Trotsky--in a series of articles later to be known as "The New Course"--delivered his most acute criticisms of the party's hierarchy to date. "A certain tendency of the apparatus to think and to decide for the

---

*"The regime established within the party is completely intolerable; it destroys the independence of the party, replacing the party by a recruited bureaucratic apparatus which acts without objection in normal times, but which inevitably fails in moments of crisis, and which threatens to become completely ineffective in the face of the serious events now impending." And like Trotsky, they insisted upon "a regime of comradely unity and internal party democracy." But what is the nature of this "internal" democracy that both Trotsky and the "Forty-Six" are clamoring for? Sapronov, one of the "Forty-Six," tells us that a "pure thorough-going democracy" obviously means "freedom of speech, Press, elections and so on. No one is advocating a pure, thorough-going inviolate democracy. We are talking about inner-party workers democracy, about a democracy the right to which is guaranteed for each party member: each may express his good or bad idea and the will of the party can accept or reject it." While all of the "Forty-Six" did not share Sapronov's "moderate" views on democracy, this was the basic position of the newly formed "Left Opposition" (Trotsky and the "Forty-Six"). Peter Jeffries, trans., Documents of the 1923 Opposition, pp. 7 and 22 and Trotsky, The Challenge of the Left Opposition [1923-25], pp. 55-58 and 399-400.

whole organization leads to seating the authority of the leading circles exclusively upon tradition." But, he warned, "history offers us more than one case of [the] degeneration of 'the old guard . . . .* We saw that on the eve of the war, the formidable apparatus of the Social Democracy, covered with the authority of the old generation, had become the most powerful brake upon revolutionary progress." How would Trotsky rememdy this situation? "The party has no other means to employ against this indubitable danger than a serious profound, radical change of course toward party democracy and the increasingly large flow into its midst of working class elements."** Having assailed the "mummified bureaucrats" Trotsky noted, however, that "it is beyond dispute that we need in our party a powerful centralized apparatus." And more importantly, "we are the only party in the country and in the period of the dictatorship, it could not be otherwise."[27] These concessions to the apparatus were not sufficient to ward off the fury of the Majority. Stalin thought that it was "rather amusing" to hear the disciplinarian Trotsky "hold forth on the subject of democracy." And he interestingly pointed out that Trotsky "needs democracy as a hobby-horse, as a strategic manoeuvre" in his quest for power. Trotsky was guilty on two counts: 1) violating the 10th Party Congress ban on factions and 2) having challenged a decision--in which he even endorsed--approved by the politbureau which acknowledged its commitment to the struggle for party democracy. Thus, a resolution of the Thirteenth Party Con-

---

*The "old guard" or "old bolsheviks" were the senior members of the party who, in collaboration with Lenin, had traversed all of the rocky roads in the quest for power in tsarist Russia. These, most notably, included Stalin, Zinoviev and Kamenev. Trotsky joined the bolshevik party in 1917. Lenin acknowledged the enormous importance of the "old guard" in the party about a year before his death. "If we do not close our eyes to reality we must admit that at the present time the proletarian policy of the party is not determined by the character of its membership [which had become less and less proletarian], but by the enormous [and] undivided prestige enjoyed by the small group which might be called the old guard of the party." Lenin, "Conditions for Admitting New Members to the Party," Vol. XXXIII, p. 257.

**Stalin would presently confound Trotsky by declaring the "Lenin levy." This recruitment drive--in principle a homage to Lenin--was, in practice, a homage to Martov since it flung open the party's doors to virtually anyone who would join it.

ference in January 1924 condemned Trotsky for having "clearly
violated the decision of the Tenth Congress of the Russian
Communist Party which prohibited the formation of factions within
the party." It went on to say that Trotsky represented "a
clearly expressed petty-bourgeois deviation." And it demanded
that there be waged "a systematic and energetic struggle of our
whole party against this petty-bourgeois deviation. . . ." This
resolution would effectively silence Trotsky's "democratic" oppositional activities until the spring of 1926.[28] During this
period, said Deutscher, "he lived as if in another world, wrapped
up in himself and his ideas. He was up to his eyes in his scientific and industrial preoccupations and literary work, which pro-
tected him to some extent from the frustration to which he was exposed. He shunned inner-party affairs. Full of the sense of his
superiority and contempt for his opponents, and disgusted with
the polemical methods and tricks, he was not interested in their
doings."[29]

Everyone, however, was not silent. An open split occurred in
early 1925 within the ruling triumvirate. Zinoviev and Kamenev--
challenging the stalinists' economic and political orientation--
in effect, adopted the essentials of the program of the Opposition.
Based in Leningrad, Zinoviev's fief, this new oppositional movement possessed considerable organizational clout. It assailed
the "new" Majority, especially its bukharinist current, as
sharply as Trotsky had assailed Zinoviev and Kamenev, members of
the "old" Majority, in 1923. But, how would Trotsky react to the
new hat now being worn by Zinoviev and Kamenev? Everybody, even
Stalin, anxiously waited. Would he join forces with them? Could
they be trusted? Trotsky would squander valuable time grappling
with these questions. In an oblique reference to the dissolution
of the triumvirate he observed that "neither classes nor parties
can be judged by what they say about themselves or by the slogans
they raise at a given moment. This fully applies to groupings
within a political party as well." And a few days later, at the
14th Party Congress in December 1925, even though Zinoviev and
Kamenev undertook a systematic and vigorous critique of Stalin's
theory of "socialism in one country"--something he had not done
up to then--Trotsky refused to come to their defense. After all,
he might have reasoned, the browbeating that the "Leningraders"
were receiving from Stalin and Bukharin was merely a continuation
of that meted out to them by him during the "literary" campaign
of 1924.*

---

*Years later Trotsky would say that "the expectation of a
struggle between Stalin and Zinoviev and Kamenev was unsuspected
at the [14th Party] Congress. During the Congress I waited in
uncertainty, because the whole situation changed. It appeared
absolutely unclear to me." Trotsky, The Case of Leon Trotsky,

After the Leningraders had been effectively broken at the 14th Party Congress--especially with the loss of their organizational base--Trotsky, awakening from a two year political slumber, in the spring of 1926 forged an uneasy alliance with Zinoviev and Kamenev in the name of the "United Opposition." Its official life-time would be barely a year. Yet, as Daniels correctly observes, this brief period represented the "hightide" of the oppositional movement in the Russian communist party. This was so not because of its program or organizational strength. Indeed, as we have indicated, zinovievists were being replaced in Leningrad as Zinoviev was critiquing the theory of socialism in one country at the 14th Party Congress. And the program of the "United Opposition" was essentially Trotsky's program of 1923.*

---

pp. 322-323 and Challenge [1923-25], pp. 385 and 390.

*In the program of the "United Opposition" there was the standard indictment of bureaucratic rule and the call for "a consistent development of workers' democracy in the party, the trade-unions and the soviets." However, unlike the previous oppositional campaigns, Trotsky, in 1927, time and again insisted upon the need for the single party system in the Soviet Union. To be sure, he--unlike Lenin--had done this before. But his 1927 statements assumed a much more principled character. He said in March 1927 that "the dictatorship of the proletariat in the Soviet Union, under conditions of capitalist encirclement, was possible only in the form of the dictatorship of the communist party." Five months later he claimed that it was an "inviolable" leninist principle that "the dictatorship of the proletariat will and can be realized only through the dictatorship of the party." And finally, barely two months before his expulsion from the communist party, he observed that "the dictatorship of the proletariat in a country which is surrounded by capitalist states does not allow either the existence of two parties or the factional splitting of a unified party." Why would these "inviolable" leninist principles become "stalinist" principles after he abandoned them in 1933? Was not the Soviet Union still "surrounded by capitalist states?" Was Stalin correct in saying that Trotsky was only using the word democracy as a "strategic manoeuvre" in his thirst for power? Trotsky, The Real Situation in Russia, pp. 100, 114-115, 117 and 193-194, On China, p. 135 and Daniels, The Conscience of the Revolution, pp. 273 and 300.

The real difference was in the intensity of the struggle and the determination of the participants. Trotsky waged a dogged campaign to win over the party's rank and file. But 1927 was not 1923. The Majority had control of all the sinews of power and influence. Thus, Trotsky was routed from the communist party in November 1927. This action symbolized the conclusion of the first phase of his "democratic" opposition to Stalin.30

Following his political defeat Trotsky was finally deported to Turkey in 1929. From his Turkish exile he sought to consolidate his forces--both inside and outside the Soviet Union--and to continue to fight against Stalin. But his situation was not quite the same. Not only was he no longer in the Russian communist party, he was not even within the borders of that state which he was so instrumental in founding. Would his ideas on democracy in the workers' state be affected by this new reality? There is no immediate evidence of it. In fact, from his arrival in Turkey until 1933, he would continue to articulate those ideas on democracy which were so characterisitic of him during the successional struggle in the Soviet Union.* And he did this despite a crescendo of voices among his followers inviting him to undertake a reassessment of the nature of the Soviet state.31

---

*But events were moving at a fast pace in the Soviet Union. And this required an assessment by Trotsky. Stalin, as was mentioned earlier, in 1928 had embarked upon a campaign of collectivization and industrialization. This campaign was so swift and bloody that by early 1930 most peasant households had been collectivized. What was Trotsky's reaction? Had Stalin finally come around to the economic program of the Opposition? There was confusion in the trotskyist ranks. Trotsky forthwith blasted Stalin's "racetrack-gallop approach to industrialization" and the "unnecessary sacrifices" imposed upon the Soviet population. Nevertheless, he was quick to point out that "the working class of Russia has the right to be proud of the truly great technical achievements accomplished within the last few years [1928-32]. These achievements became possible only when the pressure of events forced the bureaucracy to make use of the platform of the Left Opposition, although after a delay and in distorted and twisted form." Therefore, though Stalin transformed the Opposition's economic program "into a fetish," Trotsky felt that he "won in a certain sense" because Stalin was forced to make "belated borrowings" from his program for the industrialization of the Soviet Union. Was Stalin a "rightist" or "leftist?" Had "Thermidor" arrived (identified until 1935 as a counterrevolutionary overturning of the "gains" of the October Revolution)? Trotsky responded time and again in these first years of exile that "our course is one of internal reform." He noted that he was

He would not begin to take a second look at the Soviet Union until 1933. And, according to Trotsky, the event which compelled him to take a second look was the "collapse" of the stalinist Communist International (Comintern) following its refusal to initiate a "complete review" of its "fatal" policy which led to the victory of Hitler and the defeat of the working class in Germany. Until the summer of 1933 Trotsky and his movement--officially known as the "International Left Opposition" but very shortly the "International Communist League"--considered themselves as a "faction" within the Comintern. Of course, this was devoid of any practical meaning since Stalin expelled, from both the Comintern and the Russian communist party, anyone who smacked of "trotskyism." In theory, however, it signified that the October revolution had neither been "betrayed" nor "overthrown." Thus, Trotsky informed his followers to engage in "critical work" and to struggle for "bold reforms." This policy, he wrote in July 1933, though it was a "necessary stage" in the development of the Opposition, "is bereft of all content today." He charged that the German "catastrophe" basically resulted from the failure of the Stalin led Comintern to seek out--as he had recommended--a tactical alliance with the German social democrats so as to prevent the victory of Hitler. "The idea of reform is to be rejected, nationally and internationally, for the Comintern in its entirety, because it is nothing more than an unscrupulous, bureaucratic caste that has become the greatest enemy of the world working class. It is absolutely necessary to free the proletarian vanguard from the dictatorship of the stalinist bureaucracy. What does this turn mean in essence? We cease to be a faction; we are no longer the Left Opposition; we become embryos of new parties." The word "revolution" came increasingly to replace the

---

"for the regeneration of the [Russian] communist party" and not the creation of a new one. And Trotsky invariably emphasized-- on this he would brook "no vacillations or doubts" within his ranks, especially in exile--that he would unconditionally defend the "gains" of the October Revolution (nationalization of the means of production and planning) "tooth and nail." Trotsky, Writings [1929], pp. 29, 79, 251 and 359, Writings [1930], pp. 131, 150 and 173, Writings [1930-31], pp. 225 and 230-231, Writings [1932], pp. 66 and 259 and Sherman, The Soviet Economy, p. 83.

word "reform" in Trotsky's vocabulary on the Soviet Union.[32]
And announcing the "struggle for the Fourth International"--
though it would not be officially "proclaimed" until 1938--Trot-
sky declared that it was now "necessary to pour new wine into
new bottles."[33]

This marked the beginning of what we have refferred to as the
second phase of his "democratic" opposition to Stalin. Until
now Trotsky had essentially sought to democratize the Russian
communist party. But from the middle of 1933 and more explicitly
from the fall of the same year he argued that "in the USSR it is
necessary to build a bolshevik party again." What were the implications of this statement? Was the Soviet Union no longer a
workers' state? If not, when did "thermidor" occur? Should he
now apologize to those who had said this long ago? Trotsky began his new analysis of Soviet reality by declaring, as previously, that "the nationalization of the land, the means of
industrial production, transport and exchange, together with the
monopoly of foreign trade, constitute the basis of the Soviet
social structure. Through these relations, established by the
proletarian revolution, the nature of the Soviet Union as a
proletarian state is for us basically defined." In short, there
was no new ruling class in the Soviet Union. "A class," he said,
"is defined not by its participation in the distribution of the
national income alone, but by its independent role in the general
structure of the economy and by its independent roots in the
economic foundation of society. Each class (the feudal nobility,
the peasantry, the petty bourgeoisie, the capitalist bourgeoisie
and the proletariat) works out its own special forms of property."
Thus, the stalinist bureaucracy was a social "excrescence" or
"tumor" rather than a new ruling class since it was not the
bearer of a new system of property "peculiar to itself and impossible without itself."[34] And though he saw a "deadly similarity" between Stalin's and Hitler's bureaucratic regimes,
Trotsky pointed out that the Soviet bureaucracy was "something
more than a bureaucracy" since "in no other regime has a bureaucracy ever achieved such a degree of independence from the domi-
nating class." Unlike other bureaucracies--including the fascists
who are basically "united with the big bourgeoisie"--the Soviet
bureaucracy, atop proletarian property, has "expropriated the
proletariat politically" and is completely separated from the
lives of working people. In short, said Trotsky, however contradictory it might appear, the Soviet working class was "simultaneously a ruling and an oppressed class."*

---

*This is one of the principal difficulties with Trotsky's
analysis. He partly recognizes this while saying that in the
Soviet Union "the means of production belong to the state. But

What is the origin and nature of this bureaucracy? How does its existence weigh on the future of the workers' state? And finally, how can it be eliminated? Trotsky responded by saying that "the historical justification for the very existence of the bureaucracy is lodged in the fact that we are still very far removed from socialist society, in the fact that the present transitional society is full of contradictions, which in the sphere of consumption, the most immediate and vital sphere for everyone, bears a character of extreme tension and always threatens to cause an explosion in the sphere of production." He went on to say that the isolation and extreme backwardness, materially and culturally, of the revolution lie at the root of bureaucratic rule in the Soviet Union. "Raising itself above the toiling masse" the bureaucracy, in its own way, acting as a sort of "policeman" regulates social contradictions and scarce resources. But, Trotsky cautioned, the role of this "gatekeeper" is a "dual one: on the one hand it protects the workers' state with its own peculiar methods; on the other hand, it disorganizes and checks the development of economic and culutral life by repressing the creative activity of the masses."* And he concluded by saying that "it is

---

the state, so to speak, 'belongs' to the bureaucracy." It appears to us to be more than a question of "so to speak." To say, as he does, that the stalinist bureaucrat is not a member of a new class because he possess no "special" property and "cannot transmit to his heirs his rights in the exploitation of the state apparatus" is an inadequate explanation of the problems of proletarian rule in the Soviet Union. Indeed, he seems to have made a fetish out of juridical norms. After all, the working class is unlike any other social class in history--especially the bourgeoisie. As possessors of "labor power" the working class--unlike the bourgeoisie--can neither rule nor effectively shape policy until it assumes political power. How can a working class, which has been "expropriated" politically, exercise its rule when it owns nothing but mere "labor power?" Trotsky's analysis provides little asisstance here. Trotsky, The Revolution Betrayed, pp. 245-252 and 278 and Writings [1937-38], pp. 69-71.

*"Its own interests [since it possessed no "special" property] constrain it to safeguard the new economic regime created by the October revolution against the enemies at home and abroad. This work remains historically necessary and progressive. In this work the world proletariat support the Soviet bureaucracy without closing their eyes to its national conservatism, its appropriate instincts and its spirit of caste privilege." Trotsky was also prepared to recognize--it would have been difficult not to do so-- that the bureaucracy "gave a mighty impulse to [the Soviet] economy." But he hurriedly added that "the source of this impulse

otherwise in the sphere of the international working class movement where not a trace remains of this dualism, here the stalinist bureaucracy plays a disorganizing, demoralizing and fatal
role from beginning to end."[35] Therefore, even though the stalinist bureaucracy performs "a necessary function," it does so "in
such a way as to prepare an explosion of the whole system which
may completely sweep out the results of the revolution." And
he maintained that the longer the isolation of this "traditional
regime"--which "stands much closer to the regime of capitalism
than to future communism"--the more ominous the prospects are
for a "restoration of capitalism" in the Soviet Union. Flowing
from this analysis the Soviet state must be considered a "sick"
or "degenerated" workers' state. And he argued that although
the process of degeneration began to set in as early as 1924,
it was not until 1933 that the "events" had demonstrated--speci-
fically the German "catastrophe"--the impossibility of seeking to
reform the existing political structures in the Soviet Union.
Thus, the "plague" of stalinism must be "burned out with a hot
iron" lest it quite possibly "facilitate the victory of the
enemy tomorrow."[36]

The coming Russian revolution--like the October revolution--
would be majoritarian and require the use of force.* But--unlike

---

was the nationalization of the means of production and the planned
beginnings and by no means the fact that the bureaucracy usurped
command over the economy." The bureaucratization of society, he
said, leads to the "suffocation of all initiative and all creative urge." Having said this, Trotsky, nevertheless, acknowledged that "within limits" a bureaucracy was a "social necessity"
in the Soviet Union. He felt that "equality of general poverty"--
as he characterized the period of Lenin's rule--would serve as "a
break upon the development of the productive forces" since it
would destroy the "personal interestedness" of the Soviet people.
What he essentially opposed was the arrogating by the bureaucracy
of "unlimited powers." Trotsky, Writings [1934-35], pp. 118-119,
124-125 and 171, In Defense of Marxism, pp. 6-7 and The Revolution
Betrayed, pp. 112-113 and 133.

*After denouncing all the party congresses from 1924 as
"bureaucratic parades," Trotsky pointed out that the stalinist
bureaucracy "can be compelled to yield power into the hands of the
proletarian vanguard only by force." But he was no less explicit
on the point that "the question of seizing power will arise as a
practical question for the new party only when it will have con-
solidated around itself the majority of the working class." He
was engaged in the political and not the technical preparation
for the removal of the stalinist "excrescence." And to drive this

the October revolution--it would leave untouched the existing forms of property. The difference between the two revolutions stems from the fact that the October revolution as been "betrayed" but not yet "overthrown." Thus, the coming Russian revolution--even though it will have "deep social consequences"--will be a "political" and not a "social" revolution.* "History has known elsewhere not only social revolutions which substituted the bourgeois for the feudal regime, but also political revolutions which, without destroying the economic foundations of society, swept out an old ruling upper crust (1830 and 1848 in France, February 1917 in Russia, etc.)." And he said that the aim of this "political" revolution was a total reorganization of the Soviet political apparatus:

> It is not a question of substituting one ruling clique for another, but of changing the very methods of administering the economy and guiding the culture of the country. Bureaucratic autocracy must give place to Soviet democracy. A restoration of the right of criticism, and a genuine freedom of elections, are necessary conditions for the further development of the country. This assumes a revival of the freedom of Soviet parties, beginning with the party of the bolsheviks, and a resurrection of the trade unions [our emphasis].

---

point home he noted, as if in passing, that "if marxists categorically condemned individual terrorism [during the fight against tsarism], obviously for political and not mystical reasons, even when the shots were directed against the agents of the tsarist government and of capitalist exploitation, they will even more relentlessly condemn and reject the criminal adventurism of terrorist acts directed against the bureaucratic representatives of the first workers' state in history." Trotsky, Writings [1934-35], pp. 122-123 and 183, Writings [1933-34], pp. 117-118 and The Revolution Betrayed, pp. 251-254 and 287.

*It is precisely because the coming revolution will only be "political" that Trotsky always maintained that he would unconditionally "remain on the last barricade" in defense of the social conquests of the October revolution. But, he argued, the best defense for the maintenance and extension of the revolutionary gains resulting from "the greatest overturn of property relations in history" is the removal of the stalinist "cancer." Is it possible, however, to be prepared to defend the Soviet Union "no matter what crimes Stalin may be guilty of" while at the same time seeking to overthrow the Stalin regime? Trotsky's explanation, as we indicated earlier, lacks a certain realism. Trotsky, The Revolution Betrayed, pp. 288-289, In Defense of Marxism, pp. 11-

With his call for "a revival of the freedom of Soviet parties"
we arrive effectively at the conclusion of the second phase of
Trotsky's "democratic" opposition to Stalin as the concept of
political revolution would henceforth assume this emphasized
meaning.

IV. Summary

We have examined the emergence of Trotsky's concept of the
political revolution. And this was undertaken around the themes
of "socialism in one country" and Trotsky's use of "democracy"
as a weapon in his struggle with Stalin. Most importantly,
the message that pervades our whole assesment of his concept of
the political revolution is that its emergence--as will now be
seen in the case of his universalizing the theory of permanent
revolution--was the direct result of his quarrels with Stalin
rather than a thoroughgoing analysis of Soviet reality. Had
he taken the latter course, he no doubt would have had to bring
into question not only Stalin's "betrayals" but also leninism
and even trotskyism.

18, 20, and 176 and Writings [1933-34], p. 121.

V. Notes to Chapter III

[1] In singling out the "two characteristic features of Stalin's outlook" Carr finds a clear "anti-theoretical bias" in him: "The first was a reaction against the predominantly 'European' framework in which the revolution had hiterto been cast, and a conscious or unconscious reversion to Russian national traditions. The second was a turning away from the highly developed intellectual and theoretical approach of the first years of the revolution, and a renewed emphasis on the practical and empirical task of administration. This new attitude had set in after the introduction of NEP, and was well established at the time of Lenin's death." And in 1929 Trotsky, as might be expected, would describe Stalin as "stubbornly empirical and devoid of creative imagination." He later appears to temper this remark with the observation that Marxism and the National Question (written in 1912) is "undoubtedly Stalin's most important--rather, his one and only--theoretical work" but even here Trotsky hastened to add that this work "was wholly inspired by Lenin, written under his unremitting supervision and edited by him line by line." Carr, Socialism in One Country, Vol. I, p. 177, Tucker, ed., The Lenin Anthology, p. 727, Deutscher, Stalin, p. 36 and Stalin, pp. 156-157.

[2] Despite his stormy and occasionally bitter relations with Lenin, Bukharin was recognized over the years as one of the bolsheviks' leading intellectuals. And this was especially true in matters of economic doctrine. With his background in economics and marxist theory in general, Bukharin--who began to develop ideas on "building socialism" in isolated and backward Russia almost simultaneously with Stalin--was able to remove some of the rough edges from the doctrine of socialism in one country as it was then (1924-27) being presented by Stalin. Though in an uneasy political and ideological alliance with Stalin against the "Oppositionists" during this time, Bukharin, himself, would be declared a "rightist" in 1928 and ultimately executed by Stalin ten years later. Stephen F. Cohen, Bukharin and the Bolshevik Revolution, p. 187, Carr, Socialism in One Country, Vol. II, p. 43, Deutscher, Stalin, p. 299 and Stalin, "Report to the 18th Party Congress," Selected Writings, p. 470 and "Speeches at the Sixth Congress of the R.S.D.L.P.(B.)," Works, Vol. III, p. 200.

[3] It should be pointed out that this debate was initially a one-sided affair as Trotsky refused to participate until 1926. Indeed, two of the members of the ruling "triumvirate" in 1924 (Zinoviev and Kamenev) would soon "break" with Stalin and subsequently take up the issue of socialism in one country before Trotsky. Yet, on the very eve of Stalin's launching of the idea

of socialism in one country Trotsky would publish his Lessons
of October which, for all practical purposes, was a frontal attack
on Zinoviev and Kamenev (less so on Stalin) for their "conservatism" and lack of decisiveness in exploiting via the Communist
International an alleged revolutionary situation in Germany in
1923. Trotsky would even ressurect the old debates in order to
prove his points. He said that "even within this party among its
leaders on the eve of the decisive action there was formed a group
of experienced revolutionists, old bolsheviks, who were in sharp
opposition to the proletarian revolution and . . . adopted on all
fundamental questions an essentially social democratic [non-marx-
ist] position. . . .This must never be forgotten if we wish other
communist parties to learn anything from us [our emphasis]." Let's
recall here that Lenin did indeed denounce and even called for
the expulsion of "Mr. Zinoviev and Mr. Kamenev" from the bolshevik party for their "strike-breaking" activity on the eve of the
October insurrection. But more importantly, he said from his
deathbed in his so-called testament that "the October episode with
Zinoviev and Kamenev was, of course, no accident, but neither can
the blame for it be laid upon them personally, any more than non-
bolshevism can upon Trotsky [our emphasis]." Thus, it was Trotsky
who first charged that the sins of the "old bolsheviks" must
"never be forgotten" even though Lenin was apparently prepared
to live and let live. So when Stalin dug up Trotsky's "non-
bolshevik" past and especially his feud with Lenin on the "democratic dictatorship"--however irrelevant the issue might be in
1924 as Trotsky had not and would not universalize his theory of
permanent revolution until late 1927--the ground had already been
prepared by Trotsky himself. And the confounding fact is that
Trotsky had prepared this ground with an ideological and political
barrage not so much against Stalin but against his future, even
if shortlived, allies Zinoviev and Kamenev. Trotsky, "The
Lessons of October" and "Our Differences," The Challenge of the
Left Opposition (1923-25), pp. 226-238, 254 and 276-278, Tucker,
The Lenin Anthology, p. 727 and Ann Bone, trans., The Bolsheviks
and the October Revolution: Minutes of the Central Committee
of the Russian Social-Democratic Labor Party (Bolsheviks), pp. 89-
95 and 114-116.

[4]"The possibility of completely building socialism in our
country is one thing; the possibility of guaranteeing our country against encroachment by international capital is another."
Stalin, "Concerning Questions of Leninism" and "The Possibility
of Building Socialism in Our Country," Vol. VIII, pp. 69-70 and
102-103 and "To Comrade Demyan Bedny," Vol. XIII, p. 25.

[5]Stalin, "The Social Democratic Diviation in Our Party," Vol.
VIII, pp. 261-262 and "The Seventh Enlarged Plenum of the E.C.C.I."
Vol. IX, p. 36. That Lenin's theory of revolution was shaped in

the context of an acceptance of the "law of uneven development"
is incontestable but that he drew the conclusion from this that
it was possible to build a "complete socialist society" in a
single country--much less "backward" Russia--is open to question.
We believe, however, that on the basis of his last writings a
sound case could be made that Lenin did believe that a socialist
society could be built in Russia in the absence of supportive
revolutions in the West provided the Eastern peoples supported
Soviet Russia until the workers in the West had risen in revolt.
After the "class truce" had set in on the Western revolutionary
fronts, Lenin gave increasing attention to the national liberation
movements in the East and the consolidation of the worker-peasant
alliance in Russia under the auspices of the NEP which was introduced in 1921 at the 10th party congress. While the NEP was
initially considered as merely a "retreat" towards capitalism--
since it sanctioned private trading and invited foreign con-
cessions--within the broad framework of state control of the
"commanding heights" of the economy, its initial success at
reviving Russia's war torn economy led Lenin to proclaim in his
last public speech that "NEP Russia will become socialist Russia"
in a matter of a few years. And a few weeks later he would write
--more correctly, dictate--that "the power of the state over all
large-scale means of production, political power in the hands of
the proletariat, the alliance of this proletariat with the many
millions of small and very small peasants, the assured proletarian leadership of the peasantry, etc.--is this not all that is
necessary to build a complete socialist society out of coopera-
tives alone. . . . Is this not all that is necessary to build a
complete socialist society? It is still not the building of
socialist society, but it is all that is necessary and sufficient
for it." He goes on to say that the European invasion during the
Civil War had prevented the Soviet state from being able to
"develop the productive forces with enormous speed" which "would
have produced socialism" in Russia. And rather than looking to
the Western working class for supportive revolutions in Russia's
quest for a "complete socialist society," Lenin, in these last
writings, turns his eyes Eastward. "In the last analysis, the
outcome of the struggle [between Soviet Russia and the West] will
be determined by the fact that Russia, India, China, etc., account
for the overwhelming majority of the population of the globe. And
during the past few years it is the majority that has been drawn
into the struggle for emancipation with extraordinary rapidity,
so that in this respect there cannot be the slightest doubt what
the final outcome of the world struggle will be. In this sense,
the complete victory of socialism is fully and absolutely assured"
[our emphasis]. Despite Trotsky's later claim that "either Lenin
slipped in his dictation or. . . the stenographer made a mistake
in transcribing her notes" Lenin's last writings--if isolated
from the main body of his work--can be found to support the theory
of socialism in one country. But, as we suggested in Chapter II,

when considered in its totality there is no basis, for example, to Cohen's assertion that Lenin must be credited with "legitimate paternity" of the theory of socialism in one country. Lenin, "Speech at the Plenary Session of Moscow Soviet," "On Cooperation" and "Better Fewer, But Better," Vol. XXXIII, pp. 443-467-471 and 498-500 and "Concession and the Development of Capitalism," "Third Congress of the Communist International" and "Tax in Kind," Col. XXXII, pp. 342-343, 368 and 488-492, Trotsky, The Third International After Lenin, p. 31, Cohen, Bukharin and the Bolshevik Revolution, pp. 138 and 187, Marcel Liebman, "Bukharinism, Revolution and Social Development," The Socialist Register 1975, pp. 86 and 90 and Charles Bettelheim, Class Struggles in the USSR, p. 501.

[6]"We proceed from the fact that the Party, the Communist Party, is the principal instrument of the dictatorship of the proletariat, that the leadership of one party, which does not and cannot share this leadership with other parties, constitutes that fundamental condition without which no firm and developed dictatorship of the proletariat is conceivable." Ten years later (1936) Stalin would bluntly state that "several parties and consequently freedom for parties can exist only in a society in which there are antagonistic classes whose interests are mutually hostile and irreconcilable. . . . " But, since the "exploitation of man by man" had just been abolished in the Soviet Union "there is no ground. . . for the existence of several parties and consequently for freedom for these parties. In the U.S.S.R. only one party can exist, the Communist Party." Stalin, "The Seventh Enlarged Plenum of the E.C.C.I.," Vol. IX, p. 49 and "Report on Constitution," SW, p. 395. There is, as we shall shortly see, no specific reference in Lenin's writings--unlike Trotsky's --in which he says "only one party can exist" either in the Soviet Union or any other workers' state. On the other hand, however, there is no specific reference in which he says that the ban imposed on "factions" at the 10th Party Congress in 1921 (over which he presided) was only a "temporary measure." Lenin, as usual, left his followers in a grey area on the question of the party's attitude towards democratic principles.

[7]In 1952, on the eve of his death, Stalin appears to have redefined his earlier conception of communism. Passing over such questions as the existence of state power under communism, he tackles issues such as the relationship between mental and manual labor, industry and agriculture, town and countryside, etc. And he concludes--contrary to his 1927 statement--that all distinctions will not be removed. "Inessential distinctions" will no longer exist under communism, he says, but "essential distinctions" will continue to exist. Stalin, Economic Problems of Socialism in the U.S.S.R., pp. 33-34.

[8]"Marxism takes its point of departure from world economy, not as a sum of national parts but as a mighty and independent reality which has been created by the international division of labor and the world markets, and which in our epoch imperiously dominates the national markets." Trotsky, The Permanent Revolution, pp. 46 and 52 and The Third International After Lenin, pp. 51-52.

[9]We now see that whereas Trotsky saw two sides to the law of uneven development Stalin would acknowledge only one. This is important because while they both claimed that the "final" victory of Russia's socialist revolution could only be concluded after the socialist revolution had been victorious in the advanced West, Stalin--with his focus on the "military" side of the threat from the West--argued that a fully developed socialist society could be established within Russia's borders even while awaiting the "final" victory in the West or more correctly, protection against foreign military assaults upon socialist Russia. As Stalin put it, "the final victory of socialism is the full guarantee against attempts at intervention and hence against restoration, for any serious attempt at restoration can take place only with serious support from outside, only with the support of international capital. Therefore, the support of our revolution by the workers of all countries, and still more the victory of the workers in at least several countries, is a necessary condition for fully guaranteeing the first victorious country against attempts at intervention and restoration, a necessary condition for the final victory of socialism." Yet, there are some writers who see this debate between Stalin and Trotsky on the theory of socialism in one country nothing more than hairsplitting over how best to industrialize Russia's backward economy. Carr says that the arguments advanced by Stalin and Trotsky looked like "the differences between two moods of the same verb, the one denoting the process, the other the completed act of building." To the contrary, however, we believe that on this particular theoretical issue there were real differences between Trotsky's and Stalin's formulations. Carr, Socialism in One Country, Vol. I, p. 305 and Vol. II, p. 51, Stalin, "Concerning Questions of Leninism," Vol. VIII, p. 68 and Richard B. Day, Leon Trotsky and the Politics of Economic Isolation, pp. 6-10.

[10]Trotsky, The Revolution Betrayed, pp. 45-64 and 248.

[11]Lenin, "Ninth All-Russia Congress of Soviets," Vol. XXXIII, p. 160 and Carr, The Bolshevik Revolution, Vol. II, pp. 290-293. As we have said, it is not entirely clear that Lenin--when his works are considered in their totality--reconciled with the fact of building a complete socialist society in isolated and back-

ward Russia on the basis of the NEP. Yet a case can certainly
be made from his last writings that he did. This is leninism in
all of its ambiguousness.

[12]"Up to the end of 1920, when the civil war was virtually
over, an officially tolerated, but in practice persecuted, political opposition continued to play some part in Soviet political
life." Leonard B. Schapiro, The Origin of Communist Autocracy,
p. 170 and Carr, The Bolshevik Revolution, Vol. I, pp. 160-190.

[13]Let's note here that while Lenin called for the abolition
of all organized opposition within the communist party, he did
not call for the banning of opposition and free discussion in
general. Moreover, the two groups specifically aimed at in the
resolution on factions--the workers' opposition and the democratic centralists--were even invited to place representatives
on the central committee. However, apart from the famous "point
7" of the resolution on factions in which the central committee
of the party as an "extreme measure" is authorized to expel party
members, there is no specific reference which suggests that the
basic decision on all organized opposition was merely an extreme
measure. Lenin, "Tenth Congress of the R.C.P.(B.)," Vol. XXXII,
pp. 224 and 257-258 and Daniels, The Conscience of the Revolution,
p. 149. Lenin's general attitude towards political democracy was
rather mixed. Both before and after the revolution and up to the
dissolution of the constituent assembly in January 1918, Lenin
seems to have been favorably inclined towards certain democratic
institutions. To be sure, he assailed "bourgeois democracy."
But at the same time he had a keen interest in the establishment
of a multi-party state and proportional representation in the
soviets with the right of recall. We will limit ourselves to
cite a few of his observations after the revolution. "There
must be no government in Russia other than the Soviet Government.
Soviet power has been won in Russia, and the transfer of government from one Soviet party to another is guaranteed without any
revolution, simply by a decision of the Soviets, simply by new
elections of deputies to the Soviets." After noting that he
favored the "conduct of elections by organized parties," Lenin
said that the "Soviets shall. . . have the right to set the date
for the reelections . . . in strict conformity with the principles of the system of proportional representation." And so that
all parties could get some print time he pointed out that "for the
workers' and peasants' government freedom of the press means liberation of the press from capitalist oppression and public ownership of paper mills and printing presses; equal right for public
groups of a certain size (say, numbering 10,000 to a fair share
of newsprint stocks and a corresponding quantity of printers'
labor" [our emphasis]. Yet, it must be said again that these
observations were made just after the October revolution and prior

119

to the dispersing of the Constituent Assembly. And there were not a few contradictions during this period of "democratic" inclinations in Lenin's statements. For instance, after the victory of the bolsheviks Lenin let it be known that his "provisional government" would merely "govern the country until the Constituent Assembly is convened." And more importantly he said that "even if the peasants continue to follow the [peasant oriented] Socialist-Revolutionaries, even if they give this party a majority in the Constituent Assembly, we shall still say--what of it?" Lenin's assumption, of course, was that the coming elections to the Constituent Assembly would reflect the new relations of forces in the country--particularly the split between "left" and "right" social-revolutionaries. When this did not happen and the right social-revolutionaries--the smaller of the two social-revolutionary parties--won a majority of the votes in countryside, Lenin, arguing that the social-revolutionary victory was based on confusion and outdated electoral lists, demanded that the Constituent Assembly (in which the bolsheviks obtained only 25 percent of the vote) submit to the Soviets--where Lenin's party had a clear majority. When it refused, Lenin declared that the "Constituent Assembly could only serve as a screen for the struggle of the counterrevolutionaries to overthrow Soviet power" and is "hereby dissolved." From here to 1921 when he decrys "will-o'-the-wisps like 'freedom of the press'" it would all be downhill for Lenin's "democratic" inclinations. Lenin, "From the Central Committee of the R.S.D.L.P.(B.)," "Draft Resolution on Freedom of the Press," "Draft Decree on the Right of Recall," and "Report on the Right of Recall," Vol. XXVI, pp. 283, 303 and 336-340, "The Proletarian Revolution and the Renegade Kautsky," Vol. XXVIII, pp. 242-243, "The Second Congress of the Communist International" and "Letter to Austrian Communists," Vol. XXXI, pp. 254-255 and 268-269, "Draft Decree on Dissolution of Constituent Assembly," Vol. XXVI, pp. 434-436 and "A Letter to G. Myasnikov," Vol. XXXII, pp. 504-509, Liebman, The Russian Revolution, pp. 314-316, Carr, The Bolshevik Revolution, Vol. I, p. 121, Anweiler, The Soviets, pp. 208-211 and Radkey, The Sickle Under the Hammer," pp. 461-465.

[14]Lenin, who played no small part in its consolidation, would likewise train his guns from late 1922 on the growing bureaucracy within the party and state apparatus. And he would aim especially at Stalin. Though not mentioning Stalin by name he said that "everybody knows that no other institutions are worse organized than those of our Workers' and Peasants' Inspection and that under present conditions nothing can be expected from this People's Commissariat [under Stalin's leadership and whose responsibility it was to stamp out bureaucracy in the governmental machinery] . . . . Let it be said in parentheses that we have bureaucrats in our party offices as well as in Soviet offices." Furthermore, following the Red Army's conquest of independent Georgia in 1921, an action initiated by Stalin, Lenin--with a certain delay which

can be attributed primarily to his having been misinformed on the actual course of events--assailed Stalin's campaign at forcibly associating the Georgian national minority with the newly proclaimed Union of Soviet Socialist Republic. "I think that Stalin's haste and his infatuation with pure administration . . . played a fatal role here." He then appealed to Trotsky, with whom he would ally on numerous questions at this time and who had already reached a similar position on the Georgian question, to defend their common position against Stalin at the upcoming 12th party congress. "It is my earnest request that you should undertake the defense of the Georgian case. . . . This case is now under 'persecution' by Stalin and Dzerzhinsky [head of the secret police] and I cannot rely on their impartiality. Quite to the contrary. I would feel at ease if you agreed to undertake its defense." Apart from the fact that Trotsky would not be up to the task at the 12th party congress, neither he nor Lenin considered the possibility of overturning Stalin's fait accompli; namely, the restoring of genuine independence to the Georgian people. They merely sought to soften the blow of Stalin's brutality. As a result of these and related reasons, Lenin, in his so-called testament, would call for the removal of Stalin from his position as secretary-general of the party. Indeed, Lenin threatened to break off relations with Stalin because of the latter's rudeness towards his wife. "I have no intention of forgetting so easily what has been done against me, and it goes without saying that what has been done against my wife I consider having been done against me as well. I ask you, therefore, to think it over whether you are prepared to withdraw what you have said and to make your apologies, or whether you prefer that relations between us should be broken off." Lenin, however, would not live to see the outcome of his appeals to Trotsky and the party in general against Stalin. Lenin, "To L.D. Trotsky" and "To Comrade Stalin," Vol. XLV, pp. 601-608, "Better Fewer, But Better," Vol. XXXIII, pp. 487-494 and "Questions of Nationalities or 'Autonomiszation,'" Vol. XXXVI, pp. 605-611, Tucker, The Lenin Anthology, pp. 725-728 and Deutscher, Stalin, pp. 228-267.

[15]Howard J. Sherman, The Soviet Economy, pp. 63-64 and Carr, The Interregnum, pp. 28031. The "scissors" were partly closed in 1924 as a result of the Stalin led government making further concessions to the peasantry, especially the rich peasants. But the "scissors" would continue to haunt the Soviet government right up to the grain crisis of 1928.

[16]Trotsky first came forward as a serious proponent for a single economic plan in 1920. Indeed, the 9th party congress in 1920 adopted his proposal recommending the need for such a plan. But the Gosplan or State Planning Commission which was established in early 1921 would soon be relegated to a back seat as a result

of the open-ended economic system which was implied by the introduction of the NEP. Trotsky, while accepting this development for
a short time, would soon begin to agitate for the broadening of
the powers of Gosplan. He wrote in early 1922 that "the State
Planning Commission must be made into a lever for putting the
economy in order, and for this a stop must be put to disrupting
the economy as a result of lack of foresight and improvisation
with regard to this central problem. No achievement in the field
of economy is to be expected from propaganda and retributive
methods if this economy is pulled in all directions without
system and without a plan." His ideas would be rebuffed by Lenin
for some time. However, in December 1922 Lenin changed positions
and adopted Trotsky's idea. "This idea [for granting legislative
functions to the State Planning Commission] was suggested by
Comrade Trotsky, it seems, quite a long time ago. I was against
it at the time, because I thought that there would then be a fundamental lack of coordination in the system of our legislative
institutions. . . . I think that we must now take a step towards
extending the competence of the State Planning Commission. . . .
In this respect I think we can and must accede to the wishes of
Comrade Trotsky. . . ." Yet, it is unclear whether we can iden-
tify Lenin with Trotsky's overall program for the industrialization of the Soviet Union. But more importantly, however, the
Stalin led government--apart from a certain verbal commitment--
would progressively edge away from Lenin's new found interest in
planning until the late 1920s. Trotsky, The Trotsky Papers, Vol.
II, pp. 733-737, Lenin, "Granting Legislative Functions to the
State Planning Commission," Vol. XXXVI, pp. 598-602 and Carr,
The Bolshevik Revolution, Vol. II, pp. 358-380.

[17]Trotsky, Tasks Before the Twelfth Congress of the Russian
Communist Party, pp. 5-7 and Daniels, ed., A Documentary History
of Communism, Vol. I, pp. 235-237.

[18]It was Preobrazhensky--a long time bolshevik, leading
economist and ally of Trotsky during these industrialization de-
bates--who provided much of the theoretical basis for the idea
of primitive socialist accumulation. "Primitive socialist accumulation. . . means accumulation in the hands of the state of
material resources mainly or partly from sources lying outside
the complex of state economy. This accumulation must play an
extremely important part in a backward peasant country, hastening
to a very great extent the arrival of the moment when the technical and scientific reconstruction of the state economy begins
and when this economy at last achieves purely economic superiority over capitalism." This program will be carried out primarily
as a result of the direct taxation of "pre-socialist economic
forms," a monopoly price policy and an appeal for the "self-re-

straint" of the working class. "Taxation of the non-socialist [economic] forms not only must inevitably take place in the period of primitive socialist accumulation, it must inevitably play a very great, a directly decisive role in peasant countries such as the Soviet Union. . . . [And] the concentration of all the large-scale industry of the country in the hands of a single trust, that is, in the hands of the workers' state, increases to an enormous extent the possibility of carrying out on the basis of monopoly a price policy which will be only another form of taxation of private economy" [since the peasantry must buy their goods and equipment from the state sector]. Furthermore, he said, "in this period the law of wages is subrodinated to the law of socialist accumulation which finds its expression in conscious self-restraint by the working class. . . . Socialist accumulation is a necessity for the working class, but now it proceeds as a consciously understood necessity. . . ." And Preobrazhensky insists that a period of primitve socialist accumulation must be traversed "as quickly as possible" as it "is a question of life and death" for the socialist state. Let's recall here that Marx had described the period of primitive capitalist accumulation as one of plunder and colonialism which was symbolized above all by the "historical process of divorcing the producer from the means of production." Would the period of primitive socialist accumulation entail so much "blood and dirst?" The very thought of such a policy made Preobrazhensky cringe. He always stressed that there was only a "formal similarity" between primitive capitalist accumulation and primitive socialist accumulation since the methods opened to the former are banned by the socialist state "from the very start and forever." Yet, and this is extremely important, neither Preobrazhensky nor Trotsky ever seriously considered what would be the significance of a rejection of their industrialization program by the peasantry and the working class. Would it then be necessary for a forced march towards socialist accumulation? Would this then signify--as Trotsky suggested in 1920--that the whole of the Soviet order was a "broken reed?" Having said this, however, there was one significant difference between Preobrazhensky's and Trotsky's approach to Russia's industrialization. Unlike Trotsky, the flow of Preobrazhensky's arguments--though he does not say so specifically--suggests that the internal resources of the Soviet Union would be sufficient for it to become fully industrialized in the absence of supportive revolutions in the West. This would become quite clear in 1928 when Preobrazhensky hurriedly made peace with Stalin after the latter under the banner of "socialism in one country" made a "left" turn and adopted, however bloodily, numerous planks from the Opposition's economic program in an effort to rapidly industrialize the Soviet economy. Trotsky, as we have seen, linked his industrialization program--no doubt partly to avoid the forced march that would subsequently be undertaken by Stalin--with the breaking of the "equilibrium" in the

West. E.A. Preobrazhensky, The New Economics, pp. 77-146, Marx, Capital, Vol. I, pp. 786 and 834, Daniels, ed., A Documentary History of Communism, Vol. I, pp. 267-269, Carr, Socialism in One Country, Vol. I, pp. 203-206, Alexander Erlich, The Soviet Industrialization Debate 1924-1928, pp. 43-52, Sherman, The Soviet Economy, pp. 70-72 and Deutscher, The Prophet Unarmed, pp. 234-238.

[19]Trotsky, "Toward Capitalism or Socialism," The Challenge of the Left Opposition [1923-25], pp. 359 and 375-376 and The Real Situation in Russia, pp. 70 and 85-93.

[20]According to Cohen, "the linchpin of his [Bukharin's] program was the encouragement of private peasant accumulation, thereby broadening the rural demand for industrial products and increasing the marketable surplus of peasant agriculture." Cohen, Bukharin and the Bolshevik Revolution, pp. 173-176, Daniels, ed., A Documentary History of Communism, Vol. I, !!. 264- 287-288 and 314-316, Stalin, On the Opposition, pp. 35-36, M. Fichelson and A. Derischebourg, ed., La Question Paysanne En U.R.S.S. De 1924 a 1929, pp. 176-177, Sherman, The Soviet Economy, pp. 71-73, William L. Blackwell, The Industrialization of Russia, pp. 92-93, Erlich, The Soviet Industrialization Debate, 1924-1928, pp. 15-23 and 30-31 and Deutscher, The Prophet Unarmed, pp. 238-240.

[21]Sherman, The Soviet Economy, pp. 75-89, Daniels, ed., A Documentary History of Communism, Vol. I, pp. 301-305, Trotsky, The Real Situation in Russia, pp. 60-79, Erlich, The Soviet Industrialization Debate 1924-1928, p. 170 and Naum Jasny, Soviet Industrialization 1928-1952, pp. 92-93.

[22]Tucker, ed., The Lenin Anthology, p. 727.

[23]Carr, The Bolshevik Revolution, Vol. I, p. 219. Unless otherwise indicated, when we use the words Opposition or Majority--though the alignments frequently changed during this time-- we refer to Trotsky and Stalin as they were the chief inspirers of both groups. However, it should be noted that the trotskyist Opposition--known historically as the Left Opposition so as to distinguish it from a Majority subdivided into a Center and Right--was not the first group within the party to call attention to the derailing of the revolutionary process. Several groups, including the Workers Opposition, from 1920 had already launched a campaign against the growing bureaucratic seizure of the party and later against the ugly influence of the NEP. They said that "the Workers Opposition considers that bureaucracy is our enemy, our scourge, and the greatest danger for the future existence of the Communist Party itself. . . . Wide publicity, freedom of

opinion and discussion, right to criticize within the party and among the members of the trade unions--such is the decisive step that can put an end to the prevailing system of bureaucracy." Later, Workers Truth was to point out that "the Communist Party, which during the years of the revolution was a party of the working class, has become the ruling party, the party of the organizers and directors of the governmental apparatus and economic life on capitalistic lines, with the general backwardness and lack of organization of the working class." Though Trotsky would never accept the argument that the Soviet economy operated "on capitalistic lines," he, nevertheless, came increasingly to adopt many of the themes broached by these groups--against whom he had previously vented his rage--in his struggle with Stalin for the mantle of leninism. Daniels, The Conscience of the Revolution, p. 128 and A Documentary History of Communism, Vol. I, pp. 202-203 and 221, Deutscher, The Prophet Unarmed, p. 51 and Carr, The Bolshevik Revolution, Vol. I, pp. 203-204.

[24]This approach would generally characterize Trotsky's actions during the successional struggle (1923-1927). Even though he had no chance at convincing the central committee and the all-powerful politbureau (together comprising fewer than seventy-five people in a party approaching one million members) of the correctness of his views, Trotsky would steadfastly refuse--until virtually the last hour--to appeal directly to the party's rank and file or, much less, the masses of workers and peasants against the "secretarial hierarchy." Had he done so would he not have exposed himself to the charge of violating the principles of "democratic centralism" and, thereby, inviting immediate expulsion from the party? Indeed, his expulsion from the party in 1927--when he belatedly appealed to the party's rank and file--flowed from this charge. Trotsky was clearly in a difficult position. However, there were more important reasons--to which we will shortly turn--for his dilemma.

[25]Trotsky's writings--as we saw with Lenin--right up to the dissolution of the Constituent Assembly are marked by a certain "democratic" inclination. To be sure, he always denounced bourgeois or "hypocritical democracy." But, during the first months after the revolution he was a fervent advocate of both a multi-party system and a free press for the Soviet state. It was only during the Civil War (1918-192) that Trotsky began to speak of the "exclusive role" of the communist party in the Soviet state. He referred to the "dictatorship of the proletariat" as the "most ruthless form of state which embraces the life of the citizens authoritatively in every direction." And he would always justify these anti-democratic views on the basis of the extreme situation imposed on the Soviet state by the Civil War. Yet, when the Civil War ended, Trotsky would continue to adhere to many of these

anti-democratic views--more and more justified on the basis of the "capitalist encirclement" of the workers' state--until 1933. We can detect, however, a moderate shift in his authoritarian views from late 1922 which would assume an organized form from the fall of 1923. Trotsky, "Results and Prospects," PR, pp. 75-76, 1905, pp. 141, 226 and 252, The Age of Permanent Revolution: A Trotsky Anthology, pp. 44-45, 59 and 219, Terrorism and Communism, pp. 107 and 168-170, Writings of Leon Trotsky [1930], p. 165, Writings [1937-38], pp. 417-419, Tasks Before the Twelfth Congress of the Russian Communist Party, pp. 29 and 37 and Challenge [1923-25], pp. 55-58 and Deutscher, The Prophet Armed, pp. 336-337 and The Prophet Unarmed, pp. 30-31.

[26]It should be recalled that Trotsky, a leader of the 1905 revolution, had rejected the tsar's "Manifesto" as a mere "scrap of paper." He had said in 1905, "here it is before you [while showing the "Manifesto" to the crowd]--here it is crumpled in my fist. Today they have issued it, tomorrow they will take it away and tear it into pieces, just as I am now tearing up this paper freedom before your eyes!" Was not the "Manifesto" of the triumvirate a "scrap of paper?" Trotsky, Challenge [1923-25], p. 408 and 1905, pp. 116-117.

[27]Trotsky, The New Course, pp. 24-27 and 90-97.

[28]To be sure, there were the stormy events surrounding the "literary debate" but, as we have seen, the issues raised were not specifically related to the theme of democracy. Daniels, A Documentary History of Communism, Vol. I, pp. 2470248 and Stalin, "Thirteenth Conference of the R.C.P.(B.)," Works, Vol. VI, p. 29.

[29]Deutscher, The Prophet Unarmed, p. 249. While it is true that Trotsky shunned "democratic" oppositional activities during this period, it is not quite correct to say that he "shunned inner-party affairs." We will provide two examples. The first concerns his speech to the 13th Party Congress in May 1924. After recognizing that the "bureaucratization of the party apparatus" was responsible for the existence of factions in the party, he expressly noted that "I believe from the political point of view it is sufficient. . . to say that I have never recognized freedom for groupings inside the party, nor do I recognize it now. . . ." And then he went on to say that "none of us wants to be or can be right against the party. In the last analysis, the party is always right, because the party is the sole historical instrument that the working class possesses for the solution of its fundamental tasks. . . . I know that no one can be right against the party. It is only possible to be right with the party and

through it since history has not created any other way to determine the correct position. The English have a proverb: My country right or wrong. We can say with much greater historical justification: whether it is right or wrong in any particular, specific question at any particular mement, this is my party." Souvarine correctly observed that "this abstract reasoning ⌐my party right or wrong⌐ amounted to giving a free hand to Stalin. . . ." Even stalin was taken aback. "The party, Trotsky says, makes no mistakes. That is wrong." Trotsky's granting of infallibility to the party--however much he might have been "jeering at the party," as Stalin suggests--served to strengthen those forces which he sought to undermine. The second example concerns his denunciation of some of his close international supporters in 1925. Max Eastman, then in sympathy with the Opposition and communism, was denounced for having just published a book, Since Lenin Died, which, said Trotsky, was based "on completely rotten foundations." Eastman's book contained, thanks to Trotsky's active assistance, the essentials of Lenin's "testament." Among other things, Lenin, in his "testament" had called for the replacement of Stalin as general secretary of the party. Trotsky, nevertheless, signed a statement--which he later said was "foisted upon me"--declaring that "there is no sincere worker who will believe in the picture painted by Eastman. It contains within itself its own refutation. Whatever Eastman's intentions may be, this botched piece of work is nonetheless objectively a tool of the counterrevolution, and can only serve the ends of the enemies incarnate of communism and of the revolution." Even while recognizing that the Opposition had been shackled since January 1924 and threatened with expulsion if it engaged in "petty bourgeois" activities, it seems clear to us that Trotsky's participation in internal party affairs is beyond doubt. We might question, however, whose interests were served through this participation. Trotsky, Challenge [1923-25], pp. 154-155, 161 and 310-317, Boris Souvarine, Stalin: A Critical Survey of Bolshevism, p. 363 and Stalin, On the Opposition, p. 95 and Political Report of the Central Committee to the Fourteenth Congress of the C.P.S.U.(B.), p. 108.

[30]Why did Trotsky fail in the struggle for power? We attribute the basic reason to what we have previously described as the exhaustion of the revolutionary process in the Soviet Union and on the Western fronts. Trotsky's tactical mistakes, as we have seen, were important but they do not carry the political weight that Daniels suggests. In short, Stalin did not have to play a very good hand in order to secure victory. While in Turkish exile, Trotsky would say that had he acted swiftly "at the beginning of 1923" he would have been victorious. Yet he immediately questioned how "solid" such a victory would have been in the existing political climate in the Soviet Union. "Here I must come back to the decisive importance of objective conditions.

Without a correct strategy victory is impossible. But even the most correct strategy cannot give victory under unfavorable objective conditions." Trotsky, My Life, pp. 481-482 and Writings [1932], p. 289 and Daniels, The Conscience of the Revolution, pp. 399-403.

[31]Trotsky wrote in 1931 that "the contradictory processes in the economy and politics of the USSR are developing on the basis of the dictatorship of the proletariat. The character of the social regime is determined first of all by the property relations. The nationalization of land, of the means of industrial production and exchange, with the monopoly of foreign trade in the hands of the state, constitute the bases of the social order in the USSR. . . . These property relations, lying at the base of class relations, determine for us the nature of the Soviet Union as a proletarian state." Two years earlier--with regard to his attitude towards democracy in the Soviet Union--he noted that "it is not a question of winning the 'freedom to organize' [which some of his followers were calling for] against a hostile class government, but the struggling for a regime under which the trade unions will enjoy--within the framework of the dictatorship--the necessary freedom to correct their own state by words and deeds." After observing that the freedom to organize "is inconceivable without freedom of assembly, freedom of the press and all the other 'freedom,'" he went on to conclude that "it is necessary to reject and condemn the program of struggle for 'the freedom to organize' and all other 'freedoms' in the USSR--because this is the program of bourgeois democracy." A few years hence, however, Trotsky would weigh his remarks on democracy in the Soviet Union a little more soberly. Trotsky, Writings [1929], pp. 290-292 and 303 and Writings [1930-31], p. 204.

[32]Stalin's German policy flowed from his general analysis of the international situation from 1928-1933. He divided the period from the first World War to 1933 into three distinct "periods" with each taxing the communist movement with a distinct task. The first period--representing an "extremely acute crisis of the capitalist system"--lasted from the end of the war to 1923. The second period--representing a "gradual and partial stabilization of the capitalist system"--lasted until 1928. And "finally came the third period," said Stalin, of "gigantic class battles" [perhaps he had in mind the veritable civil war that his government was currently waging against the peasantry]. With regard to Germany during the "third period" Stalin rejected "the liberal idea of a basic difference between fascism and bourgeios democracy." Indeed, he considered the latter to be the more dangerous of the two since it was not "openly fascist." Thus, he sought to "mobilize the [German] masses on the basis of the

united front below" [which, in effect, meant against the leadership of the social democratic party, the SPD]. Trotsky, on the other hand, rejected Stalin's "stupid" and "false schemata" of the "third period." And he said that he could "look calmly" at Stalin's charge that he was now a "rightist." Looking at Germany, Trotsky wrote--before Hitler's triumph--that "at the moment that the 'normal' police and military resources of the bourgeois dictatorship, together with their parliamentary screens, no longer suffice to hold society in a state of equilibrium--the turn of the fascist regime arrives." Having said this, however, he emphasized--with an eye towards Stalin--that "when a state turns fascist it doesn't only mean that the forms and methods of government are changed,. . . it means, primarily and above all, that the workers organziations are annihilated; that the proleatariat is reduced to an amorphous state; and that a system of administration is created which penetrates deeply into the masses and which serves to frustrate the independent crystallization of the proletariat. Therein precisely is the gist of fascism." This policy would not be carried out against the leadership of the German social democratic movement but in tactical alliance with it. Trotsky, The Struggle Against Fascism in Germany, pp. 132-141 and 155-159, Writings [1930], pp. 36, 66 and 364, Writings [1930-31], pp. 230-31, Writings [1932-33], pp. 304-305 and 308-309 and Writings [1933-34], pp. 26-27 and Degras, ed., The Communist International, Vol. II, pp. 455-457 and Vol. III, pp. 27-30, 54, 159 and 296.

[33]It should be noted, however, that his "orientation towards a new International"--though he didn't emphasize it--also stemmed from his recognition of the political, and presently physical, liquidation of his followers in the Soviet Union. Despite all of what he would say about the the coming political revolution in the Soviet Union, Trotsky turned his attention more and more towards the West. The following statement is characteristic of his new attitude towards the Soviet Union: "The leninist current [trotskyist] in the Soviet Union can, from now on, only be revived by great revolutionary successes in the West [our emphasis]. Those Russian bolsheviks who remain true to our cause under the unheard-of pressure of national reaction. . . will be recompensed by the further course of development. But now the light will come not from the East but from the West." If he were assured of "great revolutionary successes in the West," the issue of the coming political revolution in the Soviet Union would be academic. But, what if he weren't? Trotsky, Writings [1933-34], pp. 44, 120-121 and 273-278 and Writings [1934-35], pp. 127, 131 and 164.

[34]Trotsky always recognized the privileged and exploitative nature of the Stalin regime, but, for him, "the privileges of the bureaucracy by themselves do not change the bases of Soviet

society, because the bureaucracy derives its privileges not from
any special property relations peculiar to it as a 'class,'
but from those property relations that have been created by the
October revolution and that are fundamentally adequate for the
dictatorshipof the proletariat." Trotsky, Writings [1933-34],
pp. 20 and 112-115, Writings [1934-35], p. 119, The Revolution
Betrayed, p. 248 and In Defense of Marxism, pp. 7 and 26.

[35]Trotsky charged that rather than utilizing the Soviet Union
as "a drill ground for the world revolution" the stalinist bu-
reaucracy--in the interest of maintaining its privileges--was
utilizing the international working class movement, through the
Comintern, "as so much small change" in its deals with imperialist
powers. The "leprosy of stalinism" was now "the principal
obstacle on the historic road of the working class." Having
condemned Stalin's foreign policy "from beginning to end" in 1934,
he would nevertheless make a modest adjustment--as he had done
when Stalin sent the Red Army into Georgia some 18 years earlier--
when a revolutionary "impulse" was provided by those "missionaries
with bayonets" in Eastern Poland on the heels of the Hitler-Stalin
pact. To be sure, Trotsky continued to decry the "general reactionary character" of Stalin's foreign policy and even the
"secondary importance" of the social overturns when measured
against the conditions under which they were obtained. But, as in
the case of Georgia in 1921, he did not denounce the seizure of
Eastern Poland by the Red Army in 1939. Taking "the facts as they
are" he would more characteristically observe that "the strangled
and desecrated October revolution served notice that it was still
alive." And the most important fact for Trotsky was that "the
safeguarding of the socialist revolution comes before formal
democratic principles." Trotsky, Writings [1934-35], pp. 124-125,
295 and 306-309, Writings [1932-33], p. 234, Writings [1933-34],
p. 312, Writings [1938-39], pp. 200-202 and 217, Writings [1939-
40], p. 197 and In Defense of Marxism, pp. 19-20, 27-28, 130-133
and 173-176.

[36]Trotsky undertook a revision of his "thermidorean"
analogy at this time. Until 1935 he had maintained that a
thermidorean victory would signify the liquidation of the "gains"
of the October revolution. However, a rereading of the French
revolution suggested to him that the downfall of Robespierre did
not lead to the reintroduction of feudal property in France. It,
instead, signified a turning to the right of the French revolution. Thus, "the smashing of the Left Opposition implied in the
most direct and immediate sense the transfer of power from the
hands of the revolutionary vanguard into the hands of the more
conservative elements among the bureaucracy and the upper crust
of the working class. The year 1924--that was the beginning of
the Soviet thermidor." Trotsky, Writings [1930-31], pp. 71-78,
[1932-33], pp. 304-305, [1933-34], pp. 104-105 and 116, [1934-35],
pp. 170, 173-174 and 313 and The Revolution Betrayed, pp. 285-

286 and 300-301.

[37]Why was democracy "a life and death need" of the Soviet
Union in 1936? Why was it not so in 1926? Trotsky simply forgot
what he had written during the first phase of his "democratic"
opposition to Stalin and now called for "a revival of the freedom
of Soviet parties." Without even mentioning the fact that the
only party that ever had any genuine freedom under Lenin's govern-
menet from 1918-21 was the communist party, did Trotsky not say
earlier that the single party system was a necessity for a
workers' state "surrounded by capitalist states?" Was the Soviet
Union no longer isolated? Furthermore, if opposition parties are
going to exist, why not permit anti-Soviet parties the right to
organize? Finally, where did Lenin--much less himself--ever say
that the ban on "factions" adopted at the 10th Party Congress was
merely a "temporary measure?" Again, on the theme of democracy,
it seems that Trotsky is more concerned with making ends meet
than with developing a coherent point of view. Trotsky, Writings
[1933-34], pp. 114-116, [1934-35], p. 172, [1935-36], pp. 224-225,
The Revolution Betrayed, pp. 95-97, 266, 276 and 288-289 and In
Defense of Marxism, p. 31.

CHAPTER IV

TROTSKY AND CHINA: UNIVERSALIZING

THE THEORY OF PERMANENT REVOLUTION

I. Moscow and the Second Chinese Revolution

The policy of the Communist International towards colonial
liberation movements was defined by Lenin during the early congresses of this international working class organization. More
specifically, this occurred at the Second and Fourth World Congresses of this organization.[1] Indeed, from the war years,
themselves, Lenin had begun to pay increasing attention to the
theme of self-determination for oppressed nations and, especially, the significance that the latter could have for proletarian
revolutions in the West. However, it was not until 1920 that
Lenin sharply outlined his perspective on colonial liberation
movements and, most importantly, the attitude that all national
parties adhering to the Communist International (Comintern)
must take toward them.[2] Why was this so? As we have seen, 1920
was somewhat of a turning point in Soviet history. It signaled
to the Soviet leaders that the revolution was isolated and was
going to remain so for some time. This international reality
of being encircled by capitalist regimes--combined with severe
internal difficulties in the workers' state--pushed Lenin more
and more to seek an Eastern outlet so as to break the capitalist
ring surrounding the Soviet state.[3] Furthermore, the colonial
liberation movements, themselves, thanks to the war to make the
world safe for "democracy" and the October revolution, were on
the march. It was against this background and the appearance of
Asian delegates at the Second Comintern Congress in 1920 that
Lenin advanced his ideas on colonial liberation movements.

The immediate context for Lenin's ideas was a dispute within
the colonial commission of the congress between him and M.N. Roy,
the Indian delegate, over the role of the national bourgeoisie
in the colonies. Roy's "theses," moreover, contained a clearly
defined Asian coloration:

. . . the fate of the revolutionary movement in
Europe depends entirely on the course of the revolution
in the East. Without the victory of the revolution in
Eastern countries, the communist movement in the West
would come to nothing. World capitalism draws its main
resources and income from the colonies, principally

from those in Asia. If it comes to the worst,
the European capitalists can give the workers the full
surplus value from their efforts and in this way win
them over to their side, having killed their revolutionary aspirations. And these same capitalists will
continue to exploit Asia, with the help of the proletariat. Such an outcome would suit the capitalists
very well. This being so, it is essential that we
divert our energies into developing and elevating the
revolutionary movement in the East, and accept as our
fundamental thesis that the fate of world communism depends on the victory of communism in the East. . . .

Roy's views left very little room for the bourgeois democratic
movement in the East which, he said, merely seeks "political
independence under a bourgeois order."* After rejecting Roy's
contention that the European revolutionary movement "depends entirely" on the East as "unfounded" Lenin--who in an earlier draft
of his theses had referred to the revolutionary possibilities of
bourgeois democratic movements in the East--arrived at a sort of
"compromise" with him on the nature of the movements in the East
and the attitude that communists should take toward them. Rather
than refer to the revolutionary possibilities of bourgeois democratic movements Lenin now spoke of the "national-revolutionary
movements" in the East. What's more, he insisted that a determined struggle be waged against "bourgeois democratic trends"
operating either under the guise of national-revolutionary movements or even, he said, dressed up "in communist colors." But
this was essentially a play on words since Lenin continued to
argue that in predominantly peasant countries--as in the East--
the colonial liberation movements must necessarily assume a
basically bourgeois character. The central question, then, was
not so much the nature of these movements as the attitude that
communists, local and foreign, should take toward them. For
Lenin therefore, even if only "provisionally" and with the aim of
"rallying the constituent elements" for the communist future,
organizations adhering to the Comintern--while maintaining their
independence from the national-revolutionary movements--"must
support by action" the movements for national unification and independence in the East. "The Communist International should

_____

*It should be noted, however, that despite Roys' Asian
standpoint he was quite clear on the fact that "the masses in
the backward countries" could reach communism only if they were
"led by the class conscious proletariat of the advanced countries."
Hélèn Carrère d'Encausse and Stuart R. Schram, eds. Marxism
and Asia, pp. 151 and 160-162.

collaborate provisionally with the revolutionary movement of the colonies and backward countries, and even form an alliance with it, but it must not amalgamate with it; it must unconditionally maintain the independence of the proletarian movement, even if it is only in an embryonic stage."* Yet, Lenin's theses were stamped with ambiguity. Where does one draw the line between a "bourgeois democratic trend" and a national-revolutionary movement? How does one really distinguish between independence and amalgamation when both the form and the duration of the alliance between the communist and bourgeois movements are to be determined concretely? Lenin's theses provide no answer to these and other questions. Nevertheless, both Roy's and Lenin's theses were adopted by the Comintern. But it was Lenin's theses which would henceforth be interpreted as official communist policy towards the East.[4]

How were these policies carried out under Lenin's rule? Lenin's Eastern policy seems entangled between his efforts to create an anti-British Asian front and his determined desire to win the favors of British industrialists and bankers. And from the standpoint of Soviet national interests--even if this was a bit contradictory--there was in the early 1920s much to be said for his position. Was not Britain the Soviet's chief rival in Central Asia? Was it not also Britain--and France--which was spearheading the anti-Soviet movement on the European continent? And was not Britain, even if somewhat incorrectly, still regarded as the principal economic force in the world? The isolated and backward workers' state was faced with the difficult choice of choosing between its own national interests and the survival of local communist movements in the Eastern countries. And it seems clear that Lenin was prepared to sacrifice local communist movements in the interest of maintaining alliances with anti-French and especially anti-British bourgeois movements. This was unmistakably so in the cases of Persia and Turkey. Both the Persian and Turkish communist parties were founded in 1920.

---

*At the Fourth Comintern Congress in 1922--the last attended and presided over by him--he reiterated his basic position of the colonial question. After emphasizing that the "chief task" of national-revolutionary movements was "to bring about national unity and achieve political independence," he insisted that the embryonic communist parties in the East "must take part in every movement which gives them access to the masses." Lenin, "The Second Congress of the Communist International," Vol. XXXI, pp. 242-243 and Degras, ed., The Communist International, Vol. I, pp. 139-144, 385 and 389.

In the case of Persia, Moscow chose the anti-British but fiercely anti-communist Riza Khan's government over the tiny Persian communist government. Indeed, Lenin abandoned the tiny Soviet Republic of Gilan on the Persian coast--which had been established under Moscow's auspices--so as to show his good intentions to the persecutor of the Persian communist movement. The diplomatic product of this collaboration between Lenin and Riza Khan was the Soviet-Persia treaty of February 26, 1921. Developments in Turkey were remarkably similar. Right on the heels of the butchery of the leadership of the local communist movement in 1920 Moscow signed a "treaty of friendship and fraternity" with the butcher, himself, Kemal Pasha (later named Ataturk). Commenting on this affair Carr noted that "for the first, though not for the last, time it was demonstrated that governments could deal drastically with their national communist parties without forfeiting the goodwill of the Soviet government. . . ." And interestingly--again reflecting the duality of Lenin's British policy--at about the same time that the Soviet-Turkey treaty was signed, an Anglo-Soviet trade agreement was reached. The salient feature in the latter agreement was Lenin's endorsement of a strong statement against the use of hostile propaganda against the British Empire:

> [Noting specifically] that each party refrains
> from hostile action or undertakings against the other
> and from conducting outside of its own borders any
> official propaganda, direct or indirect, against the
> institutions of the British Empire or of the Russian
> Soviet Republic respectively, and more particularly
> that the Russian Soviet Government refrains from any
> attempt by military or diplomatic or any other form
> of action or propaganda to encourage any of the peoples
> of Asia in any form of hostile action against British
> interests or the British Empire, especially in India
> and in the independent state of Afghanistan.*[5]

---

*It is interesting to note that the Third Comintern Congress--which was held three months after the Anglo-Soviet trade agreement of March 16, 1921--gave virtually no attention to the Eastern question. Trotsky typified the flow of events at this congress by pointing out that the colonial movement--after Europe and America--represented the "third source" of the world revolution. Roy, in any event, registered an "energetic protest" against the Comintern's "liquidating of the Eastern question." Was Lenin testing the British waters? Carrere d'Encausse and Schram, eds., Marxism and Asia, pp. 172, 187 and 194-195, Fernando Claudin, The Communist Movement, Vol. I, pp. 242-253, Franz Borkenau, World Communism, pp. 292-295, Carr, The Bolshevik Revolution, Vol. III,

How did Lenin apply his Eastern policy towards China? Was he motivated by the same concerns as in the case of Persia and Turkey. We do not know what his China policy would have been in 1927. We can only surmise on the basis of what he did do in other areas of the East--though the situation in Turkey in 1920 was not that of China in 1927--and on his general appreciation of developments in China through the early 1920s. Prior to the October revolution, Lenin, especially after the Chinese revolution of 1911, had expressed considerable interest in developments in China. He wrote several articles on the Chinese political situation. This was most notably the case on the question of the role of the bourgeoisie in the Chinese revolution. After referring to Sun Yat-sen, leader of the revolution of 1911, as a "revolutionary democrat" he wrote in 1913 that "one could hardly quote a more striking example of this rottenness of the entire European bourgeoisie than the support it gives to reaction in Asia in aid of the selfish interests of financiers and capitalist swindlers. Throughout Asia a mighty democratic movement is growing, spreading and gaining in strength. The bourgeoisie there still sides with the people against reaction." Would he have said this during the hightide of the Chinese revolution of 1925-27? What is clear is that following the October revolution, Lenin's government, on several occasions, sought to come to terms with the Chinese people and their leaders. In 1919 the Soviet government, then beseiged by "white" forces, addressed an important document to "the governments of North and South China"--itself somewhat revealing since the government of the North, or Peking, consisted of militarists--declaring that it "has renounced the conquests made by the tsarist government which deprived China of Manchuria and other areas. Let the people living in those areas themselves decide within the frontiers of which state they wish to dwell and what form of government they wish to establish in their own countries. The Soviet government returns to the Chinese people without any compensation, the Chinese Eastern Railway, and all the mining, timber, gold and other concessions seized by Russian generals, merchants and capitalists under the tsarist government. . . ." Two facts stand out concerning the passage

---

pp. 275-293 and 301, Brandt, Stalin's Failure in China, pp. 14-15, Marcel Liebman, Leninism under Lenin, pp. 374-384, Lazitch and Drachkovitch, Lenin and the Comintern, Vol. I, pp. 412-413, Warren Lerner, Karl Radek, pp. 91-125, Degras, ed., The Communist International, Vol. I, pp. 105 and 368-370 and Trotsky, The First Five Years of the Communist International, Vol. I, pp. 222-223.

emphasized in the preceding statement: 1) when it was declared
--despite the highly favorable impact it had upon the Chinese
people, especially intellectuals--it could not have been implemented since much of the area in question was in the hands of
the white troops and 2) when it could have been implemented,
following the defeat of the white troops in late 1920, it was
not since Lenin's government--though not the Chinese--denied its
existence. Was he seeking new allies but without wanting to make
too many concessions? Indeed, the whole tenor of Lenin's China
policy suggests that he was seeking an anti-British and, this
time, an anti-Japanese front. If this could be established via
a revolutionary movement in China, so much the better. But the
China of the leninist years was not what it would become by 1927.
The two principal political organizations in the revolution of
1927--the kuomintang and the communist party--were just being
forged. Thus, as Isaacs correctly observed, the first Soviet
officials or agents reaching China in 1920 "came looking not for
new revolutionary currents to swim in but for a deal with any
likely looking band of militarists and politicians who might
serve Russian diplomatic interests. . . . The puny nationalist
movement led by Sun Yat-sen in the south [without mentioning the
communist party which was not founded until 1921] did not impress them as a point of support for Soviet interests."6 Lenin's
Eastern policy was certainly a victim of the isolation and
backwardness of the workers' state. But, and this must not be
forgotten, it was visibly stamped with a Soviet first label.
And it was this problematical heritage that Stalin and Trotsky
would quarrel over during the Chinese revolution of 1925-27.

What were the origins of the Chinese revolution? The events
that ultimately led to the revolution of 1925-27 began unfolding
against the background of the birth and agitation of the working
class, the influence of the October revolution and the highly
nationalistic May Fourth Movement. Prior to the 19th century
China possessed an essentially self-contained and self-sufficing
agrarian economy. To be sure, she remains primarily agricultural
even today. Still, the "opening" of China by the Great Powers in
the 19th century provided the basis for the emergence of a small
but influential "modern industry" sector in the economy. But
this nascent and heavily foreign owned industry remained almost
completely hamstrung throughout the turn of the century as the
Western countries--producing cheaper and better quality manufactured goods--were able to inundate their "spheres of influence"
in the Chinese market with their products. It was the First
World War--compelling the Great Powers to concentrate primarily on
military production--which provided the necessary respite so as to
allow Chinese industry to undertake a considerable spurt. And it
was this situation that gave impetus to the birth of the Chinese
bourgeoisie and especially the tiny working class population
concentrated in the coastal cities and in the rice-milling,

textile, mining and transport industries. The second major factor in the background of the Chinese revolution was the impact of the October revolution. There are several reasons why Chinese nationalists and revolutionaries would be attracted to the October revolution. Was not the red flag of labor hoisted above a huge, underdeveloped and predominantly peasant country? Indeed, Lenin consistently stated that "in very many and very essential respects, Russia is undoubtedly an Asian country and, what is more, one of the most benighted, medieval and shamefully backward of Asian countries." Furthermore, the Western countries --especially Britain--and Japan were the common enemies of Russia and China. Britain, for instance, was the chief inspirer of the anti-Soviet movement both in Europe and Asia and possessed the largest "sphere of influence" in China. It seems, however, that Lenin's increasing interest in the problems of Eastern countries from 1920--as reflected in his "theses" on the colonial question at the Second Comintern Congress--and especially his indications that he was prepared to break with the tsarist past on relations with his Chinese neighbors were the most important reasons, at least initially, why Chinese nationalists and revolutionaries were attracted to the October revolution. With regard to the impact of the October revolution on China, Isaacs stated that "the invasion of its ideas, its spokesmen, its representatives was the most fateful invasion of China since the arrival of Western merchants and warriors nearly a century before." The final major factor in the background of the Chinese revolution was the highly nationalistic May Fourth Movement. This refers to the social, political and intellectual ferment that rocked China from the First World War until roughly 1921. It issued from the humiliations wrought upon China by the West and Japan and from the limitations of the Chinese revolution of 1911.[7] Yet, while the response of the Chinese intellectual community* was marked by anti-Western nationalism, it was at the same time pro-Western culturally:

---

*Although the May Fourth Movement was primarily a movement of intellectuals, it attracted broad sectors of the Chinese population. This can be seen in the response to an appeal of the students in 1919 from which the movement actually received its name. According to Harrison, "more than 100,000 people in sixteen of the twenty-one provinces of the time actively responded to the demonstration of some 5,000 students in Peking on May 4, 1919 [against the anti-China decisions at Versailles]. For the first time on a national scale, the anger of the intellectuals, born of despair at the plight of China, significantly reached other sections of the population--professional people, merchants, and even certain segments of labor and the peasantry." Harrison, The Long March to Power, pp. 8-9 and 13-14.

The May Fourth Movement was actually a combined intellectual and Sociopolitical movement to achieve national independence, the emancipation of the individual, and a just society by the modernization of China. Essentially, it was an intellectual revolution in the broad sense, intellectual because it was based on the assumption that intellectual changes were a prerequisite for such a task of modernization, because it precipitated a mainly intellectual awakening and transformation, and because it was led by intellectuals. This also accelerated numerous social and political and cultural changes. The most important purpose of the movement was to maintain the existence and independence of the nation. . . . In order to do this, the intellectual reformers, unlike the previous generations, advocated the modernization or Westernization of China in all important aspects of her culture, from literature, philosophy, and ethics to social, political and economic institutions and customs. They started by attacking tradition and re-evaluating attitudes and practices in the light of modern Western civilization, the essence of which they thought to be science and democracy. The basic spirit of the movement, therefore, was to jettison tradition and create a new, modern civilization to 'save China.'[8]

These three factors--the birth and agitation of the working class, the October revolution and the highly nationalistic May Fourth Movement--with war and revolution in the air, provided the background for the unfolding of the powerful events of 1925-27. And the two principal political formations during the revolution of 1925-27--the kuomintang (kmt) and the communist party (ccp)-- were spawned directly by this social and political ferment which preceded the revolution. Although the kuomintang or nationalist party dates ideologically from the turn of the century, it was not officially proclaimed until 1912. The communist party was founded in 1921. During the summer of 1922 (June-July), the communist party outlined its attitude towards the bourgeois or nationalist party:

The proletariat's support of the democratic revolution is not (equivalent to) its surrender to the capitalists. Not to prolong the life of the feudal system is absolutely necessary in order to raise the power of the proletariat. This is the proletariat's own class interest. It would be no liberation for the proletariat if a successful democratic revolution brought it only some minor liberties and rights. . . . The ccp is the party of the proletariat. Its aims are to organize the proletariat and to struggle for (the

establishment of) the dictatorship of the workers
and peasants, the abolition of private property, and
the gradual attainment of a communist society. At
present the ccp must, in the interest of the workers
and poor peasants, lead the workers to support the
democratic revolution and forge a democratic united
front of workers, poor peasants, and petty bourgeoisie
. . . . However, the workers must not become the
appendage of the petty bourgeoisie within this democratic united front, but must fight for their own
class interests. Therefore, it is imperative that
the workers be organized in the party as well as in
labor unions. Ever mindful of their class independence,
the workers must develop the strength of their
fighting organization (in order to) prepare for the
establishment of soviets in conjunction with the poor
peasantry and in order to achieve (the goal of) complete liberation. The ccp is a section of the CI
[Comintern] . The party calls the Chinese workers and
peasants to rush to its banner for the (coming) struggle:
it asks the oppressed masses of all China to fight in
common with the workers and poor peasants under the
party banner; and it hopes that the revolutionary masses
of the whole world will march forward shoulder-to-shoulder
[our emphasis].

Three significant points stand out in the preceding citation:
1) while maintaining its "class independence," the communist party
--the "vanguard" of the proletariat--expressed its willingness to
"act jointly" with the nationalist party in the formation of a
"united front," 2) the relevancy of soviets for China is openly
acknowledged and 3) though this is more important as a re-
flection of communist attitude than a reality of the nationalist
party, there is no mention of the bourgeoisie in the united
front.[9] Within the span of a few weeks, these positions would
be completely reversed. And the impetus for this volte-face
would come primarily from Moscow. In August 1922 the Comintern's
representative in China, Maring--having failed to convince the
kuomintang's leadership to form an alliance of equals with the
communist party and seeking to bolster the Soviet position in
China--insisted that members of the communist party enter the
kuomintang as individuals. He rationalized this by declaring
that the kuomintang was unlike other parties in that it was a
multi-class party. Stalin would later describe it as a "bloc
of four classes;" that is, a bloc of the bourgeoisie, petty
bourgeoisie, proletariat and peasantry. Would this not be a
breach in the class independence of the proletarian party? Did
not Lenin say in 1920 that "even if it is only in an embryonic
state" the communist party must not "amalgamate" with non-

141

proletarian movements? When disgruntled voices were raised Maring promptly invoked the discipline of the leninist Comintern.* With this the communist party dutifully proclaimed its readiness to submit to Moscow's line.** However, official relations between the communist party and the kuomintang would not

---

*"All the decisions of the congresses of the Communist International, as well as the decision of its Executive Committee, are binding on all parties belonging to the Communist International. . . . Those members of the party who reject in principle the conditions and theses put forward by the Communist International are to be expelled from the party." Having recently adhered to the Comintern, the Chinese communist party-- under the pain of expulsion--was obliged to acknowledge the preceding statute. Moreover, words such as "independence" and "amalgamation"--as defined in Lenin's theses on the colonial question--lend themselves to a variety of interpretations. Degras, ed., The Communist International, Vol. I, pp. 114 and 171-172 and Brandt, et al., eds., A Documentary History of Chinese Communism, pp. 52-53.

**At the Fourth Comintern Congress in November 1922-- attended and presided over by Lenin--the Chinese delegate stated that "on the assumption that the anti-imperialist united front is necessary to get rid of imperialism in China, our party has decided to form a national front with the national revolutionary party of the kuomintang. Members of the communist party joined the kuomintang as individuals. . . . If we do not enter this party we shall remain isolated, preaching a communism which is, it is true, a great and sublime ideal, but which the masses do not follow. . . . If we enter the kuomintang we shall be able to show the masses that we too are for revolutionary democracy, but that for us revolutionary democracy is only a means, although we do not ignore the daily demands of the masses. . . . We can rally the masses round us and split the kuomintang party." The communist party has now advanced its rationale for submitting to the line of the Comintern. Even these positions would be toned down over the next few years. Degras, ed., The Communist International, Vol. I, p. 383.

be officially sealed until January 1923. This occurred not as
a result of negotiations between the kuomintang and the communist party but between the Soviet government and the kuomintang.
The "Joint Manifesto of Sun Yat-sen and A.A. Joffe" declared
that "Dr. Sun is of the opinion that, because of the non-existen-
ce of conditions favorable to their successful application to
China, it is not possible to carry out either communism or even
the soviet system in China. M. Joffe agrees entirely with this
view;* he is further of the opinion that China's most important
and most pressing problems are the completion of national unification and the attainment of full national independence" [our
emphasis].10 Sun and the kuomintang would not have had it any
other way.11 He insisted not only that the members of the
communist party enter the kuomintang as individuals but that
they pledge allegiance to the principles and discipline of the
kuomintang. Thereafter the communist party observed that "the
kmt should be the central force of the national revolution and
should assume its leadership." And it expressed the hope that
"all the revolutionary elements in our society will rally to
the kmt, speeding the completion of the national revolutionary

---

*A few years earlier Lenin noted that "it has . . . been
definitely established that the idea of the soviets is understood by the mass of the working people in even the most remote
nations, that the soviets should be adapted to the conditions
of a pre-capitalist social system and that the communist parties
should immediately begin work in this direction in all parts of
the world." And barely two months before the Joffe-Sun statement he said that "for backward countries the soviet system
represents the most painless transitional form from primitive
conditions of existence to the advanced communist culture which
is destined to replace capitalist methods of production and
distribution throughout the world economy." It should be pointed
out, however, that Lenin's role in the shaping of the Comintern's
China policy from late 1922--when it took concrete form--is not
entirely clear. That he favored some form of an alliance between the Chinese communist party and the kuomintang is un-
questionable. But that he endorsed, for instance, the Joffe-Sun
statement has not been established. Indeed, in January 1923,
Lenin--bedridden as a result of his second stroke--seemed much
more concerned with Soviet domestic policy. Lenin, "The Second
Congress of the Communist International," Vol. XXXI, pp. 242-
243, Degras, ed., Soviet Documents on Foreign Policy, Vol. I, pp.
370-371 and The Communist International, Vol. I, pp. 138-139 and
388 and Vol. II, p. 5, Claudin, The Communist Movement, Vol. I,
p. 276 and Brandt et al., eds., A Documentary History of
Chinese Communism, p. 70.

movement." As Isaacs noted, "the Chinese communist party. . .
confined itself religiously to building the kuomintang and
propagating its program. Its members were the most indefatigable
party workers, but they never appeared as communists nor presented any program of their own. The communist party became in
fact and in essence, in its work and in the manner in which it
educated its own members, the left-wing appendage of the
kuomintang."[12]

Neverthless, under the impact of the "tide of May 4th" and as
a result of this alliance--albeit orchestrated in Moscow--both
the communist party and the kuomintang experienced spectacular
growth from its consummation in 1923. The communist party was
gaining influence in kmt areas of the south and the kuomintang
was especially benefiting from the organizational and military
skills of the Comintern. All of this was taking place in the
midst of increasing agitation among the workers and peasants.
Harrison observed that "continuing inflation, rampant taxes and
warlordism, and increased foreign penetration of China all contributed to a new surge of mass discontent, culminating in the
great anti-imperialist and anti-warlord movements of 1925-27."
By the summer of 1925, and especially in 1926, strikes, demonstrations and property seizures were common-place undertakings by
the Chinese working people. The second Chinese revolution had
begun.[13] The summer of 1926 witnessed the biggest "anti-warlord"
and "anti-imperialist" movement to date in China. Under the
leadership of Chiang Kai-shek, who succeeded Sun as one of the
leaders of the kmt and soon to become its undisputed leader, this
Northern Expedition brought the kuomintang a tremendous reception
from the workers and peasants who were under the false assumption
that Chiang was at the head of "liberation" armies. Much of the
confusion in the ranks of the working people--and even among
rank and file communist party members--can be attributed to the
fatal policies pursued by the Moscow-directed communist party
leadership. Isaacs correctly stated that "the kuomintang marched
its forces northward to replace the power of the older militarists with its own. It marched not to fight imperialism but to
compromise with it. Deluded by their own leaders into believing
that a kuomintang victory would bring about a great improvement
in their conditions of life and livelihood, the masses of ordinary people rose in a veritable tidal wave that swept the ex-
peditionary armies to the banks of the Yangtze." What's more,
said North, the communists failed "to harness or exploit the
peasant discontent they had stirred up. The countryside was on
the edge of revolt. . . . " And alongside this peasant discon-
tent--and perhaps more importantly--waves of economic and political strikes were occurring in the cities. For instance, in
Shanghai--a city which contained about half the Chinese industrial proletariat--the union movement was strong enough to consider taking and holding the city on at least three occasions.

Indeed, on one of these occasions Shanghai was actually taken and held for a brief period--until, of course, the communist bosses cooled things out--in early 1927 just prior to the bloody arrival of Chiang's "revolutionary armies."[14] A combined labor-peasant revolt in 1926-27 had been prepared and was now ready to be harnessed.

II. Which Way Trotsky?

What was Trotsky saying on all these events? The period from April 1926 to April 1927 comprised the beginning of the northern campaign--though not officially proclaimed until July 1926-- to its bloody conclusion in the Shanghai disaster.[15] This, indeed, was the most crucial phase of the Chinese revolution. Was Trotsky openly and vigorously opposing the Stalin-Bukharin policy on China? He would claim in 1929 that "long before Chiang Kai-shek crushed the Shanghai workers. . . we issued warnings that such a consequence was inevitable." The facts, however, are somewhat more complicated than this. Prior to 1927 China was not a central issue in the struggle between Stalin and Trotsky for Lenin's man-tle.[16] This, in itself, is not entirely surprising since the Chinese revolution--as we have already indicated--didn't reach its crucial phase until well into 1926. There were, however, other reasons for an absence of sharp struggle over China in the Soviet Union prior to 1927: 1) the central issues in the struggle between Stalin and Trotsky from 1923 had centered on the questions of party democracy and industrialization in the Soviet Union and to a lesser extent on European affairs; 2) the delicate balance within the United Opposition--flowing from Trotsky's apparent concessions to Zinoviev in order to maintain the alliance against the Majority--and the weight of the Stalin government, especially on matters of information, were such that Trotsky's response to the China policy being pursued would almost certainly have been a measured one;[17] 3) finally, there was no basic difference between the assessments of Stalin and Trotsky--in spite of the polemical exaggerations on both sides--on the class nature of the Chinese revolution. And this would remain so until the fall of 1927 or after the revolution's defeat.

Having said this we should nevertheless make it clear that there were important differences between Stalin and Trotsky on China both before 1927 and before the fall of 1927. These differences stood out in two important areas: 1) on the nature of the alliance between the kuomintang and the communist party and 2) on the role of soviets in the Chinese revolution. With re-gard to the question of the alliance Trotsky clearly favored some sort of alliance between the communist party and the kuomintang during the early years of the collaboration. Unlike Stalin, however, Trotsky, from at least 1926, came to question the nature of the alliance between the communist party and the

kuomintang.* This stemmed from Trotsky's conception of the
kuomintang and his assessment of the class struggle in China.
He seems to have regarded the kuomintang organization in the
early 1920s as an alliance between the petty bourgeoisie and the
bourgeoisie with the latter increasingly gaining the upper hand.
Along with this development he felt that the Chinese communists--
even if victimized by national oppression and, indeed, because
of that fact--must begin to reckon with the sharpening of the
class struggle between the bourgeoisie and the oppressed masses
of workers and peasants.[18] He wrote in the fall of 1926 that
"as far as China is concerned, the solution to the problem of
relations between the communist party and the kuomintang differs
at different periods of the revolutionary movement. The main
criterion for us is not the constant fact of national oppression
but the changing course of the class struggle both within
Chinese society and along the line of encounter between the
classes and parties of China and imperialism." A few months later
he wrote that "the wider the territory under nationalist rule
and the more the kuomintang takes on the character of a govern-
ing party, the more it becomes bourgeois. . . . There can be no
doubt that the nationalist government in China, upon seizing
huge territories and finding itself face to face with gigantic
and extremely difficult problems, upon experiencing the need
for foreign capital and clashing daily with the workers, will
make a sharp turn to the right, toward America to a certain extent and Britain." And he left no doubt that he felt the kuomin-

----

*Stalin would consistently support the kuomintang either in
its entirety or its "left wing" until the latter expelled the
communists from the organization in July 1927. He wrote in late
1926 that "it is said that the Chinese communists should withdraw
from the kuomintang. That would be wrong, comrades. The with-
drawl of the Chinese communists from the kuomintang at the present time would be a profound mistake. The whole course, character and prospects of the Chinese revolution undoubtedly testify
in favor of the Chinese communists remaining in the kuomintang and
intensifying their work in it." And barely a week before
Chiang's anti-communist massacre in April 1927 Stalin--in a reference to the kuomintang's right wing--said that "they have to
be utilized to the end, squeezed out like a lemon and then flung
away." Was it not the communists who were "squeezed out like a
lemon and then flung away?" Nevertheless, Stalin continued to
support the "left wing" kuomintang until the latter no longer
needed his support. Stalin, "The Prospects of the Chinese Revolution," Vol. VIII, pp. 383-384 and "Questions of the Chinese
Revolution," Vol. IX, pp. 229-230, Harrison, The Long March to
Power, p. 92 and Degras, ed., The Communist International, pp.
345-347 and 391-395.

tang was becoming "more bourgeois" in the context of an intensified class struggle in China. This necessitated, he argued, a
reassessment of the Comintern's policy demanding that Chinese
communists remain in the kuomintang.* Chinese communists had not
only entered the kuomintang but were, on Moscow's instructions,
submitting to its discipline and principles. Trotsky insisted
that if the communist party were to be speared the worst form
of menshevism--as even the mensheviks had insisted upon their
organizational independence--there must be a "revising" of organizational relationship between the communists and nationalists.[19] Arguing that the "centrifugal tendencies of the class
struggle" was now tearing the kuomintang apart, he wrote in 1926
that the time had come for the "drawing of organizational lines."
The communist party must withdraw from the kuomintang and establish "an independent class party and class policy" so as to
assume the leadership of the "awakened" working class and its
peasant allies. It should be noted, however, that Trotsky was
not calling for an "immediate" withdrawal from the kuomintang
but simply a withdrawal from the kuomintang. The difference is
significant. What Trotsky favored was a sort of "transitional
formula" towards communist independence or a phased withdrawal.
This becomes clearer if it is noted that even as Chiang's troops
in their northward march struck successive blows against the
communists--most notably in the Shanghai bloodletting in April
1927--Trotsky could write on May 7, 1927 on the communist-
kuomintang alliance that "it is not a question of a break but
of preparing a bloc, not on the basis of subordination but on
the basis of a genuine equality of rights." Three days later he
said that "it is necessary to leave the kuomintang but the communist party must be allowed a certain time to prepare." How much
time? He provided no answer. Trotsky simply felt that if the

----

*Trotsky wrote in 1930 that "I personally was from the very
beginning, that is, from 1923, resolutely opposed to the communist party joining the kuomintang. . . ." Documentary support
for such a claim, however, is wanting. What's more, four years
earlier he had written that "the participation of the CCP in the
kuomintang was perfectly correct in the period when the CCP was
a propaganda society which was only preparing itself for future
independent political activity but which at the same time, sought
to take part in the ongoing national liberation struggle [our
emphasis]." There must now be a reassessment of this policy in
the light of "the rise of a mighty strike wave among the Chinese
workers." So, even if he didn't initially approve the entry of
the communist party into the kuomintang--which remains unclear--
Trotsky no less came to sanction it. Trotsky, On China, pp. 113-
114 and 125-126, Leon Trotsky Speaks, p. 202 and Writings [1930-
31], p. 87.

communist party were allowed to operate "in its own name [and] under its own banner" in a phased withdrawal policy, it would not be able to remain in the kuomintang very long.[20] Given the nature of the kuomintang this was no doubt a plausible assumption. But Trotsky's formulation lacked a certain political clarity and, thus, as will shortly be seen, would be correctly criticized by Stalin. It was not until June 23, 1927--on the eve of the expulsion of the remianing communists from the "left wing" of the kuomintang but well after this organization had tragically revealed itself to the Chinese workers--that Trotsky corrected the "serious blunder" of having called for withdrawal from the kuomintang and then not calling for it. After acknowledging that he had done so in order to avoid a further sharpening of the "contradictions within our own party" he went on to say that "our basic approach [meaning the United Opposition] on this question was correct, since we all held to the course for withdrawal from the kuomintang. Our mistake was in pedagogically watering down, softening and blunting our position on the basic question. It has yielded nothing but minuses for us: vagueness of position, defensive protestation and lagging behind the events. We are putting an end to this error by openly calling for immediate withdrawal from the kuomintang [our emphasis]."* This statement

_____

*This, however, did not mean that Trotsky was opposed to "purely practical agreements from one occasion to the next" with the kuomintang. "As was said long ago, purely practical agreements, such as do not bind us in the least and do not oblige us to anything politically, can be concluded with the devil himself if that is advantageous at a given moment. But it would be absurd in such a case to demand that the devil should generally become converted to Christianity, and that he use his horns not against workes and peasants but exclusively for pious deeds. In presenting such conditions we act in reality as the devil's advocates and beg him to let us become his godfathers." And he said about a year later in 1929 that "never and under no circumstances may the party of the proletariat enter into a party of another class or merge with it organizationally." Trotsky, On China, pp. 114-116, 182-183, 200, 249-250, 292-293 and 403 and The First Five Years of the Communist International, Vol. II, p. 96.

of June 23, 1927 finally and uniquivocably--even if belatedly--
separated Trotsky from Stalin on this issue. After all, even
Stalin was saying that it was only necessary for communists to
remain in the kuomintang "at the present time."[21]

The other important difference between Stalin and Trotsky
emerged in the spring of 1927 and centered on the question of
soviets in China. Neither Trotsky nor Stalin argued that soviets
were irrelevant for China. The question at stake was under what
circumstances should they be established and for what purpose.[22]
Trotsky began to call for the formation of soviets in March 1927.
And importantly, he did so before the fall of Shanghai to the
kuomintang. He wrote on March 29th that "I totally fail to comprehend why the call for soviets is not being raised in China.
It is precisely through soviets that the crystallization of the
class forces can keep pace with the new stage of the revolution
instead of conforming to the organizational-political traditions
of a bygone day. . . ." After linking the call for the arming
of the workers and peasants with the creation of soviets, he
wrote two days later that "it goes without saying that the
formation of soviets must be done very carefully, in accordance
with all the class relations, local conditions, and other special
features and factors, so as not to give any accidental advantage
to reactionary elements in one place or another, not to cause
disturbances among the troops, etc. Nevertheless, everything
points to the fact that this task of truly consolidating the
conquered territories by forming soviets of the working and
exploited masses of the Chinese population cannot be postponed
any longer." Soviets, he said, do not simply exist to issue the
call for the seizure of power, but lead the masses along the
necessary preparatory stages in advance of issuing the call for
the seizure of power.[23] Stalin immediately charged Trotsky with
wanting "to skip over the kuomintang phase of the Chinse revolution."[24] Moreover, said Stalin, Trotsky's arguments were stamped
with an obvious contradiction. Writing in May 1927--before
Trotsky had called for an "immediate" withdrawal from the
kuomintang--Stalin wondered "why. . . does Trotsky not propose
now that the communists should immediately withdraw from the
kuomintang and the Wuhan government [seat of the kuomintang's
"left wing"]? How can you set up soviets, how can you set up a
regime of dual power and at the same time belong to that self-
same Wuhan government you intend to overthrow? Trotsky's theses
provide no answer to this question."[25] Even after he had called
for an "immediate" withdrawal from the kuomintange Trotsky would
continue to be haunted by the contradictions and ambiguities contained in his formulations on the Chinese revolution until the
fall of 1927.

This point can be observed in several areas. What would be
the governmental form in revolutionary China emanating from a

successful policy of communists' withdrawal from the kuomintang
and the formation of soviets? Who would participate in this
victorious revolutionary government? What would be its tasks?
On the face of it these questions seem simple enough. After all,
at the very heart of Trotsky's contribution to revolutionary
thought is the theory of permanent revolution. But one would look
forever to find any explicit reference by Trotsky to this theory
during the Chinese revolution. As a matter of fact Trotsky
simply utilized Lenin's old formula of the "democratic dictatorship of the proletariat and the peasantry."* He wrote in March
1927 that a "workers and peasants' government" was on the order of

---

*Lenin had introduced the concept of the democratic
dictatorship of the proletariat and the peasantry during the 1905
revolution. It would be, said Lenin, the governmental form resulting from the victorious revolutionary alliance between the
proletariat and the peasantry in Russia's bourgeois revolution.
And he made it clear that any "idea of seeking salvation for the
working class in anything save the further development of capitalism is reactionary. In countries like Russia the working class
suffers not so much from capitalism as from the insufficient
development of capitalism. . . . That is why a bourgeois revolution is in the highest degree advantageous to the proletariat.
A bourgeois revolution is absolutely necessary in the interests
of the proletariat. The more complete, determined, and consistent
the bourgeois revolution, the more assured will the proletariat's
struggle be against the bourgeoisie and for socialism." Thus,
Lenin felt that the democratic dictatorship of the proletariat and
the peasantry "may bring about a radical redistribution of landed
property in favor of the peasantry, establish consistent and full
democracy, including the formation of a republic, eradicate all
the oppressive features of Asiatic bondage, not only in rural but
also in factory life, lay the foundation for a thorough improvement in the conditions of the workers and for a rise in their
standard of living, and--last but not least--carry the revolutionary conflagration into Europe. Such a victory will not yet
by any means transform our bourgeois revolution into a socialist
revolution; the democratic revolution will not immediately
overstep the bounds of bourgeois social and economic relationships;
nevertheless, the significance of such a victory for the future
development of Russia and of the whole world will be immense."
Lenin, "Two Tactics, "Vol. IX, pp. 49-50 and 56-57.

the day for China. And this governmental "alliance of workers
and peasants under the leadership of the proletariat" could only
result in "the further development of [the] productive forces
on the basis of capitalism" since China has no prerequisites
whatever economically for an independent transition to socialism."
Indeed, said Trotsky, "only an ignoramus of the socialist-reaction-
ary variety could think that present-day China, with its current
technological and economic foundations, can through its own
efforts jump over the capitalist phase."* He then went on to
say that the "Chinese revolution will have a genuinely democratic
worker and peasant character. In its economic life, commodity-
capitalist relations will inevitably predominate. The political
regime will be primarily directed to secure the masses as great
a share as possible in the fruits of the development of the productive forces and, at the same time, in the political and cultural utilization of the resources of the state."** Since China
currently lacked the material prerequisites for a socialist
revolution, would she inevitably have to undergo the agonizing
process of full-scale capitalist development? This, said Trotsky,

---

*He wrote in May 1927 that "the Chinese revolution has a
national-bourgeois character principally because the development
of the productive forces of Chinese capitalism collides with its
governmental customs, dependence upon the countries of imperialism. The obstruction of the development of Chinese industry and
the throttling of the internal market involve the conservation
and rebirth of the most backward forms of production in agriculture, of the most parasitic forms of exploitation, of the most
barbaric forms of oppression and violence, the growth of surplus
population, as well as the persistence and aggravation of
pauperism and all sorts of slavery."

**Trotsky also indicated that China's new political system
would be a multiparty system. "From the standpoint of the class
interests of the proletariat--and we take them as our criterion--
the task of the bourgeois revolution is to secure the maximum
of freedom for the workers in their struggle against the bourgeoisie. From this standpoint the philosophy of the leaders of
the kuomintang in regard to a single centralized party that per-
mits neither any parties nor any factions within it is a philosophy hostile to the proletariat, a counterrevolutionary philosophy which lays down the ideological foundations for Chinese
fascism in the future." The bourgeois revolution must not lead
to the "dictatorship of one party but [to] a guarantee of the
maximum democracy." Did this also apply to the proletarian revolution? He was asked? Trotsky quickly retorted that "in Russia
the one-party dictatorship is the expression of the proletarian
dictatorship." This was said, let's recall, at the same time

was "wholly dependent upon the development of the world proletarian revolution." And he elaborated on this "ABC wisdom" by
stating that:

> . . . The anticapitalist persepctive of China's
> development is unconditionally and directly depen-
> dent upon the general course of the world proletarian
> revolution. Only the proletariat of the most advanced
> capitalist countries--with the organizaed assistance
> of the Chinese proletariat--will be able to take in
> tow the 400 million atomized, pauperized, backward
> peasant economy, and through a series of intermediate
> stages lead it to socialism, on the basis of a world-
> wide exchange of commodities, and direct technical and
> organizational assistance from the outside. To believe
> that without the victory of the proletariat in the
> most advanced capitalist countries, and prior to this
> victory, China is capable with her own forces of
> 'skipping over the capitalist stage of development'
> is to trample underfoot the ABCs of marxism [our
> emphasis].*

_____

that he was struggling for "democracy" in the Soviet Union.
Trotsky, On China, pp. 129-131, 135, 142, 147-48, 154, 163 and
228.

*Stalin likewise shared this view. He also thought that "the
future revolutionary government in China will in general resemble
in character the government we used to talk about in our country
in 1905, that is, something in the nature of a democratic dictatorship of the proletariat and the peasantry, with the difference,
however, that it will be first and foremost an anti-imperialist
government. . . . It will be a government transitional to a
non-capitalist, or, more exactly, a socialist development of
China." Although he and Trotsky were in basic agreement on the
class character of the Chinese revolution, this didn't prevent
Stalin from charging Trotsky with confusing China's "bourgeois-
democratic revolution with a proletarian revolution." Trotsky
responded time and again during the spring and summer of 1927 to
this "senseless contention" by saying that in China there "is a
question not of the socialist but of a bourgeois-democratic revolution." Stalin, "The Prospects of the Revolution in China,"
Vol. VIII, p. 382 and "Revolution in China and Tasks of the
Comintern," Vol. IX, pp. 296-297 and 306 and Trotsky, On China,
pp. 129, 141-142, 147, 155 and 162.

There were, however, certain problems with Trotsky's use of
the concept of the democratic dictatorship. Who would represent
the peasantry in the new revolutionary government? Would it be
the kuomintang or a section of it. As he came to reject the
kuomintang, would a peasant party simply emerge out of the heat
of the revolution. Trotsky doesn't tell us.[26] Furthermore, why
was the democratic dictatorship inappropriate--and even dangerous
--for Russia but not for China? True enough, Russian industry
was a little more advanced and its working class was slightly
larger than was the case in China. Nevertheless, was not Russia
a "shamefully backward" and essentially Asiatic country as both
he and Lenin always described it? Did he not also say before the
October revolution--as Stalin correctly recalled--that the realization of Lenin's "naive" and "self-limiting" formula of the
democratic dictatorship would ultimately result "either in the
repression of the workers by the peasant party or in the removal
of that party from power?" What had changed since the Russian
revolution? Trotsky simply forgot what he had previously written
and undertook a wholesale adoption of Lenin's formula. On the
other hand, two important points should be kept in mind. It had
been the official policy of the leninist Comintern to link the
possibility for successful socialist revolutions in the East with
proletarian revolution in the West. The embryonic communist
movements in the East were expected to forge alliances with
the much larger bourgeois or "national-revolutionary" movements
in the interest of the "anti-imperialist"--perhaps more correctly
anti-British--struggle.* And secondly, Trotsky had not yet universalized his theory of revolution. Up to now the theory of permanent revolution was merely the product of the "peculiar
character" of tsarist Russia. At the First Comintern Congress in
1919 Trotsky said that "the emancipation of the colonies is conceivable only in conjunction with the emancipation of the working
class in the metropolises. The worekrs and peasants not only of
Annam, Algiers and Bengal, but also of Persia and Armenia, will
gain their opportunity of independent existence only in that hour
when the workers of England and France. . . will have taken state

_____

*Lenin wrote in 1920 that if they had "the aid of the pro-
letariat of the advanced countries" and the Soviet state it would
be a mistake to assume that "the backward peoples must inevitably
go through the capitalist stage of development." And the "Theses
on the Eastern Question" of the Fourth Comintern Congress--the
last of the leninist congresses--state that "the colonial revolution can triumph and maintain its conquests only side by side
with the proletarian revolution in the highly developed countries."
Lenin, "The Second Congress of the Communist International," Vol.
XXXI, p. 244 and Degras, ed., The Communist International, Vol. I,
pp. 43, 138-140 and 389-391.

power into their own hands." About a year later he noted that "in India victory is out of the question without the aid and the leadership of the English proletariat." His views on this question were most succinctly summed up in late 1922:

> It is self-understood that the colonies--Asia and Africa (I speak of them as a unity), despite the fact that they, like Europe, contain the greatest graduations--the colonies, if taken independently and isolatedly, are absolutely not ready for the proletarian revolution. If they are taken isolatedly, capitalism still has a long possibility of economic development in them. But the colonies belong to the metropolitan centers and their fate is intimately bound up with the fate of these European metropolitan centers. . . . In the colonies we observe the growing national revolutionary movements. Communists represent there only small nuclei implanted among the peasantry. So that in the colonies we have primarily petty-bourgeois and bourgeois national movements. . . . The growth of the influence of socialist and communist ideas, the emancipation of the toiling masses of the colonies, the weakening of the influence of the nationalist parties can be assured not only by and not so much by the role of the native communist nuclei as by the revolutionary struggle of the proletariat of the metropolitan centers for the emancipation of the colonies.

The colonial struggle would remain for Trotsky--as it had been for the leninist Comintern--"a mighty reserve for the world proletariat" throughout the course of the Chinese revolution.[27] Thus, his use of the concept of the democratic dictatorship--in spite of all the problems it raised--was inconsistent neither with existing Soviet policy nor with his own political development.

All of this, however, changed with the coming of the fall of 1927. Trotsky now wrote from September 1927 that "the business at hand is the dictatorship of the proletariat" and insisted that this fact should be presented "clearly and distinctly and in its full scope." Only "philistines," said Trotsky, would engage in the "abstract and lifeless" argument that "China has not yet matured for a socialist revolution." Considering what he had said earlier about the current absence of the material prerequisites in China for a socialist revolution, we might wonder what had really changed. He stated that "it is precisely the epoch of imperialism that has led to such a sharpening of class relations in China and made the solution of the most important tasks of the revolution impossible, not only under the leadership of the bourgeoisie, but also through the democratic dictatorship of the petty bourgeoisie and the proletariat; and by so doing the task

of establishing the dictatorship of the proletariat supported by
the rural and urban poor has been put on the agenda." Trotsky
was now substituting politics for the absence of economics. He
simply exchanged The German Ideology for Results and Prospects.
No longer was there a need for a preliminary socialist victory in
the West. Now invoking the "law of uneven development," Trotsky
affirmed that "the concrete, historical, political, and actual
question is reducible not to whether China has economically matured for 'its own' socialism, but whether China has ripened politically for the proletarian dictatorship."[28] As a result of this
development and the "opportunist" policy of the Comintern, Lenin's
concept of the democratic dictatorship has "hopelessly outlived
its usefulness." The coming "third" Chinese revolution, Trotsky
now contended, "will win as a dictatorship of the proletariat or
it will not win at all."[29]

II. Summary

    We have sought to show the relationship between the theory
and practice of the leninist Comintern on the colonial question
as a necessary point of departure in our assessment of the
struggle between Stalin and Trotsky over the meaning of the
Chinese revolution from which ultimately emerged a universalization of Trotsky's theory of permanent revolution. Lenin's
"theses" on the colonial question stated that "all communist
parties must support by action the revolutionary liberation
movements in these countries. . . . The Communist International
should collaborate provisionally with the revolutionary movement
of the colonies and backward countries, and even form an alliance
with it, but it must not amalgamate with it; it must unconditionally maintain the independence of the proletarian movement,
even if it is only in an embryonic stage." But when was a
bourgeois or national revolutionary movement "genuinely revolutionary?" Could a national revolutionary movement which was
as much, if not more, anti-communist as anti-British be considered
"genuinely revolutionary?" What should be the nature and duration of an alliance between the communist movement and the
national revolutionary movement? On these and other questions
Lenin's theory and practice left room for a variety of responses.
And they would not be long in coming from Stalin and Trotsky
in the context of their struggle over the Chinese revolution.
But were there real differences between Stalin and Trotsky over
the Chinese revolution? The differences were quite real but the
line separating Stalin from Trotsky was not nearly as clear as
they both claimed. Both acknowledged that neither a socialist
revolution nor a dictatorship of the proletariat was currently
at stake in China. And both favored at some point the withdrawal
of the communist party from the kuomintang, the arming of the
workers and peasants and the formation of soviets which, they
claimed, would lead to the establishment of a democratic dicta-

torship of the proletariat and peasantry in China. No doubt the
question of timing was all important.[30] Even here, however,
Trotsky did not call for the "immediate" withdrawal of the
communists from the kuomintang until well after Chiang's anti-
communist massacre in Shanghai. Yet, it was out of this maze of
ambiguities and contradictions that beset his assessment of the
Chinese revolution that Trotsky would come to universalize his
theory of permanent revolution. He wrote in early 1928 that the
Chinese experience had "revealed the hollowness of the slogan of
the bourgeois-democratic revolution." And a few months later he
declared that "with regard to countries with a belated bourgeois
development, especially the colonial and semi-colonial countries,
the theory of permanent revolution signifies that the complete and
genuine solution of their tasks of achieving democracy and
national emancipation is conceivable only through the dictatorship
of the proletariat as the leader of the subjugated nation, above
all its peasant masses." This, indeed, was the "central idea"
of the theory of permanent revolution.[31]

IV. Notes to Chapter IV

[1] During the first four congresses of the Communist International--those attended and presided over by Lenin, 1919-1922--and to a certain extent its fifth in 1924, there was considerable room for free, lively and passionate debates. However, its last two congresses in 1928 and 1935--without mentioning decisions undertaken in the name of the organization--clearly reflected the bureaucratic apparatus that had become all-powerful in the Soviet Union. Yet, it is our contention that even the leninist congresses--despite Lenin's occasional criticisms--reflected the Russian orientation of the Communist International. Not only was the organization based in the capital of the only workers' state but the powerful Executive Committee of the Communist International (ECCI) was headed by Zinoviev and Karl Radek, the latter coming to bolshevism after the October revolution. Moreover, most of the important resolutions and manifestoes adopted by the leninist Communist International (Comintern) were written by Lenin and Trotsky. Thus, when we speak of Comintern policy or Soviet policy--unless otherwise stated--we do not mean two fundamentally distinct entities.

[2] See Chapter II for an examination of Lenin's views on the interrelationship between imperialism, self-determination of oppressed nations and proletarian revolution in the West.

[3] Trotsky said that the "March Action" of the German communist party in 1921 had "sounded the alarm" to the Soviet leaders about the lack of revolutionary readiness of the Western working class. "The signal for a review of the international tasks of communism was given by the March 1921 events in Germany. . . . During the March days of 1921 in Germany we saw a communist party--devoted, revolutionary, ready for struggle--rushing forward, but not followed by the working class." Trotsky no longer asserted that "civil war is on the order of the day throughout the world." From 1921 he contended that communist parties "must win the confidence" of the majority of the working class rather than seeking immediately to capture political power. This was now symbolized by the Comintern's call for a "proletarian united front" in the West and an "anti-imperialist united front" in the East. Degras, ed., The Communist International, Vol. I, pp. 43, 177, 215-227, 316 and 390 and Trotsky, The First Five Years of the Communist International, Vol. II, pp. 91-109.

[4] While we have centered our examination of Lenin's views around the debate between him and Roy, there was another point of view manifested at the Second Comintern Congress that deserves mentioning. This view was expressed by Serrati, the Italian

communist leader. His was an extreme European outlook which declared itself "hostile to all forms of class collaboration." With regard to the colonial liberation movements, he contended that "the genuine liberation of the oppressed peoples can be carried out only by the proletarian revolution and the Soviet regime, and not by a temporary and accidental alliance of the communist parties with bourgeois parties which are said to be revolutionary. Such alliances can, on the contrary, lead only to the weakening of the class consciousness of the proletariat, above all in the countries which as yet are scarcely accustomed to the struggle against capitalism." Conrad Brandt, Stalin's Failure in China, pp. 3-4, Brandt, Schwartz and Fairbank, A Documentary History of Chinese Communism, p. 68, Carr, The Bolshevik Revolution, Vol. III, pp. 255-258, Branko Lazitch and Milorad M. Drachkovitch, Lenin and the Comintern, Vol. I, pp. 385-389 and Carrère d'Encausse and Schram, eds., Marxism and Asia, pp. 151-152 and 165-167.

[5]Lenin was clearly prepared to do whatever was necessary in order to defend Soviet national interests which, for him and Trotsky, was to a certain extent interchangeable with the idea of international revolution. However, the Anglo-Soviet trade agreement of 1921 did not lead to the level of economic contact that Lenin had anticipated. And this became even clearer at the Genoa conference in April 1922. The basic aim of this conference was the reintegration of Russia and Germany, the two outcasts of the "Great War," within Europe's economic and political framework. But what came out of the conference was an agreement between Russia and Germany--the Rapallo treaty--in which the two European outcasts would assist one another economically and especially militarily. What is important here is not so much the Rapallo treaty--though it raises certain political questions--but the general proposal for world disarmament introduced by Lenin's representative at the conference. This is important because it indicates how far Lenin was prepared to go in order to woo the capitalist powers. Chicherin, Commissar for Foreign Affairs and Lenin's personal representative, at the opening session of the conference stated that "the economic reconstruction of Russia, the largest state in Europe, with its incalculable natural resources, is an indispensible condition of universal economic reconstruction. Russia, on its side, declares itself fully prepared to contribute to the solution of the tasks confronting the conference by all the means at its disposal, and the means are not negligible. To meet the needs of world economy, and of the development of its productive forces, the Russian government is ready to open its frontier, deliberately and voluntarily, for international transit trade; to grant for cultivation millions of acres of most fertile land; to grant rich timber, coal and mining concessions, particularly in Siberia, and a number of other concessions throughout the territory of the RSFSR." This,

as we have seen, is consistent with the foreign component of
Lenin's NEP. But Chicherin interestingly concluded that "all
efforts made to restore world economy are vain so long as the
threat of new wars hangs over Europe and the world, wars perhaps
even more destructive and devastating than that we have just
lived through..... The Russian delegation intend, in the course
of this conference, to propose the general limitation of armaments,
and to support every proposal designed to lighten the burden of
militarism, on the condition that this limitation is applied to
the armies of all countries, and that the rules of war are
supplemented by the absolute prohibition of its most barbarous
forms, such as poison gas, aerial warfare, etc., and in particular
the use of means of destruction against peaceful populations. It
follows that Russia is equally ready to limit its own armaments,
on condition of full and unconditional reciprocity, and on condition that the necessary guarantees are provided against any sort
of attack and against interference in its domestic affairs."
Does this statement not sow illusions among the masses about the
nature of bourgeois states? Is not militarism an inevitable
feature of "imperialism?" Even if one accepts that Lenin was
playing upon the contradictions within the capitalist camp, it
seems clear that he was more concerned with establishing good relations with the capitalist states than with promoting world revolution. We need only recall that Lenin once wrote that "their
principal argument [that of socialist advocates of disarmament] is
that the disarmament demand is the clearest, most decisive, most
consistent expression of the struggle against all militarism and
against all war. But in this principal argument lies the disarmament advocates' principal error. Socialists cannot, without
ceasing to be socialists, be opposed to all war. . . . One of
the main features of imperialism is that it accelerates capitalist
development in the most backward countries, and thereby extends
and intensifies the struggle against national oppression. That
is a fact, and from it inevitably follows that imperialism must
often give rise to national wars." If so, did he now subscribe
to "bourgeois pacificism?" Had he also gone over to "European
chauvinism?" Louis Fischer, The Soviets in World Affairs, pp.
273-319, Carr, The Bolshevik Revolution, Vol. II, pp. 355-357,
371-378 and 422-423, Deutscher, The Prophet Unarmed, pp. 56-58,
Degras, ed., Soviet Documents on Foreign Policy, Vol. I, pp. 233-
235, 237-247, 298-301 and 304 and Lenin, "Military Program of Proletarian Revolution," and "The 'Disarmament' Slogan," Vol. XXIII,
pp. 77-79, 83 and 96-97.

[6]James P. Harrison, The Long March to Power, p. 48, Jacques
Guillermaz, A History of the Chinese Communist Party, p. 68,
Robert C. North, Moscow and Chinese Communists, pp. 25-26 and 45,
Harold R. Isaacs, The Tragedy of the Chinese Revolution, p. 61,
Carrère d'Encausse and Schram, eds., Marxism and Asia, pp. 135-

139, Brandt, Stalin's Failure in China, pp. 14-15, Borkenau, World Communism, pp. 302-303, Allens S. Whiting, Soviet Policies in China, pp. 258-262, Shao Chuan Leng and Norman D. Palmer, Sun Yat-sen and Communism, pp. 52-53 and 172-173 and Degras, ed., Soviet Documents on Foreign Policy, Vol. I, pp. 92, 159-161 and 214.

[7]This refers to the revolution that brought about the over-throw of the Manchu dynasty in 1911. However, the fall of the monarchy led neither to national independence nor national unification. Indeed, with the demise of the central government, China came to endure the "reign of the generals" and, thereby, exposed herself to even more foreign penetration as the Great Powers could play off one warlord against another. The key to the problem confronting China, as Isaacs correctly observed, was that "no class or group emerged from it [the revolution of 1911] capable of directing the transformation of the country, of solving the agrarian crisis, of regaining national independence and building strength to resist the pressure and incursions of the imperialist powers." The struggle for national independence and national unification would be undertaken again--and with mixed results--during the "second" Chinese revolution of 1925-27. Isaacs, The Tragedy of the Chinese Revolution, pp. 20-21, 29-30, 33-34 and 43-45, Guillermaz, A History of the Chinese Communist Party, pp. 28-45 and North, Moscow and Chinese Communists, pp. 44-46.

[8]Chow Tse-tsung, The May Fourth Movement, pp. 1-2, 7-8, 15, 84, 289, 293-294 and 358-359 and Lucien Bianco, Origins of the Chinese Revolution, pp. 27-28, 32, 39-41 and 43.

[9]Brandt, et al., eds., A Documentary History of Chinese Communism, pp. 62-65.

[10]Moreover, two weeks earlier a Comintern resolution after declaring that the "only serious national-revolutionary group in China is the kuomintang" went on to say that "it is expedient for members of the ccp to remain in the kuomintang." Degras, ed., The Communist International, Vol. II, pp. 5-6.

[11]Moscow readily agreed to Sun's demands. After all, the kmt was the larger of the two Chinese organizations and possessed a more deeply rooted tradition of radicalism. Fairbank, for instance, correctly noted that "it [the ccp] numbered hardly more than 300 members in 1922 . . . whereas the kuomintang in 1922 already had 150,000 members." Moscow, it seems, with its policy of creating a "bloc within" sought to "split" the kmt and ultimately capture the organization. Sun Yat-sen had an interest in this "marriage of convenience" as well. Could not his organi-

zation which seemed all but spent in 1921 benefit from some of the discipline and ideology of the October revolution? Having failed in his attempt to obtain material and political support from the West, apparently disappointed over the limitations of the 1911 revolution and with a certain sympathy for the October revolution, Sun found it useful to establish a practical alliance with the Soviet Union. But, as he was wont to do, Sun insisted that "if Russia wants to cooperate with China, she must cooperate with our party and not Chen Tu-hsiu [leader of the Chinese communist party]. If Chen disobeys our party, he will be ousted." John K. Fairbank, The United States and China, p. 174, Shao Chuan Leng and Norman D. Palmer, Sun Yat-sen and Communism, pp. 52-53, 59 and 91-95, Alfred D. Low, The Sino-Soviet Dispute, p. 33, Brandt et al., eds., A Documentary History of Chinese Communism, pp. 68 and 72-73 and Guillermaz, A History of the Chinese Communist Party, pp. 44-45.

[12]Isaacs, The Tragedy of the Chinese Revolution, pp. 56-57 and 64, Brandt et al., eds., A Documentary History of Chinese Communism, pp. 71-72, North, Moscow and Chinese Communists, p. 70, Harrison, The Long March to Power, p. 48 and Degras, ed., The Communist International, Vol. II, p. 25.

[13]Harrison, The Long March to Power, pp. 59 and 83-84, Guillermaz, A History of the Chinese Communist Party, p. 80, Low, The Sino-Soviet Dispute, p. 36 and Isaacs, The Tragedy of the Chinese Revolution, pp. 55, 104 and 111.

[14]North, Moscow and Chinese Communists, pp. 89-90 and Guillermaz, A History of the Chinese Communist Party, p. 121.

[15]This refers to the surprise attack and beheading of the Shanghai labor movement on April 12, 1927 by Chiang's "liberation" armies. Harrison noted that "at a stroke the Shanghai radical movement was crushed. . . . [And] shortly after the events in Shanghai,. the axe struck successive heavy blows elsewhere." Chiang's entry into the city had been well prepared. He was portrayed by both the Comintern and the Chinese communist party as a defender of the people's causes. Stalin, for example, in late 1926--after cautioning the Chinese communist party against making excessive demands against the landlords--stated that "the advance of the Canton troops [the reference is to Chiang's Northern Expedition] meant a blow aimed at imperialism, a blow aimed at its agents in China. It meant the freedom of assembly, freedom to strike, freedom of the press, freedom of coalition for all the revolutionary elements in China and for the workers in particular. . . ." This was said even though Chiang's "revolutionary armies"--in a dress rehearsal of the Shanghai massacre--had

liquidated the labor movement and ousted all communists from
the leading bodies of the kuomintang in Canton, the traditional
revolutionary center of China and then the nationalist capital,
on March 20, 1926. Is there any wonder why the Shanghai workers
were "surprised?" Carrère d'Encausse and Schram, eds., Marxism
and Asia, p. 53, Harry Schwartz, Tsars, Mandarins and Commissars,
pp. 92-111, Charles B. McLane, Soviet Strategies in Southeast
Asia, pp. 45-64, Harrison, The Long March to Power, pp. 91-96,
Bianco, Origins of the Chinese Revolution, p. 58, Guillermaz,
A History of the Chinese Communist Party, pp. 99-101 and 124-125,
Isaacs, The Tragedy of the Chinese Revolution, p. 119, North,
Moscow and Chinese Communists, pp. 96-97 and Degras, ed., The
Communist International, Vol. II, pp. 337-339.

[16]Trotsky, My Life, p. 529 and Deutscher, The Prophet Unarmed, pp. 321-327.

[17]Brandt noted that "undoubtedly Trotsky did make concessions
to his more cautious allies, but what he conceded was still, at
the time, of minor importance to him." Brandt, Stalin's Failure
in China, pp. 156-157, Trotsky, On China, pp. 210, 217 and 220
and Stalin, p. 398 and Daniels, The Conscience of the Revolution,
pp. 283-284.

[18]Trotsky had consistently expressed his lack of confidence
in the Eastern bourgeoisies from the Russian revolution of 1905.
He said in 1921 that since the colonial bourgeoisie was essentially an "instrument of foreign domination" it could not be
expected to wage a "consistent or energetic" struggle against
imperialism. Thus, any attempt to subsume the class struggle
under national oppression was anathema to Trotsky. He wrote in
early May 1927 that "a policy that disregarded the powerful
pressure of imperialism on the internal life of China would be
radically false." And he went on to say that it would be
"profound naivete to believe that an abyss lies between the so-
called comprador bourgeoisie, that is, the economic and political
agency of foreign capital in China, and the so-called national
bourgeoisie. No, these two sections stand incomparably closer
to each other than the bourgeoisie and the masses of workers
and peasants." As the class struggle was on the upswing in China,
Trotsky saw no reason to place confidence in an organization that
from the mid-1920s had increasingly become merely an instrument
in the service of the "national" bourgeoisie. Trotsky, The
First Five Years of the Communist International, Vol. I, pp. 223
and 250 and On China, pp. 159-160.

[19]Trotsky often likened Stalin's alliance policy in China
to the "organizational tailendism" that was manifested with re-

gard to the Anglo-Russian Trade Union Unity Committee. This refers to Stalin's decision not to break with British union officials in May 1926 when the latter--in the midst of a powerful
coal miners strike--utilized the authority of the October revolution to crush the strike movement. Degras, ed., Soviet Documents
on Foreign Policy, Vol. II, pp. 240-241 and The Communist International, Vol. II, pp. 298-302, Stalin "The Anglo-Russian Unity
Committee," Vol. VIII, pp. 186 and 193, Trotsky, On Britain,
pp. 259-263 and Deutscher, Stalin, pp. 401-403.

[20]Stalin likewise insisted that the communist party be an
independent party. "The party must maintain its independent
organization with a strictly centralized apparatus. The most
important specific tasks of the CCP are to organize and educate
the working masses, to build trade unions and thus establish a
basis for a powerful mass communist party. In this work the CCP
should appear under its own colors, distinct from any other group,
while avoiding any conflict with the national-revolutionary movement [our emphasis]." This latter phrase is typical of Stalin's
statements on the independence of the Chinese communist movement. The communist party must avoid "any conflict" with the
kuomintang while at the same time rejecting the "dubious" independence contained in Trotsky's call for a withdrawal from
the kuomintang. Stalin, "Talk with Students of Sun Yat-sen University," Vol. IX, pp. 270-271 and Degras, ed., The Communist
International, Vol. II, pp. 6 and 278.

[21]Stalin, "The Prospects of the Revolution in China," Vol.
VIII, p. 383.

[22]It should be recalled that a few years earlier the Soviet
government, then controlled by the "triumvirate," in an effort
to establish an alliance with the kuomintang had agreed with Sun
that "it is not possible to carry out either communism or even
the soviet system in China." Stalin now wrote in May 1927 and
in response to Trotsky's challenge that "the whole question
[of Soviets in China] is when to form them, in what circumstances
[and] in what situation." Brandt, et al., eds., A Documentary
History of Chinese Communism, p. 70 and Stalin, "Concerning
Questions of the Chinese Revolution," Vol. IX, p. 239.

[23]As he had always done, Trotsky gave special importance
to the winning over of the soldiers to the revolution. "The
first and most important thing they [the soviets] will do is
provide an organization for the workers and help them in organizing their fraternization with the soldiers. The first order of
business for the soviet of workers' deputies of a given industrial city or region should be to draw into its ranks soldiers'

deputies, representatives from the garrisons. . . . Failure to organize soviets of workers' and soldiers' deputies will mean turning the soldier into canon fodder for Chiang Kai-shek and setting the stage for a bloody massacre of the workers like the one that occurred in Shanghai." About a year later in June 1928 he summed up his position on the importance of soviets in the revolutionary process: "Soviets must be set up not on the eve of the insurrection, not under the slogan of immediate seizure of power--for if the matter has reached the point of the seizure of power, if the masses are prepared for an armed insurrection, without a soviet, it means that there have been other organizational forms and methods that made possible the performance of the preparatory work to insure the success of the uprising. . . . The task of the soviets is not merely to issue the call for the insurrection or to carry it out, but to lead the masses toward the insurrection through the necessary stages. At first the soviet rallies the masses not to the slogan of armed insurrection, but to partial slogans, so that only later, step by step, the masses are brought toward the slogan of insurrection without scattering them on the road and without allowing the vanguard to become isolated from the class." Trotsky, On China, pp. 129-130, 133-134, 152-153, 164 and 319-320.

[24]As we will presently see, the charge that Trotsky sought to "skip over" the bourgeois-democratic revolution in China is even less correct than it was in the case of the Russian revolution. Nevertheless, Stalin's conception of the Chinese revolution--at least formally--differed from that of Trotsky. It was Stalin's contention that the Chinese revolution must go through "three stages." These are the "anti-imperialist," "bougeois-democratic" and "soviet" stages. The first two stages would be led by the kuomintang and the last by the communist party. Thus, to call for soviets--as Trotsky was doing--during the spring and summer of 1927 was both theoretically incorrect and dangerous. As Stalin put it in May 1927, "when the moment of the complete victory of the bourgeois democratic revolution approaches [Chiang's April coup had marked the end of the first stage], and when in the course of the bourgeois revolution the paths of transition to the proletarian revolution become clear, the time will have arrived when it is necessary to set up soviets of workers', peasants' and soldiers' deputies, as elements of a dual power. . . . When that time comes the communist must replace the bloc within the kuomintang by a bloc outside the kuomintang and the communist party must become the sole leader of the new revolution in China." Stalin, therefore--though he came to agree with Trotsky on the need for arming the workers and peasants--disagreed with Trotsky on the question of soviets during the Chinese revolution.. For Stalin, soviets--as organs of power--must inevitably clash with the kuomintang. And this is exactly what Stalin sought to avoid during the "kuomintang phase"

of the revolution. He proposed to establish instead workers'
and peasants' "committees" which would serve to deepen the
"kuomintang phase" of the revolution and thereby prepare for the
soviet future. Stalin, "Questions of the Chinese Revolution,"
Vol. IX, pp. 226 and 229-234, "Concerning Questions of the
Chinese Revolution," Vol. IX, p. 241 and "Revolution in China
and Tasks of the Comintern," Vol. IX, pp. 314-315 and "Joint
Plenum of the C.C. and C.C.C. of the C.P.S.U. (B.)," Vol. X, pp.
10-15, Degras, ed., The Communist International, Vol. II, pp. 337,
344, 363-365, 387 and 391 and Isaacs, The Tragedy of the Chinese
Revolution, pp. 119-120 and 191-193.

[25]According to Stalin, "only ignoramuses can combine the
existence of soviets with the possibility of communists belonging
to the kuomintang party." But the formation of soviets "at the
present moment" would involve more than the question of Trotsky's
"stupidity" as their introduction would be "playing into the hands
of the enemies of the Chinese revolution." Stalin, "Questions
of the Chinese Revolution," Vol. IX, pp. 233-234, "Revolution in
China and Tasks of the Comintern," Vol. IX, pp. 304-306 and
"The Political Complexion of the Russian Opposition," Vol. X,
pp. 159-162.

[26]Curiously, on one occasion he suggested that the communists
might be obliged to join the bourgeois kuomintang government.
"The communists cannot . . . relinquish support for the nationalist army and the nationalist government, nor, it appears, can they
refuse to become part of the nationalist government." Years
earlier he had written that "it is one thing when representatives
of the democratic strata of the people enter a government with
a workers' majority, but it is quite another thing when representatives of the proletariat participate in a definitely bourgeois-democratic government in the capacity of more or less
honored hostages." Did he now approve, even if momentarily, of
the Chinese communists becoming "more or less honored hostages"
of the bourgeois kuomintang government? Would he thus permit
the kuomintang to join the future revolutionary government as
the peasants' representative? Again, Trotsky remains unclear.
Degras, ed., The Communist International, Vol. I, pp. 425-427 and
Trotsky, "Results and Prospects," PR, p. 69 and On China, pp.
126 and 148.

[27]Trotsky, 1905, pp. 316-317, "Results and Prospects," PR,
pp. 36-37, The First Five Years of the Communist International,
Vol. I, pp. 25, 125, 139 and 222-223 and Vol. II, pp. 316-317.

[28]It should be noted that Trotsky was no longer calling for soviets in China under the existing circumstances of revolutionary defeat. As the "historical ascension is exhausted" in China he now insisted that "the communist party can and should formulate the slogan of the constituent assembly with full powers, elected by universal, equal, direct and secret suffrage." Stalin, however, was now calling for the formation of soviets. The revolutionary tide, he argued, was on the rise. Stalin's views were tragically realized when he instructed the Chinese communists to stage a rising in December 1927 in order to establish the "Canton Commune." After Shanghai, Wuhan and elsewhere the results were not unexpected. Guillermaz observed that "the movement was quelled with the utmost brutality, involving more loss of life than the insurrection itself. The communist cadres were hunted down mercilessly. . . . The crushing of the Canton Commune, coming as it did after the liquidations in Wuhan, Shanghai and other towns, completed the collapse of the Chinese proletariat as an effective revolutionary force." And while the Comintern in 1928 was prepared to acknowledge--as it was quite obvious by then--that "the Chinese communist party has suffered a grave defeat" over the last two years, it was not prepared to accept the responsibility for this "undeniable fact." Recognizing that "errors" were committed, a Comintern resolution on China in 1928 expressly declared that the errors were "situated not in the basic tactical line [of the Comintern] but in the political acts carried out and in the line adopted in practice in China." In short, the Chinese communist leadership led the party down the road of defeat. This, as we have seen, was not quite the case. Carrère d'Encausse and Schram, eds., Marxism and Asia, pp. 232-233, Bianco, Origins of the Chinese Revolution, p. 57, Borkenau, World Communism, pp. 306 and 316, Degras, ed., Soviet Documents on Foreign Policy, Vol. II, p. 287, North, Moscow and Chinese Communists, p. 113, Trotsky, On China, pp. 268-269, 360, 370, 373 and 400, Stalin, "The Fifteenth Congress of the C.P.S.U. (B.)," Vol. X., p. 290, Isaacs, The Tragedy of the Chinese Revolution, p. 273 and Guillermaz, A History of the Chinese Communist Party, pp. 162-165.

[29]Once Trotsky had emerged in September 1927 with the concept of the dictatorship of the proletariat for China, he would stick with it throughout the 1930's in his assessment of the "coming third Chinese revolution." And his analysis of class forces would remain essentially unchanged throughout the decade. He would again and again emphasize the necessity of a worker-peasant alliance under the leadership of the working class. However, with the decapitation of the urban movement in 1927 and the increasing importance of hte peasantry in the revolutionary process, Trotsky often felt that it was necessary to

lecture the increasingly peasant-oriented Chinese communist
party on the "petty bourgeois" nature of the peasantry. He wrote
in 1932 that "it is one thing when a communist party, firmly
resting on the flower of the urban proletariat, strives through
the workers to lead a peasant war. It is an altogether different
thing when a few thousand or even tens of thousands of revolutionists, who are truly communists or only take the name, assume
the leadership of a peasant war without having serious support
from the proletariat. This is precisely the situation in
China." And he wrote further that "the peasant movement is a
mighty revolutionary factor insofar as it is directed against
the large landowners, militarists, feudalists and usurers. But in
the peasant movement itself are very powerful proprietary and
reactionary tendencies, and at a certain stage it can become
hostile to the workers and sustain the hostility already equipped
with arms. He who forgets about the dual nature of the peasantry
is not a marxist." Trotsky was expressing his concern about the
possibility of a confrontation between the armed, property-
oriented peasantry and the prostrated working class. The basic
principle underlying this concern is not new. Trotsky had always
argued that once the proletarian state began to make "deep inroads" into bourgeois property it would inevitably enter into
"hostile conflict" with the peasantry. As fas as Trotsky was
concerned, however, what made the present situation all the more
dangerous was not only that the prostrated Chinese workers were
not in power but the fact that the Chinese communist party was
basing itself upon an armed peasantry to the virtual exclusion
of the working class. The actual outcome of the "third" Chinese
revolution would be somewhat more complicated than Trotsky's
assessment allows. Trotsky, 1905, p. vi, On China, pp. 275, 305
and 525-528 and Writings [1938-39], p. 366.

[30]Trotsky wrote in September 1927 that "the call for a
democratic dictatorship of the proletariat and peasantry, if it
had been advanced, let us say, at the beginning of the Northern
Expedition, in connection with the call for soviets and the
arming of the workers and peasants, would have played a tremendous role in the development of the Chinese revolution, would
have completely assured a different course for it. It would
have isolated the bourgeoisie and thereby the conciliationists,
and it would have led to the posing of the question of the
dictatorship of the proletariat under conditions infinitely more
favorable than in the past." Yet, Brandt correctly wonders
whether Trotsky's proposals would have "stayed the hand of
Chiang Kai-shek." And Dunn contended that Trotsky's approach
to the Chinese revolution was generally not "at all convincing."
He noted that "the Chinese proletariat was not only very concentrated geographically and thus very easy to suppress militarily . . . as Chiang Kai-shek showed all too graphically in

1927. It was also the product of a very much less developed and
. . . a much smaller industrial sector than had existed in
Russia by 1914." Was Trotsky correct then in boldly asserting
that had his policies been adopted "we would have obtained the
necessary running start, would have disintegrated the armies of
the enemies, obtained our own army and we would have assumed
power--if not in the whole of China at once, then in a very considerable section of it?" Trotsky, On China, pp. 265, 286 and
385, Brandt, Stalin's Failure in China, p. 163, Lenin, "The Second Congress of the Communist International," Vol. XXXU, p. 242,
Wei, China and Soviet Russia, pp. 77-81, Low, The Sino-Soviet
Dispute, pp. 231-233, Chesneaux, Peasant Revolts in China, p. 103,
Schram, Mao Tse-tung, p. 97, North, Moscow and Chinese Communists,
p. 90, John Dunn, Modern Revolutions, p. 87 and Degras, ed., The
Communist International, Vol. I, pp. 143-144 and 368.

[31]Trotsky, On China, pp. 279, 290, 313 and 412 and The
Permanent Revolution, pp. 132 and 276.

CHAPTER V

SUMMARY AND CONCLUSIONS

I.   Marxism

The marxist theory of revolution is composed of three
interconnected components. The first of these is that social
revolution is justified only on the condition of the existence
of modern large-scale industry. As Engels put it:

> The separation of society into an exploiting class,
> a ruling and oppressed class, was the necessary consequence
> of the deficient and restricted development of production
> in former times. . . . But if upon this showing, a
> division into classes has a certain historical justifi-
> cation, it has this only for a given period, only under
> given social conditions. It was based upon the in-
> sufficiency of production.

Marx and Engels maintained, espeically towards their last years,
that there was no question of an "insufficiency of production"
in the West. Indeed, it was argued that the endless search for
profits now constituted a brake on the further development of
the West and the world in general. It therefore followed, according to Marx and Engels, that a foundation for soviet revolution
had been firmly established in the West. But what was true for
the West was not necessarily so for the East. Their basic
case against undertaking social revolution in the East--unless,
of course, it occurred simultaneously with that in the West--
centered around their conception of the future society. In its
main features socialism/communism implies a classless and
stateless society whose realization is possible only upon the
preliminary existence of an abundance of goods and services.
Therefore, social revolution in the East would lead, at best, to
a "monastic economy" or equality in poverty. The more likely
outcome, however, would be the replacing of the existing exploitative society by another. They wrote that modern large-scale
industry "is an absolutely necessary practical premise because
without it want is merely made general and with destitution
the struggle for necessities and all the old filthy business
would necessarily be reproduced." The problem of the backwardness of the Eastern countries which are now being "forcibly
dragged out of their isolation" can be resolved either through
full-scale capitalist development or by their being swept along
in the wake of revolutionary winds blowing from the West.
Socialism was unthinkable outside of a Western frame of reference.[1]

The second component of the marxist theory of revolution is the need for a large working class population. This in fact was implied by the very existence of modern industry. "In proportion as the bourgeoisie, i.e., capital, is developed, in the same proportion is the proletariat, the modern working class, developed--a class of laborers, who live only so long as they find work, and who find work only so long as their labor increases capital." The "historical mission" of the increasingly majoritarian working class movement* was not only self-emancipation but the emancipation of all humanity from the grip of class history. According to Marx and Engels, "it is not a question of what this or that proletarian, or even the whole proletariat itself, imagines the goal to be for the moment. It is a question of what it is and what, conformable to the proletariat's essence, it will be compelled to be historically. Its goal and historical action are perceptibly and irrevocably predetermined in its own life situation, as well as in the whole organization of modern bourgeois society." Yet, even though the working class is revolutionary "by its inner nature" it will require the assistance of a political party if it is to win political power. But this party would be neither vanguardist nor conspiratorial and emanate directly from the economic struggles of the working class.[2]

And lastly, the third component of the marxist theory of revolution recognizes the necessity of an economic crisis springing from the "fetters" which prevent the further development of the productive forces. This "crisis" is an acknowledgement that "the mode of production is in rebellion against the mode of exchange, the productive forces are in rebellion against the mode of production which they have outgrown. . . . The whole mechanism of the capitalist mode of production breaks down under the pressure of the productive forces, its won creation."** The

---

*As we have seen Marx and Engels came more and more to recognize the necessity of forging an alliance with the peasantry as England was the only European country with a majority working class population.

** Engels, Anti-Dühring, pp. 327-328 and Marx, Capital, Vol. I, pp. 836-837. Marx and Engels, as we indicated in Chapter I, in their last years acknowledged that in some countries the working class might find a parliamentary resolution of this "crises."

existence of these three interconnected "elements"--modern large-scale industry, a large working class movement independently and self-consciously organized as a result of its economic struggles against the capitalist class, and an economic crisis--are the "sole conditions" in which Marx and Eegels would countenance social revolution as their primary concern was the abolition of class distinctions "once and for all." Yet it was exactly these objective conditions that did exist towards the turn of the century. Why was there no revolution? At the very moment when marxism began to penetrate the powerful German labor movement the latter was no longer prepared to storm the heavens. 1895 was not 1848. Why should this "bourgeois proletariat"--whose standard of living had improved considerably since 1848--risk its present for an uncertain future? Again, as was suggested in Chapter I, an oversimplification of the complex relationship between social consciousness and material reality haunts the marxist theory of revolution.[3] And it was this "contradiction" between the theory of marxism and the reality of the Western working class movement that led directly to the leninist theory of revolution.

II. Leninism

As in the case with marxism, the leninist theory of revolution is composed of three basic components. The first and most important of these is the recognition of the necessity of a "vanguard" political party as the instrument of socialist consciousness which directs the working class movement both organizationally and ideologically. "Disunited by the rule of anarchic competition in the bourgeois world, ground down by forced labor for capital, constantly thrust back to the 'lower depths' of utter destitution, savagery, and degeneration, the proletariat can, and inevitably will, become an invincible force only through its ideological unification on the principles of marxism being reinforced by the material unity of organization. . . ." But this "grounded down" proletariat can reach these marxist principles only "from without" as the "history of all countries shows that the working class, exclusively by its own efforts, is able to develop only trade union consciousness." And most importantly, under conditions of tsarist Russia only a small, secret and tightly disciplined organization of professional revolutionaries is capable of bringing socialist consciousness to the working class.* These statements represent a substantive break

---

*"The only serious organizational principle for the active workers of our movement should be the strictest secrecy, the strictest selection of members and the training of professional revolutionaries. . . . This is absolutely essential for us be-

with the marxist conception of the relationship between socialist consciousness and the working class movement.

The second component of the leninist theory of revolution is
the idea that Russia's belated bourgeois revolution would be
accomplished by the "democratic dictatorship of the proletariat
and the peasantry" which, itself, would be the victorious conclusion of a revolutionary alliance between the proletariat and
peasantry under the leadership of the proletariat and its van-
gurad party. "All social democrats are convinced that, in its
social and economic content, the present revolution is a bourgeois
revolution. This means that it is proceeding on the basis of
capitalist production relations, and will inevitably result in a
further development of those same production relations. To put
it more simply, the entire economy of society will still remain
under the domination of the market, of money, even when there
is the broadest freedom and the peasants have won a complete
victory in their struggle for the land." This observation clearly reflects Lenin's assessmen of the class character of the 1905
revolution and the coming 1917 revolution. More importantly,
however, he drew the conclusion from 1905 that the "congenital
counterrevolutionism" of the Russian bourgeoisie--a position
he would not stubbornly cling to--made it imperative that the
proletariat seek a firm alliance with the land-thirsty peasant
majority in the interest of carrying out a bourgeois revolution
without the bourgeoisie. But time and again Lenin insisted that
"hegemony" in this alliance between the proletariat and peasantry
must belong to the proletariat as the peasantry "counts for
nothing" without its revolutionary partner. Indeed, he would
later say that "one proletarian has more strength than 200 peasants." Yet there are some problems with Lenin's argument. Why
is the proletariat prevailed upon to exercise "hegemony" in its
revolutionary alliance with the peasantry before the revolution
but not after it? After all, Lenin did say that the peasant
partner in the "democratic dictatorship" would "inevitably" turn

---

cause there can be no question of replacing it by general democratic control in Russia." Lenin is ackowledging that the form
that "vanguardism" assumes is dependent upon the social and political climate of each particular country. Lenin, "What Is To Be
Done?," Vol. V, pp. 375, 452-454, 466-467 and 480 and "One
Step Forward, Two Steps Back," Vol. Vii, p. 412.

against the workers when the latter began to struggle for a transition away from the victorious bourgeois revolution and towards the socialist revolution. This is especially important since he occasionally gave the impression that this transitional struggle would not be long in coming.[4] The bankruptcy of the concept of the "democratic dictatorship" would soon reveal itself before the reality of revolution in 1917.

The final component in the leninist theory of revolution is the idea that the objective basis for revolution springs from the existence of a "revolutionary situation." The essential feature of a revolutionary situation is a serious political and economic crisis in which "revolutionary mass action" is capable of being undertaken by the working class in order to overthrow the existing government. Lenin's concept is anchored more to political and international relations than it is to national productive forces. Indeed, his concept of "imperialism" seems to provide the economic basis that would otherwise be wanting for revolution in Russia. In doing so, to be sure in the name of "marxism," this allowed Lenin to depart from the essentially Western orientation of the marxist theory of revolution.* There are three basic components to the leninist theory of revolution: the necessity of a vanguard party in the working class movement, the concept of a democratic dictatorship in Russia's bourgeois revolution and the idea that the objective basis for revolution springs from the existence of a revolutionary situation.

Lenin, however, "modified" his theory of revolution on two occasions. The first occurred in 1917 and the second around 1920. Sensing the World War spawned revolutionary possibilities in the West and facing the default of the much heralded democratic dictatorship--even if only partially formed--in Russia's bourgeois revolution Lenin, for the first time, raised the slogan of the dictatorship of the proletariat for Russia in April 1917. As the democratic dictatorship had become an "appendage of the bourgeoisie" he noted that "the specific feature of the present situation in Russia is that the country is passing

---

*Lenin's departure from the Eurocentrism of marxism was, however, a conditional one. As we have seen, the Eastern struggles could only serve to "kindle" the necessary revolutionary flames in the West. Lenin, "The Collapse of the Second International" and "Several Theses," Vol. XXI, pp. 213-214 and 402-404.

from the first stage of the revolution . . . to its second stage which must place power in the hands of the proletariat and the poorest sections of the peasants."* The dictatorship of the proletariat would now have responsibility for performing both bourgeois and socialist tasks. But it should be noted that even though Lenin never utilized the concept of the democratic dictator-ship after the October revolution, it was never formally repu-diated except in the context of the Russian experience. More-over, his use of the concept of the "anti-imperialist united front" in the East certainly implied an acceptance of its under-lying principle. What Lenin modified then was not so much his theory of revolution as the way that Russia's bourgeois revolution must be carried out. The second "modification" in his theory of revolution began to unfold around 1920. Against the background of the growing isolation of the Soviet state and the revolt of the peasant majority Lenin began to look more towards the East and a consolidating of the alliance between the prole-tariat and the peasantry through the introduction of the NEP. But did his increasing support for the colonial struggles in the East and implied support for the idea of "a complete socialist society" in NEP Russia suggest a real modification of his theory of revolution? Clearly there was a shift in emphasis. Still, as was noted in Chapters II and III, Lenin always placed the "salvation" of the Russian revolution--however temporarily reality pushed him in another direction--squarely in the laps of the Western proletariat.[5] Thus the leninist theory of revolution, despite occasional "modifications," remained substantively what it was prior to April 1917.

III. Stalinism

Stalin's theory of socialism in one country emerged against the background of the further deepening of the new foreign and domestic realities facing the Soviet state from around 1920. In addition to the already mentioned exhaustion of the revolutionary process both in the West and the Soviet state there was now the death of Lenin and the struggle for the mantle of leninism between the Majority and the Opposition in the communist party. This was the general setting when Stalin, however timidly at first, began to advance his ideas on socialism in late 1924. Basing himself on the "law of uneven development" and to be sure in the name of "leninism," he proceeded:

---

*While he speaks of allying with "the poorest sections of the peasants," the flow of his numerous statements at this time and right up to around 1920 suggest that the peasantry was merely a "temporary" ally as he was really "holding out" for the expected revolutionary assistance from the Western working class. Lenin,

174

Formerly, the victory of the revolution in one
country was considered impossible, on the assumption
that it would require the combined action of the
proletarians of all or at least of a majority of
the advanced countries to achieve victory over the
bourgeoisie. Now this point of view no longer fits
in with the facts. Now we must proceed from the
possibility of such a victory, for the uneven and
spasmodic character of the development of the various
capitalist countries under the conditions of imperialism, the development within imperialism of catastrophic contradictions leading to inevitable wars, the
growth of the revolutionary movement in all countries
of the world--all this leads, not only to the possibility, but also to the necessity of the victory of
the proletariat in individual countries.

Stalin, however, carefully distinguished between the "victory"
in one country and the "final" and necessary victory on the
international plane. Thus, although the Soviet state "possesses
all that is needed" to build a "complete socialist society," its
victory would not be "fully guaranteed" until the "victory of the
revolution in at least a number of countries." In this way
Stalin was able to dodge some of the shafts directed at him by
Trotsky. It would soon be quite clear though what Stalin meant
by socialism. In the midst of his crach collectivization and
industrialization program, which he later described as a "revolution from above," Stalin contended that the "building" of
socialism--in the context of the "intensification of the class
struggle" and the "capitalist encirclement"--required the
strengthening of the state "to the utmost." Indeed, even after
the official proclamation of socialism in 1936 Stalin continued
to ridicule the "rotten theory" about the abolition of the class
struggle under socialism and went on to point out that the state,
itself, might exist under communism.* Socialism in one country

---

"The Tasks of the Proletariat in the Present Revolution" and
"Letters on Tactics," Vol. XXIV, pp. 22-23 and 45-46.

*Stalin, "The Foundations of Leninism," Vol. VI, pp. 109-
111, "Concerning Questions of Leninism," Vol. VIII, pp. 68-70,
"The Results of the First Five Year Plan," Vol. XIII, p. 215 and
Marxism and Linguistics, pp. 28 and 43 and Daniels, ed., A
Documentary History of Communism, Vol. II, p. 57.

and its ideological retinue--the intensified class struggle
and the strengthening of the state--was no more than a rationale
for the construction of the social and economic foundation that
was absent at the time of the "political" victory of the
bolsheviks.

IV. Trotskyism

There were four broad stages in the evolution of Trotsky's
theory of revolution. The first of these was the theory of
permanent revolution itself. Against the background of the
"peculiar character" of the social and economic development of
tsarist Russia, the context of the 1905 revolution and with a
certain disgust for quoting Marx, Trotsky advanced the theory of
permanent revolution. "It is possible for the workers to come
to power in an economically backward country sooner than in an
advanced country." The basic idea underlying this statement
was that as a result of the development of the world economy the
Russian bourgeoisie--unlike its Western counterpart in the 18th
and 19th centuries--was neither capable nor willing to fulfill
its historic responsibilities. "The third estate," he said,
"cannot be brought back to life by weeping and wailing." Thus,
although the coming Russian revolution would be bourgeois in its
"objective aims," it could only be successful as a dictatorship
of the proletariat "supported" by the peasantry:

> The class which is capable of winnning this
> battle will have to fight it, and will then have
> to assume the role of a leading class--if Russia
> is to be truly re-born as a democratic state.
> These conditions, then, lead to the hegemony of
> the 'fourth estate.' It goes without saying that
> the proletariat must fulfill its mission, just as
> the bourgeoisie did in its own time, with the help
> of the peasantry and the petty bourgeoisie. It
> must lead the countryside, draw it into the move-
> ment, make it virtually interested in the success
> of its plans. But, inevitably, the proletariat
> remains the leader. This is not the 'dictatorship
> of the proletariat and the peasantry,' it is the
> dictatorship of the proletariat supported by the
> peasantry.*

---

*In all of this Trotsky said very little about the develop-
ment of the productive forces. "The proletariat grows and
becomes stronger with the growth of capitalism. In this sense
the development of capitalism is also the development of the

And Trotsky went on to say that "the proletariat's work will
not, of course, be confined within the limits of a single state.
The very logic of its positions will immediately throw it onto
the world arena." This was so for three interrelated reasons:
1) the proletarian regime will have the support of the provincial
and property-minded peasant majority only so long as it does
not begin the transition towards the socialist tasks of the
revolution. But, said Trotsky, "no matter under what political
flag the proletariat has come to power, it is obliged to take
the path of socialist policy. It would be the greatest utopianism
to think that the proletariat, having been raised to political
domination by the internal mechanism of a bourgeois revolution,
can. . . limit its mission to the creation of republican-democratic
conditions for the social domination of the bourgeoisie;" 2) at
the moment when the peasantry "turns its back" on the proletarian
regime, the Russian revolution would be "inevitably" crushed by
the European bourgeoisies; 3) and finally, "the social conditions
of Russia are still not ripe for a socialist economy." Therefore,
the theory of permanent revolution contains both a national and
international dimension. Backwardness is both the source and the
problem of the coming Russian revolution. It meant that the
revolution must begin on a national foundation but that it could
be consummated only in the world arena. And for Trotsky the
"world arena" meant precisely carrying the victorious revolution
"on to European soil." Having said this, however, the strength of
Trotsky's theory of permanent revolution--though he would not
universalize it until the 1920's--resides precisely in its recognition that "backward" countries are not obliged to await the preliminary socialist victory in the West. Furthermore, of the
principal revolutionary theories in the Russian social democratic
movement, Trotsky's was the most perceptive and came closest to
correctly predicting the actual course for the Russian revolution
of 1917. But its strength also proved to be its weakness. This

---

proletariat towards dictatorship. But the day and the hour when
power will pass into the hands of the working class depends
directly not upon the level attained by the productive forces
but upon relations in the class struggle, upon the international
situation, and, finally, upon a number of subjective factors:
the traditions, the initiative and the readiness to fight of
the workers. . . . . To imagine that the dictatorship of the proletariat is in some way automatically dependent on the technical
development and resources of a country is a prejudice of 'economic' materialism simplified to absurdity. This point of view
has nothing in common with marxism." As we have seen, however,
this "point of view"--unlike trotskyism--has quite a lot in
common with marxism. Trotsky, "Results and Prospects," _PR_,
pp. 36-37 and 62-66 and <u>1905</u>, pp. 49 and 309-313.

can be seen in Trotsky's acceptance in 1917 of the necessity of the leninist "vanguard" party in the revolutionary process. This step marked the beginning of the second stage in the evolution of his theory of revolution.

Prior to 1917 Trotsky contended that socialist consciousness would develop among the working class on the basis of "unceasing class struggle" and the "inexorable laws" of the dependence of social consciousness upon social conditions. To be sure, he was committed to the existence of revolutionary organization and even a measure of centralism. But what he applauded most of all was the "self activity" of the proletariat:

> The system of political substitutionism [i.e., leninism] results--consciously or unconsciously--from a false and sophistic conception of the links between the objective interest of the proletariat and its consciousness. Marxism teaches that the interests of the proletariat are determined by the objective conditions of its existence. These interests are so powerful and inevitable that, in the final analysis, the consciousness of the proletariat is obliged to take them into account; that is, the subjective interests of the proletariat result from its objective interest.

And he concluded that "political substitutionism" or vanguardism could only lead to a "dictatorship over the proletariat." Trotsky's conception of the role of the revolutionary process before 1917 was partly connected to his idea of the coming world revolution as a single process. This view of the coming world revolution as a single process was only implicit in his writings and more before the October revolution than after. He wrote in 1906 that "there is every ground for assuming that the financial crisis arising from the bankruptcy of Russia will directly repeat itself in France in the form of an acute political crisis which can end only with the transference of power into the hands of the proletariat. In one way or another, either through a revolution in Poland, through the consequences of a European war, or as the result of the State bankruptcy of Russia, revolution will cross into the territories of old capitalist Europe." His optimism was more explicitly expressed in the midst of the First World War when he declared that "a victorious revolution in Russia or England is unthinkable without a revolution in Germany and vice-versa."[6] This optimism, however, proved to be misguided on two counts: 1) the "self-activity" of the Russian working class--especially as it found expression in menshevism--proved unable to carry it beyond the February revolution and 2) the Russian revolution would find no outlet in Western Europe. The first of these realities led directly to Trotsky's acceptance of the necessity of the leninist vanguard party and the second would ultimately lead to his conception of the "degenerated workers' state." The theory of permanent revolution was now wedded to the vary idea of revolutionary organization which Trotsky had previously argued must lead to a "dictatorship over the proletariat."

The third stage in the evolution of Trotsky's theory of revolution began with his universalizing the theory of permanent revolution in 1927. In spite of the fact that the October revolution was victorious partly as a result of Lenin's last second adoption--even if only in this particular case and without ever formally acknowledging it--of the theory of permanent revolution, Trotsky had always considered this theory only as a theory of the Russian revolution. The theory of permanent revolution, he once wrote, was the product of the "peculiar character" of the social and economic development of tsarist Russia. Typical of Trotsky's position was his statement at the First Comintern Congress that "the emancipation of the colonies is conceivable only in conjunction with the emancipation of the working class in the metropolises. The workers and peasants not only of Annam, Algiers and Bengal, but also of Persia and Armenia, will gain their opportunity of independent existence only in that hour when the workers of England and France . . . will have taken state power into their own hands." His standpoint, moreover, was not inconsistent with that of the leninist Comintern. The "Theses on the Eastern Question" of the Fourth Comintern Congress clearly stated that "the colonial revolution can triumph and maintain its conquests only side by side with the proletarian revolution in the highly developed countries." Trotsky, however, would begin a reassessment of his views in the course of the Chinese revolution of 1925-27. Not long after the defeat of the Chinese revolution--which he not unexpectedly attributed to Stalin's "opportunist" policy--Trotsky declared that "with regard to countries with a belated bourgeois development, especially the colonial and semi-colonial countries, the theory of the permanent revolution signifies that the complete and genuine solution of their tasks of achieving democracy and national emancipation is conceivable only through the dictatorship of the proletariat as the leader of the subjugated nation, above all its peasant masses." He had now universalized the theory of permanent revolution. Contrary to Marx and Engels, revolution in the East would no longer have to await the preliminary socialist victory in the West. This represented a considerable advance over marxism even if socialist revolution in the East could only serve as a "bridge" to socialist revolution in the West. The problem, however, was that Trotsky was now stripping the theory of permanent revolution of much of its

179

original concreteness while universalizing it with regard to the
extremely diverse and complex state systems in the "East."
Furthermore, the basis on which it was universalized is itself
open to question. As we have seen, Trotsky's analysis of the
Chinese revolution--no less than Stalin's--was fraught with
ambiguities and contradictions. Yet it was out of this dubious
debate with Stalin that he came to universalize the theory of
permanent revolution.[7]

The fourth and final stage in the evolution of Trotsky's
theory of revolution began in 1933 with his application of the
concept of a political revolution to a degenerated workers'
state. During the first phase of his "democratic" opposition to
Stalin, Trotsky had argued that the Soviet political structure--
though he was most concerned with getting his views heard in the
increasingly stalinized communist party--could be revitalized
through the process of instituting "bold reforms." However,
Trotsky claimed that Stalin's refusal to undertake a "complete
review" of the implications of his foreign and domestic policies
following the virtually uncontested victory of Hitler in 1933
necessitated a reassessment of his perspective on the Soviet
Union. He now contended that the October revolution--even while
acknowledging the preponderant roles of backwardness and isola-
tion--had been "betrayed" by Stalin. "The proletariat of a
backward country was fated to accomplish the first socialist
revolution. For this historic privilege, it must, according to
all evidences, pay with a second supplementary revolution--
against bureaucratic absolutism." Although this coming "supplementary" revolution will have "deep social consequences" there
will be no question "this time of changing the economic foundations of society, of replacing certain forms of property with
other forms" as the "gains" of the October revolution--national-
izations, planning and state monopoly of foreign trade--have not
yet been "overthrown."[8] The essential problem here--apart from
several observations previously raised and the highly questionable claim that he was a fighter for democracy--is Trotsky's
refusal to analyze his and Lenin's role in the "betrayal" of the
October revolution. To have done so might have led him not only
to abandon leninism but even the theory of permanent revolution
which, after all, provided much of the theoretical content for
the October revolution.

[1]Marx and Engels, "The German Ideology," "The Principles of Communism" and "The Communist Manifesto," SW, Vol. I, pp. 37, 63-64, 85, 112 and 125, Bottomore, ed., Karl Marx, p. 240 and Engels, Anti-Dühring, pp. 333-335.

[2]Marx, The Poverty of Philosophy, pp. 95 and 151-152, Marx and Engels, Correspondence, p. 386, Engels, "The Role of Force in History," SW, Vol. III, p. 391 and Padover, ed., Karl Marx: On Revolution, p. 23.

[3]Plamenatz wrote that "everyone who has read Marx has often misunderstood him, for when a man writes as he did there are often several different and equally plausible interpretations to be put on his words. If we think we have good reason for preferring one interpretation to the others, we must believe that anyone who chooses one of the others has mistaken Marx's meaning." Accordingly, with the death of Engels in 1895, a variety of interpretations or "revisions" of the writings of Marx and Engels occurred. The most well-known, of course, was the self-proclaimed "revisionist" of the German social democratic party, Eduard Bernstein. Bernstein, a collaborator of Engels and the latter's literary executor, declared--barely three years after the death of Engels--that much of marxism had been falsified by the events and that the time had come for social democrats or marxists to scuttle the dialectics, the labor theory of value and the dictatorship of the proletariat from the "marxist" present. While Bernstein's approach clearly emptied marxism of much of its content, the controversy surrounding his views clearly revealed the problems involved when seeking to relate the marxist theory of revolution to the reality of the Western working class movement. Engels, "The Housing Question" and "On Social Relations in Russia," SW, Vol. II, pp. 311, 361 and 387-388, Eduard Bernstein, Evolutionary Socialism, pp. 5-15, 35-39 and 83-84, John Plamenatz, German Marxism and Russian Communism, pp. 171-172 and Peter Gay, The Dilemma of Democratic Socialism, pp. 141-164.

[4]Lenin, "Social Democracy's Attitude Towards the Peasant Movement" and "Two Tactics," Vol. IX, pp. 50, 56-57 and 237, "Report on the Unity Congress of the R.S.D.L.P.," Vol. X, pp. 334-335, "When You Hear the Judgement of a Fool," Vol. XI, p. 473, "Agrarian Question and the Forces of the Revolution," Vol. XII, pp. 333-334, "On the 'Nature' of the Russian Revolution," Vol. XV, Vol. XV, p. 27 and "The Second All-Russia Congress of Miners," Vol. XXXII, p. 58.

[5]Lenin, "On Cooperation," "Our Revolution" and "Better Fewer, But Better," Vol. XXXIII, pp. 467-474 and 499-500.

[6]It should be remembered, however, that Trotsky--especially from the 1920's when his ideas came under attack by Stalin-- explicitly rejected the idea that the theory of permanent revolution implied that the world revolution would be a "single simultaneous act." Trotsky, The Permanent Revolution, pp. 97-99, 105-108, 112-115 and 154, Nos Tâches Politiques, pp. 122-125 and 197 and La Guerre Et La Révolution, Vol. II, pp. 321-322.

[7]Trotsky, History of the Russian Revolution, Vol. III, pp. 380-381, The First Five Years of the Communist International, Vol I, p. 25 and The Permanent Revolution, p. 276 and Degras, ed., The Communist International, Vol. I, pp. 389-391.

[8]Trotsky, Writings [1930-31], pp. 230-231 and The Revolution Betrayed, pp. 288-289.

SELECTED BIBLIOGRAPHY*

Primary Sources

Lenin, V.I. Collected Works. 4th ed. Moscow: Progress Publishers, 1972.

_____. Alliance of the Working Class and the Peasantry. Moscow: Progress Publishers, 1971.

Marx, Karl and Engels, Frederick. Collected Works. New York: International Publishers, 1975.

_____. Selected Works. Moscow: Progress Publishers, 1970.

Stalin, J.V. Works. Moscow: Foreign Languages Publishing House, 1953.

_____. Marxism and Lingusitics. New York: International Publishers, 1951.

_____. Marxism and the National Question. London: Lawrence and Wisehart, 1947.

_____. Economic Problems of Socialism in the U.S.S.R. New York: International Publishers, 1952.

_____. On Opposition. Peking: Foreign Language Press, 1974.

Trotsky, Leon. 1905. New York: Random House, 1971.

_____. The Permanent Revolution and Results and Prospects. New York: Merit Publishers, 1969.

_____. The Age of Permanent Revolution: A Trotsky Anthology. New York: Dell Publishing Co., 1964.

_____. Politique de Trotsky. Paris: Armand Colin, 1968.

_____. The Intelligentsia and Socialism. London: New Park Publications, 1966.

_____

*Although a mass of literature--both primary and secondary-- was consulted in order to produce this study, we will list, however, only those works which were actually cited.

Trtosky, Leon. Nos Tâches Politiques. Paris: Pierre Belfond, 1970.

_____. La Guerre et la Révolution. Paris: Tete de Feuilles, 1974.

_____. Terrorism and Communism. Ann Arbor: The University of Michigan Press, 1961.

_____. The First Five Years of the Communist International. New York: Pathfinder Press, 1972.

_____. The Trotsky Papers. Paris: Mouton, 1971.

_____. Tasks Before the Twelfth Congress of the Russian Communist Party. London: New Park Publications, 1975.

_____. Literature and Revolution. Ann Arbor: Ann Arbor Paperbacks, 1960.

_____. The Challenge of the Left Opposition [1923-25]. New York: Pathfinder Press, 1975.

_____. The Real Situation in Russia. New York: Harcourt, Brace and Compnay, 1928.

_____. On Britain. New York: Pathfinder Press, 1973.

_____. On China. New York: Pathfinder Press, 1970.

_____. The Third International After Lenin. New York: Pathfinder Press, 1970.

_____. My Life. New York: Pathfinder Press, 1970.

_____. Leon Trotsky Speaks. New York: Pathfinder Press, 1972.

_____. Writings of Leon Trotsky [1929-40]. New York: Pathfinder Press, 1975.

_____. The History of the Russian Revolution. Ann Arbor: The University of Michigan Press, 1957.

_____. The Struggle Against Fascism in Germany. New York: Pathfinder Press, 1971.

_____. The Stalin School of Falsification. New York: Pathfinder Press, 1972.

_____. The Revolution Betrayed. New York: Pathfinder Press, 1972.

Trotsky, Leon. The Case of Leon Trotsky. New York: Merit
    Publishers, 1969.

_____. In Defense of Marxism. New York: Pathfinder Press,
    1970.

_____. Stalin. New York: Harper and Brothers Publishers, 1941.

General

Anweiller, Oskar. The Soviets: The Russian Workers, Peasants,
    and Soldiers Councils. New York: Pantheon Books, 1974.

Ascher, Abraham, ed. The Mensheviks in the Russian Revolution.
    Ithica: NY: Cornell University Press, 1976.

Avenas, Denise. Le Pensée de Leon Trotsky. Toulouse: Edouard
    Privat, 1975.

Avineri, Shlomo. The Social and Political Thought of Karl Marx.
    Cambridge: Cambridge University Press, 1972.

Avrich, Paul, ed. The Anarchists in the Russian Revolution.
    Ithica, NY: Cornell University Press, 1973.

_____. Kronstadt 1921. New York: W.W. Norton and Co., 1974.

Baron, Samuel H. Plekhanov: The Father of Russian Marxism.
    Stanford, CA: Standford University Press, 1963.

Bender, Frederick L., ed. The Betrayal of Marx. New York:
    Harper Torch Books, 1975.

Bernstein, Edward. Evolutionary Socialism. New York: Schocken
    Books, 1970.

Bettelheim, Charles. Class Struggles in the USSR. New York:
    Monthly Review Press, 1976.

Bianco, Lucien. Origins of the Chinese Revolution. Stanford,
    CA: Stanford University Press, 1971.

Blackwell, William L. The Industrialization of Russia. New
    York: Crowell, 1970.

Blanqui, Auguste. Textes Choisis. Paris: Editions Sociales,
    1971.

Bloom, Solomon F. The World of Nations: A Study of the National
Implications in the Work of Karl Marx. New York: AMS Press,
Inc., 1967.

Bober, M.M. Karl Marx's Interpretation of History. New York:
W.W. Norton and Company, 1948.

Borkenau, Franz. World Communism. Ann Arbor: Ann Arbor Paperbacks, 1963.

Bottomore, T.B. Classes in Modern Society. New York: Vintage
Books, 1966.

Brandt, Conrad. Stalin's Failure in China. New York: W.W.
Norton and Company, 1958.

Brandt, Conrad; Schwartz, Benjami; and Fairbank, John F., eds.
A Documentary History of Chinese Communism. New York:
Atheneum, 1973.

Brossat, Alain. Aux Origines de la Révolution Permanente. Paris:
Francois Maspero, 1974.

Broué, Pierre, ed. La Question Chinoise Dans l'Internationale
Communiste. Paris: EDI, 1976.

_____. La Parti Bolchevique. Paris: Les Editions de Minuit,
1971.

Carmichael, Joel. Trotsky. New York: St. Martin's, 1975.

Carr, E.H. The Bolshevik Revolution. London: Penguin Books,
1969.

_____. Socialism in One Country. New York: MacMillan, 1960.

_____. The Interregnum. Baltimore, Maryland: Penguin Books,
1969.

_____. Studies in Revolution. New York: Grosset and Dunlap,
1964.

Carrère d'Encausse, Hélèn, and Schram, Stuart, R., eds. Marxism
and Asia. London: Penguin Press, 1969.

Chamberlin, William H. The Russian Revolution. New York:
Grosset and Dunlap, 1963.

Chernov, Victor. The Great Russian Revolution. New Haven:
Yale University Press, 1936.

Chesneau, Jean. _Peasant Revolts in China_. New York: W.W. Norton and Company, 1973.

Chow, Tse-tung. _The May Fourth Movement_. Stanford, CA: Stanford University Press, 1960.

Claudin, Fernando. _The Communist Movement._ New York: Monthly Review Press, 1960.

Cliff, Tony. _Lenin_. London: Pluto Press, 1975.

Cohen, Stephen F. _Bukharin and the Bolshevik Revolution_. New York: Alfred A. Knopf, 1973.

Cole, G.D.H. _Socialist Thought: The Forerunners_. New York: St. Martin's Press, 1967.

_____. _Socialist Thought: Marxism and Anarchism_. New York: St. Martin's Press, 1969.

Conquest, Robert. _The Great Terror_. New York: Collier Books, 1973.

Dan, F.I. _The Origins of Bolshevism_. London: Secker and Warburg, 1964.

Daniels, Robert V. _The Conscience of the Revolution: Communist Opposition in Soviet Russia_. New York: Simon and Schuster, 1969.

_____., ed. _A Documentary History of Communism_. New York: Random House, 1960.

Davis, Horace B. _Nationalism and Socialism_. New York: Monthly Review Press, 1967.

Day, Richard B. _Leon Trotsky and the Politics of Economic Isolation_. Cambridge: Cambridge Uniersity Press, 1973.

Degras, Jane, ed. _Soviet Documents on Foreign Policy_. New York: Oxford University Press, 1952.

_____. _The Communist International_. London: Frank Cass and Company, Ltd., 1971.

Derischebourg, A., and Fichelson, M., eds. _La Question Paysanne en U.R.S.S. de 1924 à 1929_. Paris: Francois Maspero, 1973.

Deutscher, Isaac. _The Prophet Armed_. New York: Oxford University Press, 1954.

187

Deutscher, Isaac. _The Prophet Unarmed_. New York: Oxford University Press, 1959.

_____. _The Prophet Outcast_. New York: Oxford University Press, 1963.

_____. _Stalin: A Political Biography_. New York: Oxford University Press, 1949.

Dommanget, Maurice. _Les Idées Politique et Sociale d'Auguste Blanqui_. Paris: M. Riviere, 1957.

Dunn, John. _Modern Revolutions_. Cambridge: Cambridge University Press, 1972.

Eastman, Max. _Leon Trotsky: The Portrait of a Youth_. New York: AMS Press, Inc., 1970.

_____. _Since Lenin Died_. New York: Boni and Liveright, 1925.

_____, _Marxism: Is it Science_. New York: W.W. Norton and Company, 1940.

Erlich, Alexander. _The Soviet Industrialization Debate 1924-1928_. Cambridge: Harvard University Press, 1960.

Fairbank, John K. _The United States and China_. New York: The Viking Press, 1969.

Fervacque, Pierre. _La Vie Orgueilleuse de Trotsky_. Paris: Fasquelle, 1929.

Fischer, Louis. _The Soviets in World Affairs._ New York: Vintage Books, 1960.

Gay, Peter. _The Dilemma of Democratic Socialism_. New York: Collier Books, 1962.

Getzler, Israel. _Martov_. Cambridge: Cambridge University Press, 1967.

Gregor, A.J. _A Survey of Marxism_. New York: Random House, 1965.

_____. _The Fascist Persuasion in Radical Politics_. Princeton, NJ: Princeton University Press, 1974.

Guillermaz, Jacque. _A History of the Chinese Communist Party._ New York: Random House, 1972.

188

Haimson, Leopold H. The Russian Marxists and the Origins of Bolshevism. Boston: Beacon Press, 1955.

_____., ed. The Mensheviks. Chicago: University of Chicago Press, 1975.

Harcave, Sidney. First Blood: The Russian Revolution of 1905. New York: MacMillan, 1964.

Harrison, James P. The Long March to Power. New York: Praeger Publishers, 1972.

Haupt, Georges; Lowy, Michael; and Weill, Claudie, eds. Les Marxistes et la Question Nationale. Paris: Francois Maspero, 1974.

Henderson, W.O. The Life of Friederich Engels. London: Cass, 1976.

Hobsbawm, E.J. The Age of Revolution. New York: Praeger Publishers, 1969.

Hunt, Richard N. The Political Ideas of Marx and Engels. Pittsburgh: University of Pittsburgh, 1974.

Hunt, R.N. Carew. The Theory and Practice of Communism. London: Geoffrey Bles, 1950.

Isaacs, Harold R. The Tragedy of the Chinese Revolution. New York: Atheneum, 1968.

Jasny, Naum. Soviet Industrialization 1928-1952. Chicago: University of Chicago Press, 1961.

Keep, J.L.H. The Rise of Social Democracy in Russia. Oxford: Clarendon Press, 1963.

Krasso, Nicolas, ed. Trotsky: The Great Debate Renewed. St. Louis Missouri: New Critics Press, Inc., 1972.

Labriola, Antonio. Essays on the Materialist Conception of History. New York: International Publishers, 1940.

Laski, Harold J. On the Communist Manifesto. New York: Pantheon Books, 1967.

Lazitch, Branko and Drachkovitch, Milorad, M. Lenin and the Comintern. Stanford, CA: Stanford University Press, 1970.

Lerner, Warren. _Karl Radek: The Last Internationalist_. Stanford, CA: Hoover Institute Press, 1972.

Levine, Norman. _The Tragic Deception: Marx Contra Engels_. Oxford: Clio Books, 1975.

Lichtheim, George. _Marxism: An Historical and Critical Study_. New York: Praeger Publishers, 1961.

Liebman, Marcel. _The Russian Revolution_. New York: Random House, 1970.

_____. _Leninism Under Lenin_. London: Jonathan Cape, 1975.

Low, Alfred D. _The Sino-Soviet Dispute_. Ritherford, NJ: Fairleigh Dickinson University Press, 1976.

Mayer, Gustav. _Friedrich Engels: A Biography._ New York: Howard Fertig, 1969.

McLane, Charles B. _Soviet Strategies in Southeast Asia_. Princeton, NJ: Princeton University Press, 1966.

McLellan, David. _Karl Marx: His Life and Thought_. New York: Harper and Row, Publishers, 1973.

Meyer, Alfred G. _Leninism_. New York: Praeger Publishers, 1969.

_____. _Communism_. New York: Random House, 1967.

Molnar, Miklos. _Marx, Engels et la Politique Internationale_. Paris: Gallimard, 1975.

Nedava, Joseph. _Trotsky and the Jews_. Philadelphia: The Jewish Publication Society of America, 1971

North, Robert C. _Moscow and Chinese Communists_. Stanford: Stanford University Press, 1963.

Padover, Saul K., ed. _Karl Marx: On Revolution_. New York: McGraw-Hill Book Company, 1971.

_____. _Karl Marx: On the First International_. New York: McGraw-Hill Book Company, 1973.

Palmer, Norman D. and Shao, Chuan Leng. _Sun Yat-sen and Communism_. New York: Praeger, 1960.

Plamenatz, John. _German Marxism and Russian Communism._ New York: Longmans, Green and Co., 1954.

Plekhanov, G. Selected Philosophical Works. Moscow: Progress Publishers, 1974.

Preobrazhensky, E.A. The New Economics. Oxford: Clarendon Press, 1965.

Radjavi, Kazem. La Dictature du Prolétariat et le Dépérissement de l'État de Marx a Lenine. Paris: Editions Anthrops, 1975.

Radkey, Oliver H. The Agrarian Foes of Bolshevism. New York: Columbia University Press, 1958.

_____. The Sickle Under the Hammer. New York: Columbia University Press, 1963.

Riazanov, David. Karl Marx and Friedrich Engels. New York: Monthly Review Press, 1973.

Roth, Guenther. The Social Democrats in Imperial Germany. Totowa, NJ: Bedminster Press, 1963.

Schapiro, Leonard. The Communist Party of the Soviet Union London: University Paperbacks, 1963.

_____. The Origin of the Communist Autocracy. Cambridge: Mass: Harvard University Press, 1977.

Schwartz, Harry. Tsars, Mandarins and Commissars. Philadelphia: Lippincott, 1964.

Schwartz, S.M. The Russian Revolution of 1905. Chicago: University of Chicago Press, 1967.

Sherman, Howard J. The Soviet Economy. Boston: Little, Brown and Company, 1969.

Sukhanov, N.N. The Russian Revolution: 1917. London: Oxford University Press, 1955.

Treadgold, Donald W. Lenin and His Rivals. New York; Praeger, 1955.

Venable, Vernon. Human Nature: The Marxian View. New York: The World Publishing Company, 1966.

Venturi, Franco. Roots of Revolution: A History of the Populist and Socialist Movements in Nineteenth Century Russia. New York: Grosset and Dunlap, 1966.

Water, Mary-Alice, ed. <u>Rosa Luxemburg Speaks</u>. New York: Path-
    finder Press, 1970.

Wei, Henry. <u>China and Societ Russia</u>. Princeton: Van Nostrand,
    1956.

Whiting, Allen S. <u>Soviet Policies in China</u>. Stanford, CA:
    Stanford University Press, 1953.

Wildman, Allan K. <u>The Making of a Workers Revolution</u>. Chicago:
    University of Chicago Press, 1967.

Williams, Eric. <u>Capitalism and Slavery</u>. New York: Capricorn
    Books, 1966.

Wilson, Edmund. <u>To the Finland Station</u>. New York: MacMillan,
    1972.

Wolfe, Bertram D. <u>Marxism: 100 Years in the Life of a Doctrine</u>.
    New York: A Delta Book, 1967.

Zeman, Z.A.B. and Scharlau, W.B. <u>The Merchant of Revolution:
    The Life of A.I. Helphand (Parvus)</u>. London: Oxford
    University Press, 1965.

INDEX

ABOUT THE AUTHOR

Curtis Stokes is an Assistant Professor of Political Science at the University of Michigan, Dearborn. He received his B.A. degree from St. Mary's University in San Antonio, Texas and his M.A. and Ph.D. degrees from the University of Michigan, Ann Arbor.